FAILURE TO DISRUPT

FAILURE TO DISRUPT

Why Technology Alone Can't

Transform Education

JUSTIN REICH

HARVARD UNIVERSITY PRESS
Cambridge, Massachusetts, and London, England

Printed in the United States of America

First Harvard University Press paperback edition, 2022
First printing

Library of Congress Cataloging-in-Publication Data

Names: Reich, Justin, 1977– author.
Title: Failure to disrupt : why technology alone can't
transform education / Justin Reich.
Description: Cambridge, Massachusetts : Harvard University Press, 2020. |
Includes bibliographical references and index. |
Identifiers: LCCN 2020012257 | ISBN 9780674089044 (cloth) |
ISBN 9780674278684 (pbk.)
Subjects: LCSH: Educational technology. | Educational change. |
Computer-assisted instruction—Evaluation. | Internet in education—
Evaluation. | MOOCs (Web-based instruction)—Evaluation.
Classification: LCC LB1028.3 .R4375 2020 | DDC 371.33—dc23
LC record available at https://lccn.loc.gov/2020012257

In the memory of Sheryl Blair, who loved schools as I do, and dedicated to Elsa, Adella, and Wren.

CONTENTS

PROLOGUE

Reader, I am reviewing the copyedited manuscript of a book about technology and learning just as a pandemic has spread across the globe. By the time you download these words onto your favorite screen or, I pray, walk into your local bookstore to pick up a copy, the world will be different.

Schools and colleges are among the most durable and conservative of our social institutions. They prepare people for the future by connecting them with knowledge and wisdom from the past. Faculty make some accommodations for changing times, but for the most part, instructors teach how they were taught. Schools hold fast.

Even during history's watersheds, they hold fast. My colleagues in higher education are right now, for the most part, trying to teach as they did before, using video conferencing software to continue broadcasting their lectures. Most elementary school teachers have quickly and wisely given up on continuing a typical spring progression and shifted to "enrichment," providing weblinks and worksheet packets that families can do at home to stay busy. Secondary school teachers are somewhere in between.

These heroic, hasty efforts by teachers are working unevenly. In educational institutions serving affluent students, where instructors can assume that students all own their own devices, have access to sufficient broadband, and live in homes stable enough to weather a global recession, things are proceeding reasonably well. Not so for schools that serve rural families and poor urban neighborhoods, or for community colleges, state institutions, and for-profit colleges serving working adults. In these settings, the best efforts of teachers are being overwhelmed by the barriers of technology access, employment disruption, hunger, homelessness, stress, and disease.

Many things that happen in schools simply cannot happen at a distance. In one of the first American news articles about the shift to online learning, a parent lamented that his six-year-old required full-time supervision to participate in the remote instruction being offered by his first-grade teacher. That anyone—a parent, a first-grade teacher, a school principal, a journalist—would expect a six-year-old to have the self-control, motivation, and attention span to participate in remote instruction is strange—yet typical of our extraordinary expectations for the power of learning technologies. It should not be a surprise that a six-year-old would need direct, physical human co-presence to participate in schooling; it is more surprising that so many people might be led to believe otherwise.[1]

In the early days of a lost semester, students, parents, and teachers are rapidly discovering the possibilities and limits of distance learning technologies. In the dark days of quarantine, technology provides some light for learning. Mo Willems, the brilliant children's book author, is broadcasting weekly lessons about reading, writing, and drawing. Vast numbers of online courses and textbooks, from massive open online course (MOOC) providers and open educational resource repositories, are providing useful support to self-paced learning, especially for older learners. As children miss months of school, the loss of math instruction is one area where students face lasting detrimental effects on academic progress, and by good fortune, adaptive math learning software is one of the most well-developed categories in the field of education technology.

For all these bright points, however, it is also obvious that the gains of learning technologies are substantially offset by the loss of schools as places for camaraderie, shelter, nutrition, social services, teaching, and learning. When all the bars closed, people could still find companions and dates (even against CDC recommendations) on Tinder, Bumble, and Grindr. If the printing presses were to stop, people could still get their news online. But parents, students, administrators, governments, and pundits who thought that schools could simply pivot to online learning and finish out the semester are learning in the early days of the pandemic that the social and social service functions of schools are intimately tied to their learning outcomes.

In what follows, I attempt to explain why learning technologies work in some situations but not others, and for some people but not others. I hope that the explanations that I developed in a period of relative stability provide some insight in the wake of a terrible pandemic. I hope it becomes clear why a steady drumbeat of techno-optimism about learning technology over the last decade might lead people to believe that a first-grade teacher could remotely instruct twenty or so six-year-olds. I expect that the world will still be wrestling with COVID-19 as this book is released, and I hope that what follows can help educators and the public understand the places where learning technologies are most likely to be of service.

We will have much to rebuild, and perhaps learning technology can help. But online learning won't be an effective replacement for our old system. Rather, the best possible future will be one where we recognize the incredible importance of our formal education systems to the social order, and we provide these systems with adequate funding, support, and respect. Our learning technologies are only as strong as the communities of educators who guide their use.

—*J. R., March 21, 2020*

FAILURE TO DISRUPT

INTRODUCTION

Education Technology's
Unrequited Disruption

THE MUST-HAVE TOY OF THE 2013 holiday season was Rainbow Loom. A simple plastic board with vertical pegs, Rainbow Loom came packaged with hundreds of small, colorful rubber bands that children could weave across the pegs to make bracelets and charms. Press coverage celebrated Rainbow Loom as a back-to-basics craft toy. The *Toronto Star* reported that "parents love the toy because it's simple. It doesn't require a battery. It doesn't mean more screen time and it isn't an app." The article quoted industry expert Jim Silver: "It's an activity. You can sit down and create. . . . Parents also like it when they show creativity. And you're not done playing with it because you can wear it."[1] In an era when iPads and smartphones were ascendant, Santa brought millions of children a toy that would finally get kids to put down those damned devices.

Except it didn't. Rainbow Loom wasn't an antidote to screens; rather, screens were integral to playing with the loom. Because some of the things children could make with Rainbow Loom were quite intricate, the easiest way to learn a new design was through a video tutorial.

In 2013, two girls—Ashley, from Pennsylvania, and Steph, from Ohio—published a sixteen-minute video demonstrating how to use Rainbow Loom to make a "starburst bracelet"—an intricate, three-dimensional display of color and technique.[2] To make the video, they mounted the camera in a stationary position above the Rainbow Loom, which they placed on the carpet. As Ashley carefully demonstrates to viewers the process of weaving each band, the video moves slowly through new techniques and speeds up through repetitive motions. Within two years, the video had been viewed more than thirty million times.

The very first Rainbow Loom videos were created by the niece and daughters of Cheong Choon Ng, the inventor of the loom. Ng recognized early on that teaching and learning would be essential to the marketing and success of his crafty new toy. After kids had made all the bracelets specified in the printed instructions that came with a kit, they could continue to discover new possibilities by searching for videos posted online by people who had invented their own creations. Ng turned to his kids to help: "The problem was that people didn't understand how [the looms] worked. So, I asked my niece and my daughters to create YouTube videos explaining how to make rubber-band bracelets. These created a trend."[3] In a quintessential example of what media scholar Henry Jenkins calls the "participatory culture" of the internet, many other children and aficionados followed suit.[4] They shared videos, asked questions, offered hints, started discussion forums, posted pictures on Facebook, and sold bracelets through online stores and websites. Together, these Rainbow Loomers formed what cultural anthropologist Mizuko Ito calls "affinity networks"—online communities of enthusiasts who connect with each other around interests and hobbies for learning, comradery, support, and critique. Running alongside the global supply chains that delivered Rainbow Loom kits under millions of Christmas trees in 2013 was an extraordinary, organic, almost instantaneous global network of teachers and learners sharing ideas, designs, and techniques.[5]

For those with access to global online networks, now is the greatest time in history to be a learner. Never before have learners had such incredible access to resources and communities of tutors and apprentices. Whether they want to learn to play guitar, brew beer, identify birds, translate Cicero, throw a javelin, intubate a trauma victim, integrate a function, detonate a bomb, program in Javascript, or become a better teacher, there are online classes, tutorials, forums, and networks full of people who are excited to teach and excited to learn. If you've ever signed up for an online class, downloaded an educational app, or watched a video about how to unclog a toilet, you are part of that network.

Bold, Unfulfilled Predictions

The first two decades of the twenty-first century brought dramatic changes in informal learning practices alongside other major social changes powered by ubiquitous connectivity and mobile devices. Journalism experienced a flourishing of new voices through blogging and social media and also a collapse of local news as traditional ad revenue sources moved to internet behemoths. Streaming technologies transformed music and entertainment industries. Dating apps spawned new courtship rituals, and social networking sites redefined the word *friend*.

Against this backdrop of rapid social change, education technologists and reformers imagined a dramatic transformation in formal education institutions. In 2008, Harvard Business School professor Clayton Christensen, with colleagues Michael Horn and Curtis Johnson, published *Disrupting Class,* a book about online learning and the future of K–12 schools. They predicted that by 2019, half of all middle- and high-school courses would be replaced by online options, and "the cost will be one-third of today's costs, and the courses will be much better."[6] These dramatic changes would be driven by innovators in education technology, or *edtech*. One such educator (though he was not identified by name in *Disrupting Class*), was Salman Khan, who in 2008 founded Khan Academy with a collection of short videos explaining math concepts, which he later augmented with an extensive collection of online practice problems and introductory videos in many other subjects. In a 2011 TED talk, "Let's Use Video to Reinvent Education," Khan described a future in which students proceed through foundational content online at their own pace, freeing up teachers to provide intensive remediation or facilitate sophisticated group projects.[7] As his vision captured the attention of popular media, *Wired, Time,* and *Forbes* all featured Khan on their covers. A typical headline read, "One Man, One Computer, 10 Million Students: How Khan Academy is Reinventing Education."[8] Khan published a book, *The One World Schoolhouse: Education Reimagined,* and founded a brick-and-mortar school, the Khan Lab School in Mountain View, California, to test and demonstrate his transformational ideas.[9]

This rhetoric of disruption, transformation, and renewal was heard in higher education as well, sparked by the emergence of massive open online courses (MOOCs). In 2011, Peter Norvig and Sebastian Thrun—researchers affiliated with Google and Stanford—offered an online course called Introduction to Artificial Intelligence. The course consisted of short online videos interspersed with practice problems, a model inspired by Khan Academy. When over 160,000 learners signed up to participate in the course, elite higher education institutions took notice and began embracing online learning with staggering speed. Stanford faculty created the for-profit MOOC providers Coursera and Udacity, while Harvard and MIT created the nonprofit MOOC provider edX. As millions signed up for the first offerings from these institutions, MOOC providers promised a radical reconfiguration of higher education, and a

New York Times headline called 2012 the "Year of the MOOC." That article summed up the vision: "The shimmery hope," it explained, "is that free courses can bring the best education in the world to the most remote corners of the planet, help people in their careers, and expand intellectual and personal networks."[10] In August 2013, Udacity cofounder Sebastian Thrun talked about the prospect of offering powerful learning experiences at low cost and global scale, and he made a confident declaration: "The thing I'm insanely proud of right now is I think we've found the magic formula."[11]

Thrun was in the vanguard of MOOC enthusiasm, but he was also one of the first to dramatically revise his expectations. Three months later, in November 2013, Thrun declared in another interview that MOOCs hadn't accomplished what he had hoped: "We were on the front pages of newspapers and magazines, and at the same time, I was realizing, we don't educate people as others wished, or as I wished. We have a lousy product."[12] In the years that followed, other edtech evangelists also displayed more chastened expectations.

Millions of people have watched Khan's two TED talks, but I suspect that far fewer have read his 2019 interview with *District Administration,* a trade magazine for school superintendents and central office staff. "Now that I run a school," he told the interviewer, "I see that some of the stuff is not as easy to accomplish compared to how it sounds theoretically." Khan's recommendations in 2019 focused less on disruptive transformations of math education and more on using Khan Academy as a modest supplement to traditional classroom instruction: "More recently, we're seeing that if students put 30 minutes to an hour per week—or one class period per week—toward software-based, self-paced learning, schools will see a 20 to 30 percent greater-than-expected gain on state assessments. That's exciting because that's a dosage that's very doable in mainstream classrooms. We tell schools to give students 30 to 60 minutes of Khan Academy per week, with teachers doing traditional curriculum four days per week." When Khan's soaring vision met the complex reality of schools, disruption and transformation gave way to accommodation.[13]

The blended model that Khan espoused in *District Administration* is actually at least twenty-five years old. In 1997, Ken Koedinger and colleagues published "Intelligent Tutoring Goes to the Big City," a report describing the use of adaptive, self-paced algebra tutoring software in the Pittsburgh public schools. Students learned in traditional settings for most of their class time and then spent about one day a week using math tutoring software, which led to improvements on math tests similar to what Khan would find decades later.[14] Much of what Khan Academy discovered by 2019 about computer-assisted math instruction, after more than $100 million in philanthropic investment, could have been found in academic papers published in the 1990s.

Genres and Dilemmas

In the decades ahead, educators can expect to hear a new generation of product pitches about the transformative potential of new technologies for school systems: how artificial intelligence or virtual reality or brain scanners are the innovations that, *this time,* will actually lead to profound changes in education. These pitches will also be wrong—these new technologies will not reinvent existing school systems (though some of them may make valuable incremental improvements)—and this book is an effort to explain why.

I have two main arguments, corresponding to the two sections of this book. First, new technologies in education are not, in fact, wholly new; they build on a long history of education innovations. Second, there are certain basic obstacles that time and time again have tripped up the introduction of large-scale learning systems. A few words about each of these arguments will help to preview the territory the book will cover.

Regarding the history of new technologies, from the earliest days of computing, back when mainframes took up entire rooms, technologists have tried to use these new machines for teaching and learning. The project of teaching people with computers is at least sixty years old, as old as digital computing itself. If you know something about this history, you can look at a new technology, trace its lineage, and make well-informed predictions about how a new iteration will contribute to existing educational systems.

In exploring this history, I'll focus on technologies for learning at scale—learning environments with many, many learners and few experts to guide them. Whereas some technologies, like a calculator, easily fit into the existing structure of schools, large-scale learning technologies are the ones that reformers most often turn to when they imagine widespread transformation of educational systems. These tools are sometimes used entirely online, but they are also blended in countless ways with on-campus learning communities in classrooms, schools, and universities. Online platforms that can be used by millions of learners independently fit squarely within the definition of learning at scale, but so can tools that attempt to individualize learning in a classroom or substantially reshape the experience in a large lecture class. I primarily study how these emerging large-scale learning technologies intersect with existing educational systems, but I remain keenly interested in interest-driven learning outside of schools and what schools can glean from the experiences of Rainbow Loomers and other participants in online affinity networks.

Large-scale learning environments can be classified into three genres, based on the answer to a key question: Who creates the activity sequence for learners? Because a sequence can be created by an instructor (as in the case of MOOCs), by an algorithm (as in the case of adaptive tutoring software), or by a peer (as in the case of distributed learning networks), there are *instructor-guided, algorithm-guided,* and *peer-guided* large-scale learning technologies. Each of these genres has a history, a research literature, and a track record of success and failures in formal educational institutions. If you can figure out into which of these categories a new large-scale learning technology fits, you can do two useful things. First, based on the prior performance of similar approaches, you can make predictions about what outcomes will emerge as new technologies are integrated into complex systems of schooling. Second, understanding what is old and recycled can throw into relief what is genuinely innovative in a new product or approach. Identifying the modest innovations in emerging technologies can help predict how a new offering might offer some incremental improvement over past efforts.

Turning to the second argument, the histories of technologies in all these genres reveal some common challenges that have consistently hindered efforts at improving learning through education technology. In Part II of this book, I identify four kinds of obstacles that large-scale learning systems have encountered repeatedly over recent decades, which I call "as-yet intractable dilemmas": the *curse of the familiar,* the *edtech Matthew effect,* the *trap of routine assessment,* and the *toxic power of data and experiments.* These patterns help explain why predictions for transformative change have fallen flat, and examining these dilemmas is critical for looking forward. These four dilemmas comprise a set of grand challenges that designers, researchers, and educators need to overcome if education technology is to make learning faster, cheaper, more enjoyable, more effective, and more accessible for people around the world.

New technologies alone will not sweep away these dilemmas, because the challenges of learning at scale are not merely technical in nature. In his ethnographic study *Life in Classrooms,* Philip Jackson offers a memorable observation: "The path of educational progress more closely resembles the flight of a butterfly than the flight of a bullet." For engineers, sometimes more is just better: a bigger explosion in the chamber leads to a faster bullet; more fuel burned makes rockets fly faster. As historian Larry Cuban argues, education is not just complicated but complex. It is an interlocking system of learners, educators, technologies, and broader social contexts, with all kinds of invisible linkages and unexpected consequences. Trying to accelerate learning by ramping up technology is like putting rockets on butterfly wings. More force does not lead linearly to more progress.[15]

Educational systems are political institutions negotiated by a diverse set of stakeholders: teachers, students, families, communities, school boards, trustees, vendors, state and federal governments, and others. They exist to serve a variety of sometimes conflicting purposes: preparing people for civil society, training workers for employment, sorting and ranking students into a social hierarchy, developing moral character, providing breakfast and lunch while parents are working, and on and on. Technologists often assume that their creations can reconfigure or bypass these complex systems, but instead, they discover that school cultures (in words that I and Mizuko Ito have used before) "domesticate new technologies."[16] Rather than upending existing educational systems, new technologies get put to work serving some particular niche in schools or universities. In the second half of this book, I argue that the most promising approaches to learning at scale combine technical innovations with efforts to improve these complex systems.

Edtech Charismatics, Skeptics, and Tinkerers

In *The Charisma Machine*, anthropologist Morgan Ames contrasts two approaches to applying emerging technology to improve learning. There are "charismatic" initiatives that envision sweeping change—her case example is the "One Laptop per Child" project launched in 2002—and ascribe tremendous power to new technologies to reinvent education.[17] In the 2000s and 2010s, evangelizing technologists often adopted the rhetoric of "disruptive innovation" to describe how emerging technologies can offer a new value proposition that leads to the wholesale transformation of existing systems. One way to look at the TED conference is as an annual revival meeting for charismatic technologists; reading transcripts from TED talks about educational topics is a reliable research strategy for finding unfulfilled predictions about education technology over the last decade. The disruption of schools promised by education-technology advocates in the first twenty years of the twenty-first century has been universally unrequited.

One opposing position to the charismatic stance is skepticism, and education technology has a rich tradition of critique that designers and educators should take seriously. But there is another alternative position to the charismatic: *tinkering,* a term drawn by Ames from David Tyack and Larry Cuban's history of K–12 schooling in the United States, *Tinkering toward Utopia.*[18] Tinkerers see schools and universities as complex systems that can be improved, but they believe that major improvement is the product of many years of incremental changes to existing institutions rather than the result of one stroke of wholesale renewal. Tinkerers study past efforts at educational reform to avoid replicating past mistakes. Tinkerers harbor an optimism that technology can be used to improve teaching and learning, but they embrace research and critique as a crucial check against utopian thinking. Charismatic technologists orchestrate boom-and-bust hype cycles, cajoling local systems into making major changes and then moving on when transformation proves elusive. Tinkerers persist much longer with their designs, their partners, and their communities. Tinkering offers a middle way between the charismatic and the skeptical.

This book is a tinkerer's guide to learning at scale. For classroom instructors, school technologists, department chairs, and administrators, the history of learning at scale provides valuable guidance in selecting and tinkering with implementation of new learning technologies. For technology developers and researchers, investigating the persistent challenges faced by education technologists over the last two decades reveals important avenues for new research and development. Understanding how technologies are being adopted to improve schooling and lifelong learning empowers parents and citizens to influence the public educational systems in which all of us have a stake.

A Tinkerer's Career in Education Technology

I came to tinkering with education technology through classroom teaching. In 2003, I took my first full-time teaching job in a private school south of Boston, where I taught ninth-grade world history. In the corner of my classroom was a cart of blue and orange clamshell MacBooks loaded with web browsers and an intranet application suite called FirstClass that offered a server-based version of just about everything that Google Suite for Education now offers through the cloud. To help the school figure out what networked learning might look like, my world history class was part of a test program in which I was expected to use the laptops every day. I loved it.

Archives, governments, and museums around the world were in the midst of a massive campaign of digitizing historical material. With colleagues, we completely redesigned our world history syllabus from a traditional survey class to one in which we investigated contemporary world conflicts through journalism and then traced the peoples involved back into ancient and medieval history. My students explored primary sources available online, and they developed and demonstrated their understanding not only through traditional assignments such as essays, but also through new media including blogs and podcasts. In a place with extremely privileged access to resources—hardware, software, networks, and support staff—and well-prepared students, I found teaching with technology to be incredibly energizing for me and for my students.[19]

I went on to co-found a consultancy, EdTechTeacher, to help schools implement digital learning. In this work, I visited with faculty and school administrators from hundreds of schools across the United States and around the world. I joined a doctoral program in 2008 and studied how social media and peer production tools like blogs and wikis were finding new uses in K–12 classrooms. I graduated right before the founding of edX, and I was the first full-time researcher hired by Harvard to develop the infrastructure for researching edX MOOCs. From my office next to the video producers and project managers who developed Harvard's first edX courses, I tried to study the enterprise as both an insider and an outsider, close enough to the action to understand some of its inner workings yet distant enough to make a concerted effort at objective analysis. Eventually, I united my interests in online learning and professional development for educators, and I now run a lab at the Massachusetts Institute of Technology (MIT) called the Teaching Systems Lab, where we aspire to design, implement, and research the future of online learning for K–12 teachers.

An oddity of my career is that I am an education technologist who often writes about how education technology fails to deliver on its promises. In 2009, around the same time that Clayton Christensen and his colleagues published *Disrupting Class,* I wrote a report on education technology for a short-lived British enterprise, *Beyond Current Horizons,* a website published by the United Kingdom's Department of Children, Schools and Families. I predicted that technology would lead to only minimal or superficial changes in school practices. I saw no evidence that edtech advocates had any plans to provide the substantial investment in professional learning that teachers would need to incorporate new technologies in powerful ways. Four years later, on my first day at work at HarvardX, I published a blog post at *Education Week* with a prediction: "I think it's probably more likely that most [MOOCs] end up being talking textbooks with auto-graded worksheets, useful in some particular circumstances with particular populations, but, like every previous generation of education technology, ultimately a disappointment. . . .

And my deepest concern is that the people who will benefit from these new initiatives are those who already are privileged and advantaged." In this book, as in my past writing, I try to maintain humility when approaching the challenges of improving school systems and to show deep respect for the teachers and professors who work heroically every day to maintain the daily work of existing schools. In the face of these challenges, three ideas have sustained my interests in tinkering with technology in schools.

The first is that the needs are vast. We will soon have eight billion people in the world, and as many of them as possible should have the benefits of education. Over two hundred million people in any given year access higher education, but many millions more dream of the opportunity.[20] Nearly a quarter of all students in schools serving America's poorest children have no access to a calculus course. Large-scale learning cannot serve all learners in all places, but we should find the places where technology can expand educational opportunities or improve learning.[21]

Second, when online learning works well, it is beautiful. I love meeting students who found a new path in life after taking a MOOC or discovering an online community. I love meeting educators whose ideas about learning and instructional design were challenged and reshaped by encounters with online tools. I enjoy watching my own young daughters explore the world of learning online. My second grader's passion for math is currently being nurtured by a flashcard app, and although I hope it is not the only way she experiences math and technology at school, I am grateful that she has the opportunity to enjoy the rewards of practice, repetition, and advancement. I think the app she has is a little better than the flashcards I used as a kid, and incremental changes of these kinds are meaningful. As my colleague Ken Koedinger says, a step change is just twenty years of incremental change as viewed from a distance.

Finally, and most importantly, I remain convinced that even though technology alone will not disrupt systems, technology can abet system change. Emerging technologies help learners, educators, and other stakeholders encounter new possibilities, and they loosen the grip of education's conservatism. They invite questions about what might be possible if we rearranged curricula, schedules, goals, assessments, and other key features of educational systems to allow emerging technologies to provide more utility and opportunity. Technology will not dissolve the stubborn challenges of education, but designed thoughtfully and implemented reflectively, learning-at-scale technologies can help. The chapters that follow are my effort to share the most important lessons I have learned about tinkering with technology in the service of improving educational systems.

I

THREE GENRES OF LEARNING AT SCALE: INSTRUCTOR-GUIDED, ALGORITHM-GUIDED, AND PEER-GUIDED

I

INSTRUCTOR-GUIDED
LEARNING AT SCALE

Massive Open Online Courses

In 2011, Peter Norvig and Sebastian Thrun, computer scientists affiliated with Stanford and Google, emailed one thousand affiliates of the Association for the Advancement of Artificial Intelligence announcing a new, free, online course: Introduction to Artificial Intelligence. The course mirrored the residential class offered to Stanford students, with videos of Norvig and Thrun talking over their computer screens as they wrote snippets of code, math equations, and bullet points of important ideas. Interspersed among these videos were multiple-choice quizzes and short computer-programming assignments, which were submitted online and graded by computer. People from 190 countries signed up for the offering, and twenty-three thousand people completed the course.[1]

This startling demand for a university-level computer science class immediately prompted other courses with huge public enrollments. Stanford computer science professors launched three classes in machine learning, artificial intelligence, and databases, and each had more than one hundred thousand enrollees. At MIT, Anant

Agarwal created a new platform, called MITx, and offered his own course, Circuits and Electronics, that gathered more than 150,000 registrants. The courses became known as massive open online courses, or MOOCs (a term coined several years earlier by a group of Canadian educators experimenting with distributed learning models.)

Venture capitalists in Silicon Valley took note of the emerging opportunity, and they provided seed funding for several online learning startups, among them Udacity and Coursera. Harvard and MIT invested $60 million to create a nonprofit alternative called edX, and they created new provost-level enterprises to lead online learning initiatives. For higher education observers used to the glacial movement of universities, these institutional changes appeared with blistering speed.[2]

Online courses had been well established in higher education long before these events. At the turn of the millennium, 8 percent of undergraduates took at least one of their classes through distance education, primarily at non-selective colleges and for-profit universities. Elite institutions, too, dabbled in online learning throughout this period. By 2012, faculty at Harvard and other institutions could put new MOOCs on edX relatively quickly because of the schools' existing, largely unheralded, investments in digital learning. In its first year, HarvardX was able to launch six courses in computer science, political philosophy, public health, ancient history, and law because many of the faculty involved in these enterprises were already conducting online courses in their own schools and scholarly societies or through Harvard's Extension School.[3]

Perhaps the most immediate change sparked by MOOCs was social rather than educational. With the blessing of Ivy League universities, online learning switched from low status to high status almost overnight. Universities that bragged about how many students they rejected in each admissions cycle began to compete for how many students they could enroll online.

In 2013, soon after finishing my doctorate, I joined HarvardX as its first full-time research scientist, the Richard L. Menschel HarvardX Research Fellow. I was physically close to the teams developing MOOCs but organizationally removed, managed by faculty on the newly created Research Committee for the Office of the Vice Provost for Advances in Learning rather than by the HarvardX executive staff. My tasks were to study the enterprise, develop the infrastructure for conducting research on edX courses (verifying data packages from edX, defining measures and metrics, and creating surveys), publish research and reports, and advise stakeholders. (The perspective on these initiatives offered here is my own; it is not the official position of either Harvard or MIT.)

Three Big Bets for MOOCs

In the months that followed the founding of edX, Coursera, and Udacity, MOOC advocates offered a set of dramatic claims—three big bets—about how MOOCs would revolutionize higher education and lifelong learning.

The first big bet was that MOOCs would transform the delivery model of higher education, led by a new generation of online providers. In early 2013, Clayton Christensen, a Harvard Business School professor known for his theory of disruptive innovation, warned that within fifteen years, "maybe half the universities would be in bankruptcy." The concern was that every local college's Introduction to Biology course would be replaced by one or two Bio 101 courses taught by rockstar super-professors from elite universities. As digital providers and their partners created these mega-courses across the curriculum, the economies of scale afforded by giant courses would allow them to be better and cheaper than anything a local institution could offer. Sebastian Thrun from Udacity speculated that in fifty years, there might be only ten institutions of higher education left, and Udacity could be one of them.[4]

The second big bet was that MOOCs would dramatically expand global access to higher education. In her 2012 TED talk, Coursera cofounder Daphne Koller described her mission as creating "the best courses from the best instructors from the best universities, [and providing] it to everyone in the world for free." Her idea was that Coursera would host free online course material and charge a small fee to anyone who wished to receive an official certificate of completion upon successfully passing a course. Learners could get a valuable new kind of credential associated with the prestige of elite universities, while Coursera minted millions for investors and university partners. Students in the far reaches of the world without access to traditional higher education would join working professionals who were too busy to return to school full-time in creating a massive new population of online learners.[5]

The third big bet was that through research and continuous iteration, these new online courses would provide more engaging and effective learning experiences. The long, droning lectures of university faculty would be replaced with short, snappy videos interspersed with active-learning exercises. The vast behavioral data generated by online learning platforms would fuel new research into the fundamentals of human learning. The resulting insights would then be applied to further improve instructional design. Koller imagined that MOOCs would "turn the study of human learning from the hypothesis-driven mode to the data-driven mode, a transformation that, for example, has revolutionized biology."[6]

Together, these three bets proposed a future in which MOOCs would sweep away all the inefficiencies of a legacy system of colleges and universities. Higher education researchers sometimes describe the challenges of improving postsecondary education by referring to the "iron triangle" of cost, access, and quality. Efforts on one side—to reduce cost, broaden access, or improve quality—generally have a negative impact on at least one of the other two sides. The promise of MOOCs was that they could have positive effects on all three sides. Costs would go down as expensive faculty labor was reduced with digitized lectures and computational assessment. Access would increase because learners would not need to pass bureaucratic barriers, pay high fees, or even be physically present in a classroom. Quality would improve as a result of technological innovation and partnerships with elite institutions.

These dramatic changes have not come to pass. Instead of transforming higher education, MOOCs have been absorbed by the existing higher education system. They are now primarily supplements to existing infrastructure for professional master's degrees and executive education programs. Understanding why these three big predictions didn't pan out and what was accomplished requires drilling down into the pedagogical and technological foundations of MOOCs to reveal their capacities and limits.

New Technologies, Old Pedagogies

Given the breathless enthusiasm with which new learning technologies are introduced, one of the most useful dispositions in evaluating edtech is to regularly ask the question, "What's really new here?" Most components of new products and systems have a long history, and only occasionally do new entrants offer a genuinely novel innovation. To evaluate how MOOCs tried to revolutionize higher education, the first step is to explore what was old and what was new.

When Thurn and Norvig were developing Introduction to Artificial Intelligence, one of their most important influences was Khan Academy. In the mid-2000s, Salman Khan, working as a senior analyst at a Boston hedge fund, started making a series of video tutorials about mathematics for his young cousin in Louisiana. The aesthetics of the videos were simple: Khan drew equations and notes on a black screen with a baritone voiceover describing what he was doing and why. Viewers never saw Khan's face; the focus was on the math.

Khan Academy's platform includes both instructional videos and practice problems, but in the early 2010s, these learning resources were separated from one another—videos on one part of Khan's website and practice problems on another. The Introduction to Artificial Intelligence course, by contrast, interleaved video tutorials with practice problems. Like Khan, Norvig and Thrun talked through a segment of content with a video lasting five to ten minutes. Unlike Khan Academy, after a video, they presented their students with a few practice problems to answer, mostly multiple-choice or short-answer questions. After several of these lessons, students completed longer programming assignments that were submitted online. A computer program graded them based on whether the programs accomplished the engineering tasks for the assignment. When students ran into questions or difficulties, a discussion forum provided a space for learners to gather and answer each other's questions. This general format was replicated in Andrew Ng's first Coursera course on machine learning and in Anant Agarwal's first MITx course on circuits and electronics.

This lecture-based pedagogical approach goes back millennia. To a first approximation, there are only two primary approaches to teaching and learning. As Plutarch wrote in "On Listening" in the first century CE, "Education is not the filling of a pail, but the lighting of a fire." Of course, theories of learning and instruction can be infinitely more complex than this simple dichotomy, but these two perspectives of pail filling and fire lighting appear in various guises throughout the history of schooling and learning. Summarizing these two ideas in the American context, historian Ellen Lagemann argued, "One cannot understand the history of education in the United States during the twentieth century, unless one realizes that Edward L. Thorndike won and John Dewey lost."[7]

In twentieth-century America, philosopher John Dewey became the patron saint of the fire-lighters. Dewey famously argued, "I believe that education, therefore, is a process of living and not a preparation for future living," and he advocated for an approach to education that emphasized apprenticeship, interdisciplinary learning, and connections to the world beyond schools. *Social constructivism*—the idea that individuals construct new understandings from prior understandings in the context of learning communities—is one term used by education researchers to capture this family of pedagogies.[8]

Edward Thorndike is less well known than Dewey, but his approach to education will be recognizable readily. Thorndike believed that education could be organized as a science, in the positivist traditions that shaped sociology, political science, economics, and other social sciences. Thorndike believed that learning could be precisely measured, and he was an early developer and advocate of standardized tests and intelligence testing. With these measures of learning, best practices in the direct transfer from experts to novices could be standardized and scientifically evaluated. No single term captures all of the pail-filling intellectual decedents of Thorndike's thinking, but *instructionism* is a useful label for these ideas. MOOC developers have been overwhelmingly instructionists.[9]

New learning technologies rarely innovate on these fundamental pedagogical ideas. Instead, they reenact them. Educators and researchers who had been conducting online courses since the 1980s noted that few new MOOCs offered an improved pedagogical experience for distance learners; most courses simply recorded a professor lecturing, harkening back to the earliest days of motion pictures when the first order of business was the filming of stage plays. MOOC advocates placed their big bets on innovation in distribution rather than innovations in teaching and pedagogy. But even MOOC technologies for online dissemination had well-established histories.[10]

The Key Components of MOOCs = Learning Management Systems, Storefronts, and Autograders

The fundamental technology supporting edX, Coursera, Udacity, and other MOOC providers was the learning management system (LMS)—a platform on which instructors could arrange and deliver learning resources to learners in a sequential order. By 2012, LMSs were widely used throughout higher education both to make online materials accessible to residential students and to facilitate fully online courses. MOOC platforms added two components on top of these LMSs: storefronts and autograders.

LEARNING MANAGEMENT SYSTEMS

The essential purpose of an LMS is to organize instructional content online. The first cited references to learning management systems appear in scholarly literature in the 1960s and 70s. The first commercially successful LMS was Blackboard, released in 1997, and the first widely adopted open-source LMS was Moodle, released in 2002. The earliest LMSs were dissemination tools that provided a space for storing and distributing syllabi, readings, and other course materials. Over time, they also offered dropboxes, which allow students to upload assignments and instructors to grade and return the work on the site, and discussion forums, which serve as the primary means of peer interaction. Crucially, LMSs provide a set of authoring tools that allow faculty with no programming experience to create course sites. By dragging and dropping content and plugins and by filling in forms and textboxes, faculty can create a presentable web presence for their courses without writing a single line of HTML, CSS, or JavaScript.[11]

Learning management systems are boring. They fall into that class of infrastructure—pipes, wires, roads, authentication protocols—that are essential to everyday experience even as they are mostly invisible. But LMSs play a powerful role in shaping people's learning experiences, mostly by homogenizing them. Despite the dozens of options—Blackboard, Moodle, Desire2Learn, Schoology, Haiku, Edmodo, Canvas, and so on—they are all largely the same. The state of the LMS field is one of feature convergence, where every innovative feature that a company develops is rapidly copied by competitors. Once schools and universities adopt an LMS, administrators from the information technology department typically create course templates for faculty. These templates have a set of standard sections—a place for the syllabus, weekly readings, weekly assignments, a discussion forum, supplementary readings, and so forth. As a result, the online components of courses within an institution are usually extremely similar to one another, whether one is teaching about poetry or proteins.[12]

These organizing structures also make MOOCs extremely similar to one another, both across the courses of a single platform (like edX or FutureLearn) and between platforms. For instance, every edX course is comprised of chapters, every chapter contains a series of "horizontals," which are sequences of subunits that are further broken into "verticals," which are scrolling pages of learning objects. By default, the edX navigation system moves every student along a linear, instructor-guided pathway through these verticals, horizontals, and chapters. While with great effort, instructional designers can hack around the edges of the edX LMS to create a different pedagogical design, in practice, most instructors make do with linear learning designs that emphasize formal content dissemination from an instructor that is followed by assessments to quantitatively measure knowledge gained.[13]

STOREFRONTS

MOOCs offered two innovations on top of conventional learning management systems. The first was a business operations innovation: MOOCs put a "storefront" on top of an LMS that allowed the public to sign up for a course. This wasn't particularly technically difficult; it just had not been done much before. Historically, students registered for a college or university, and then, from within that college, they signed up for classes through a registrar, which in turn granted them access to a course LMS. At elite colleges and universities, it was impossible to buy just one course a la carte; one needed to buy a year's worth of courses, live in student housing, and eat from a meal plan. Coursera, Udacity, and EdX allowed anyone in the world to directly register for an online course and to access the course LMS without enrolling in a university or interacting with a registrar. It turned out that millions of people around the world were, initially, interested in casually exploring free courses without any formal university affiliation.[14]

AUTOGRADERS

Automated assessment is the second MOOC addition to the traditional features of a learning management system. For decades, LMSs had very simple assessment items, such as multiple-choice and fill-in-the-blank problems, as well as dropboxes and other mechanisms for students to submit essays, labs, problem sets, and other complex assignments that were then evaluated by human graders. This model was insufficient, however, once online courses became massive. With over 160,000 registrants in Intro to AI, there was no possibility that teaching staff could evaluate all the work submitted by students. Assignments had to be assessed by computer programs.

In some disciplines, educators and technology developers have made great progress in developing automated assessment of complex student performances. Computer scientists have developed tools that can evaluate the quality of students' programs along a number of dimensions: Does the submission meet engineering requirements (does it print "Hello World" to a screen or correctly identify misspelled words in a document)? How quickly does it run? How many lines of code are required? Does the code meet design specifications in its syntax, indentation, and other features to allow developers to collaborate with one another?[15] Other quantitative disciplines, including physics and math, also have developed such automated assessments when the steps to solve a problem are well defined. A crucial part of the first MITx course, Circuits and Electronics, was a circuits simulator that allowed students to connect wires, lights, capacitors, transistors, and other elements in order to perform specific engineering challenges. Since the physical laws behind these electrical components are well understood, and since these components behave predictably and consistently, the simulator can determine objectively whether or not students have a correct solution to a problem.[16]

There remain many fields of study, however, for which computers cannot validly assess complex human performance.[17] Under most conditions, computers cannot effectively evaluate unstructured text in essays or short-answer assignments (in Chapter 7, we will discuss the few conditions under which they might be able to do this). Since teaching how to reason from evidence is one of the main purposes of higher education, and since the main way of demonstrating this reasoning is through essays and similar written performances, the inability to autograde this kind of work is a critical limitation for instructor-guided online learning. MOOC developers conducted some interesting experiments with automated essay grading and peer grading, but for the most part, these systems have proved cumbersome and insufficiently reliable. Automated essay grading systems require extensive human training—through hand grading hundreds of sample submissions—before machines can take over. Peer grading systems require every submission to be evaluated by multiple course participants, so assigning students to write an essay also requires them to read and give feedback on four or five others. Few MOOC providers have continued to experiment with these systems. Since automated assessments can evaluate human performance more reliably in some domains than others, MOOCs are better suited to credential learning in those domains where knowledge is more amenable to computational assessment.[18]

Learning management systems, in use for two decades before the arrival of MOOCs, had not previously led to the three big breakthroughs that MOOC enthusiasts predicted: expanded access, transformed systems, or better teaching from data-driven research. This helps frame our investigation of MOOCs. Now that we have identified what is old, we can focus on what is new: Could the main innovations—storefronts and autograders—lead to the fulfillment of the three big bets of MOOCs?

From Storefronts to Online Program Managers

When the first few million people clicked through the new storefronts created by MOOCs in 2012, it initially appeared as if the first big bet of MOOCs—transforming the delivery model of higher education—could indeed pay off. Students around the world could take single courses through MOOC providers and earn a credential to show to prospective employers. Two problems with this model emerged. First, relatively few students who signed up for courses actually completed them. Second, the value of non-degree credentials remained ambiguous; bypassing the bureaucracy of admissions also meant giving up on the legitimacy associated with formal relationships with an academic institution. As a result, the novel delivery models that MOOC advocates imagined with their new storefronts have largely given way to more well-established arrangements in higher education.

As MOOC advocates emphasized the staggering number of people who registered for new offerings, researchers, journalists, and critics asked a logical follow-up question: "How many of them passed the class?" Early research reports showed that MOOC completion rates typically hovered around 5 percent. Debates ensued as to how substantial of a problem this was. Perhaps it was fine for leisurely browsers of online learning to sample but not complete courses, much as one might sample articles but not read the entire Sunday *New York Times*. Nonetheless, further research suggested that even committed learners often did not finish their courses; only about 20 percent of learners who declared in surveys that they intended to complete a course were successful in doing so, and completion rates among those who paid for the opportunity to earn a "verified" certificate were around 50 percent. MOOC advocates argued that these figures were not out of line with what might be found in other non-selective higher-education settings, and MOOC critics observed that most learners failed to meet their goals. Pedagogical considerations aside, low pass rates threatened the growth of a certificate-based business model; customers who failed to earn a certificate were unlikely to pay for subsequent courses.[19]

Furthermore, the value of these certificates was unclear, and no widespread evidence emerged that employers were recognizing them in hiring or promotion at any meaningful scale. In one study of sixty MOOC certificate earners, researchers found that learners had mixed views of the value of those certificates. Some described them as evidence of learning that was valuable in conversations with current and potential employers, but others declared that while they found the learning valuable, the certificates were meaningless. Perhaps the best indication of the questionable value of certificates is that after a few years, MOOC providers embraced more familiar approaches to credentialing students.[20]

With relatively few students finishing individual courses and with the value of individual course certificates in question, MOOC providers pivoted away from individual courses and toward more comprehensive programs. Udacity was the earliest to make this shift, and through a partnership with Georgia Tech and AT&T, it created the first MOOC-based degree program, an online master's degree in computer science. With a $2 million start-up investment from AT&T, Georgia Tech created thirty online courses, enrolled 380 students in its first year, and by 2019 was enrolling over two thousand new students per year. Given that just over ten thousand master's degrees in computer science are awarded every year in the United States, these are substantial numbers. With the online degree costing only $7,000, successful graduates get the exact same academic certification as students in Georgia Tech's highly regarded on-campus program. Evidence suggests that the program attracted primarily working professionals who were not applying to residential degree programs. Since students take only a few courses per semester and are allowed six years to complete the program, as of this writing, the dropout rate is not yet clear, though the dean of the School of Computing estimated it to be about 40 percent per year. Coursera, edX, and FutureLearn have followed with other fully online master's degrees, most of which are more expensive than the Georgia Tech online master's, and none of which have yet attracted as much attention, enrollment, or research interest.[21]

Some MOOC providers have experimented with a middle path between offering single course certificates and full master's degrees. edX created a new program called the MicroMasters that allows students to earn an online credential by completing a series of MOOCs and sometimes passing a proctored exam. Students can then apply those credentials as course credit toward an on-campus or online degree. For instance, people who earned a MicroMasters from MIT's supply chain management program could apply to earn an accelerated on-campus master's at MIT or at partner schools, such as the University of Zaragoza, in only one semester of residence. In the first year of the new blended program, MIT enrolled approximately forty students in the traditional one-year master's program and admitted another forty students who completed the MicroMasters and then attended one semester on campus to earn a degree. The program developers were gratified to learn that the blended-program students were well prepared by their online courses and earned spring semester grades that were slightly higher than their residential counterparts.[22]

As of 2019, edX has created over fifty MicroMasters programs. The hope is that MicroMasters might become to the master's degree what the associate degree has been to the bachelor's, an affordable stepping stone to a more complete degree. The crucial difference is that associate degrees are overwhelmingly entry points to higher education, whereas thus far, MicroMasters appear to be an extension for the already educated. In the MIT supply chain MicroMasters program, the majority of students to earn the MicroMasters credential and the majority of those who go on to earn the master's degree already had a first graduate degree and were pursuing a second one.[23]

In addition to these degrees and programs, MOOC providers also make their courses available for companies to provide through their internal professional development offerings. In some cases, corporations purchase "seats" for their learners in existing courses, and sometimes MOOC providers codevelop new programs for use within companies. For instance, Udacity has developed a variety of nanodegrees, non-credit-bearing technology credentials, in partnership with tech-sector employers; as one example, their natural language processing nanodegree is advertised as developed in partnership with IBM and Amazon Alexa. Little research has been conducted about these private offerings, but they have similarities with nondegree certificate programs that technology companies have offered for many years (for example, "Microsoft-certified" technicians).[24]

What these MOOC-based degrees, MicroMasters, and corporate training programs have in common is that they recognize the value of a formal, bureaucratic connection between a learner and a university or employer. MOOC providers have found that people willing to pay for educational services want their purchases to include some kind of recognizable credential, not just a certificate for an individual course. The course-based MOOC storefronts still exist, but rather than becoming a new pathway to higher education, they are more like try-before-you-buy teaser opportunities, where people can sample a course to see what a degree program might be like.[25]

In less than a decade, then, MOOC providers have come to look less like a disruptive force and more like a well-established player in higher education called online program managers (OPMs). Few have heard of low-profile companies such as Pearson Embanet, Wiley Education Services, or 2U, but for two decades, they have operated behind the scenes driving the expansion of online learning in higher education. My first encounter with OPMs came in 2006, when I was running a little website for teachers called the Best of History Websites. A representative from Embanet called and asked if he could place an advertisement on the site for Norwich University's online master's in military history. As we chatted, I asked him if Embanet was a marketing firm, and he explained that Embanet's purview was much broader. They would take on nearly any element of a university's online degree programs—marketing, admission, instructional design, even teaching—and perform those functions under a university's brand. Online program managers even made financing easier by paying upfront for the development costs of new programs in exchange for an ongoing fraction of the tuition revenue from subsequently enrolled students. Coursera CEO Jeff Maggioncalda, who took over the company in 2017, has been explicit that the company's strategy is to follow the trail blazed by OPMs such as 2U and assist universities in implementing online degree programs.[26]

The first big bet of MOOCs, that they would fundamentally reconfigure the business model of higher education, has not panned out. No doubt some institutions will close in the years ahead, but it is unlikely that half of all colleges and universities will be gone by 2028, and closures are more likely to be caused by declining public funding, global recession, and demographic shifts than by disruptive competition from low-cost MOOC providers. MOOCs have neither conquered the world nor gone bust. Instead, they plod along, adopting forms and business models—like OPMs or executive education—that are recognizable to those familiar with the history of online learning in higher education over the last two decades.

New storefronts did not revolutionize higher education: In the future, MOOCs will occupy particular niches within a conservative, complex higher education system. Their impact will be different in computer science versus the humanities, in professional schools versus colleges, in developed and developing countries, and for those seeking their first degree versus the already-credentialed. If storefronts are not the killer adaptation for MOOCs, what about autograders? Which students can thrive in the self-paced online learning environments that autograders enable, and which disciplines are amenable to autograding?

The Diversity and Homogeneity of People and Courses on MOOC Platforms

The second big bet of MOOC enthusiasts was that their low-cost and online format would expand access to higher education to learners around the world from diverse life circumstances. Indeed, all kinds of people in nearly every country in the world have signed up for MOOCs. The bulk of people who succeed in this kind of instructor-guided, self-paced online learning, however, are typically already-educated, affluent learners with strong self-regulated learning skills. Autograded courses allow people to proceed at their own time and pace, but the scale of the enterprise means that students need to press on alone or find their own sources of academic support.

In 2013, the *New York Times* featured the story of Battushig Myanganbayar, dubbed the Boy Genius of Ulan Bataar. Myanganbayar was a high school student in Mongolia who earned a perfect score on the first MITx MOOC about circuits and electronics and who later was admitted to MIT. The core narrative of the article was a boy on the periphery of civilization who suddenly, through the generosity of MIT and the magic of the internet, had access to the richest learning resources to be found in the core of the Ivory Tower. The full story was somewhat more nuanced. The principal of the boy's school was the first MIT graduate from Mongolia, and the principal arranged for a Stanford graduate student to spend several months running labs in the high school's physics class that would complement the MITx MOOC. One interpretation of the story, then, is that through MOOCs, MIT can reach students around the world; another interpretation is that if MIT graduates go on to become principals in every school, MIT can reach students around the world. Causality is a tricky thing.[27]

MOOCs have some remarkable young students like Myanganbayar, but most MOOC students are older, already have a bachelor's or advanced degree, and are embedded in the workforce. Two very strong predictors of registering for and succeeding in a MOOC are what social scientists call socioeconomic status (measures of access to social and financial capital) and proficiency with self-regulated learning strategies.

From the detailed data we have from HarvardX and MITx about where learners live, we know that 80 percent of people who register for these MOOCs come from the world's most affluent countries. Those who come from less developed countries tend to be among the most well educated in those countries. An early *Nature* paper titled "Online Education: MOOCs Taken by Educated Few" presented data from Coursera courses showing that 80 percent of learners had a bachelor's degree and 44 percent had a master's degree. Subsequent studies of edX found similar participation patterns. Within the United States, HarvardX and MITx students live in neighborhoods that are approximately one-half standard deviation more affluent than typical Americans. There are edX registrants from every type of neighborhood, from the very poorest to the most affluent, but the income distribution of HarvardX and MITx registrants is higher than Americans as a whole. MOOCs open a door of opportunity that anyone can walk through, but the majority of people walking through that door are already well off, financially and academically. Furthermore, once students enroll in a class, affluence is a good predictor of who finishes. MOOC researchers have identified a "global achievement gap" in which learners from the most affluent countries earn certificates at substantially higher rates than learners from the least developed countries, even adjusting for individual education level and other factors.[28]

The handful of experiments in using MOOCs with underserved populations of undergraduates in the United States have had disappointing outcomes. In 2012, Udacity partnered with San Jose State University to replace face-to-face remedial math courses with MOOCs, and the results were disastrous, with student pass rates substantially below those of residential counterparts. Seasoned observers of higher education questioned whether automating faculty labor through recorded video and autograded practice problems could solve the complex challenges of the fundamentally social enterprise of learning and education. In 2015, Arizona State University partnered with edX to create the Global Freshman Academy, a program where prospective students could take introductory courses as MOOCs and pay to transfer the credit toward an ASU degree. By the end of 2019, over 350,000 people had signed up for one of the twenty MOOCs developed for the program, but only 1,750 paid for college credit, and fewer than 150 students pursued a degree at ASU. Overall, MOOCs have created new opportunities for the already educated more than they have created new pathways into higher education.[29]

Successful MOOC learners demonstrate effective use of self-regulated learning strategies, such as goal setting, time management, help seeking, self-monitoring, and so forth. Learners who use these strategies persist longer and earn higher grades than those who don't, which is perhaps not surprising given the minimal social interactions in most MOOCs. People develop self-regulated learning strategies through direct instruction and practice, often through a long apprenticeship in formal educational systems. If self-paced MOOCs require self-regulated learning, and if self-regulated learning is most commonly developed through formal education, then this provides a learning science rationale for one of the key observations about MOOCs: they are most likely to effectively serve the already educated pursuing advanced postsecondary learning.[30]

The population of MOOC learners is also affected by the range of MOOC offerings. In their early days, Coursera and edX emphasized their interest in reproducing the full academic diversity of the modern university. Harvard's first offerings reflected this effort, including Michael Sandel's popular political philosophy class, JusticeX; David Malan's introductory computer science class, CS50X; and Gregory Nagy's course on classic literature, The Ancient Greek Hero in 24 Hours. When looked at closely, every MOOC had a different origin story, a different approach, and a different goal.

In technical fields, however, autograders and assessments work reasonably well to certify and credential learners, and in the humanities, they don't. We have not developed computer programs that can provide meaningful feedback to a student's essay on "What does it mean to be human?" In part because of these limits, and in part because of labor market returns on educational investment in technical fields, the earliest degree programs created by edX, Coursera, and Udacity have followed the contours of where autograders are most useful by offering degrees in such courses as computer science, data science, accounting, marketing, and cybersecurity. In many respects, the modal MOOC in 2019 looks a lot like Norvig and Thrun's first effort in 2011: most MOOCs are instructional sequences of short videos and autograded practice problems that teach topics in quantitative and computational fields. These kinds of courses may be valuable continuing education for already-educated workers in the white-collar tech sector, but they don't offer the full array of entry points into higher education that are available in community and state colleges.

These findings explain why the second big bet of MOOCs—that they would dramatically expand access to higher education to new populations—has not materialized. The majority of learners who sign up for MOOCs already had access to and success with higher education, and these advantages are compounded among those who go on to complete MOOC courses and earn credentials. These patterns have shaped the course offerings and strategies of MOOC providers, who have increasingly targeted their offerings toward those seeking postbaccalaureate professional degrees and executive education certificates.[31]

The present circumstances do not portend an inescapable destiny. The bulk of early MOOC research, news media, and attention has focused on elite providers, in part because of their enormous marketing power and cultural cachet, and in part because the elite providers have the resources to hire folks like me to conduct research full time about their endeavors. Research evidence is just beginning to emerge from smaller, regionally focused MOOC providers, and patterns of participation in that environment may be quite different. For instance, a recent study comparing learners in the Arab world taking HarvardX and MITx courses to learners enrolled with the Jordanian MOOC provider Edraak shows that learners in Edraak courses have better gender balance, include more people with lower levels of education, and have higher completion rates compared to their Arab counterparts on edX. A few specific features of Edraak may explain this success: their courses have instructors from Arab universities, are targeted to regional needs, and support the right-to-left writing of the Arabic language. It may be that MOOCs will be able to expand access to higher education if they are designed and hosted by institutions that support broad access to education as part of their core mission rather than by elite universities. This likely requires that governments and philanthropists make major investments in the public online offerings of colleges and universities with a proven track record of expanding access to higher education.

Terabytes of Data, Little New Insight

The servers of MOOC providers collect vast new sources of data about learning behavior from students around the globe. Every time a student submits a problem, clicks a new page, or starts or stops a video, a server records a log of the action. Researchers can then aggregate millions and millions of individual actions to study the complex patterns of learners across the world.

The third big bet of MOOCs was that these new sources of data—vaster, more global, and finer grained than almost anything ever collected by education researchers—would lead to new insights about how humans learn, both in general and online specifically. Despite considerable effort over many years trying to make this bet pay off, progress here has been disappointing.

Researchers have developed a variety of useful, policy-relevant findings about the MOOC enterprise, but this information is largely limited to descriptive evidence of MOOC learners, not *how* they learn. We know how many learners register, what background levels of education they have, what courses they take and complete, and so forth. These data are useful for understanding who might benefit from taking MOOCs, the value of MOOCs for postsecondary professional education, and how MOOCs might perpetuate inequality. But despite the efforts of a global network of researchers studying MOOCs, very little has been discovered about *learning* in MOOCs.[32]

I have jokingly summarized the bulk of MOOC learning research as proving Reich's Law: "People who do stuff do more stuff, and people who do stuff do better than people who don't do stuff." One of the earliest MOOC papers, by Jennifer Deboer and colleagues, involved taking every measure of behavior and outcome that they could think of (such as grades, number of problems answered, and time spent watching video) and correlating each of those measures in a giant matrix with every other measure in a MOOC. The central finding was that almost all of the measures were correlated—people who answered more problems were likely to watch more videos, people who watched more videos got higher grades, and so forth. That students who do more go on to learn more is not an insight requiring millions of dollars of research investment.[33]

It turns out that one can have terabytes of data about what people do online and very little understanding of what changes inside their heads. Rather than building lots of courses and hoping that data-driven insights appear downstream, a far more promising approach is to invest in online courses that are designed from the beginning not just for student learning but also for conducting research about learning. The Open Learning Initiative (OLI), from Carnegie Mellon University and Stanford, is one of the best examples of how we might pursue such a path.

The OLI, which predates the halcyon years of MOOCs, was an organization of researchers, instructors, and learning designers who created a set of openly licensed online courses in introductory topics like statistics and biology for use in traditional higher education settings. The OLI team also sought to demonstrate a methodology for course development that would advance research and student learning simultaneously. Open Learning Initiative course development was an iterative, multidisciplinary enterprise. The OLI team brought together experts in assessment, instructional design, course subject matter, and learning science. Collaboratively, the team identified key concepts, developed assessment items, and produced learning materials. Both assessment and learning materials were tagged using the key concepts such that assessment items could be connected with the relevant learning materials. As learners participated in the course, researchers examined assessment items to understand where students were performing well and where they were struggling, and they refined the instructional materials and assessments to continuously improve those outcomes.[34]

The development model for OLI courses is quite different from the development process for typical MOOCs, which are usually designed by a single professor with the support of one or two instructional technologists. Funding rarely supports upgrades to MOOCs once the course is completed. As a result, most MOOCs have tended to be transliterations of residential classes to online settings, with minimal improvements to take advantage of online tools and only modest improvements between runs of a course.

An OLI course costs at least an order of magnitude more to develop than a typical MOOC, but research results from this approach have been promising. Independent researchers used the OLI statistics course in a rigorous experiment in which students at six nonselective colleges were randomly assigned to take either a typical introduction to statistics course taught in a typical manner—in-person lectures, recitations, and so forth—or to take the online OLI statistics course with optional weekly recitations with an instructor. Students assigned to either condition did equally well on the final exam, but students in the OLI course reported spending 18 percent less time on the course than their counterparts in the in-person courses. For typical college students, the self-paced course developed their initial statistics fluency as well as a traditional lecture class, but required less time. Of the thousands of MOOCs that have been developed, virtually none has a research base supporting its effectiveness comparable to that of OLI.[35]

Tinkering with MOOCs in the Teaching Systems Lab

I have described a somewhat disappointing picture above—MOOCs primarily serve already-educated students in professional programs who already possess strong self-regulated learning skills, they have been absorbed into existing higher education systems rather than disrupting them, and we haven't learned much about learning from them.

Nonetheless, my colleagues and I in the MIT Teaching Systems Lab labor away at tinkering with new approaches to MOOCs, primarily about teacher and school leadership. In our field of K-12 professional education, the needs are vast; educators around the country are disappointed with the professional development they are offered, yet their success as teachers is intimately linked to the very future of the nation. We are working to create a new generation of open online learning that builds upon the successes and failures of the past. We offer courses such as Launching Innovation in Schools, Design Thinking for Leading and Learning, Envisioning the Graduate of the Future, and Becoming a More Equitable Educator that provide learners with the skills and inspiration to lead learning initiatives in their local schools.[36]

Our designs attend to findings from MOOC research. Our entire enterprise of serving teachers is premised on the research showing that already-educated professionals are among the groups best prepared for self-paced online learning. Since self-regulated learning remains a challenge for many learners, we do, however, encourage our participants to join "learning circles," small groups of educators at the same school taking the course together, and we provide facilitator guides and other resources to try to make collaboration easier. Since we know that most people who register for a course drop out soon after enrollment, we start our courses with short "capsule" units that summarize the most important ideas of the course. Our assessment and research efforts are focused not on course completion or clicks, but rather on whether our courses actually change the behavior of our educators when they are back in their classrooms. We follow our learners out in the field through surveys and interviews to understand whether and how they apply what they learn. We raise substantial funding to support interdisciplinary teams of designers, education experts, software developers, learning scientists, and evaluation researchers working together to make courses that simultaneously advance practice and research.

Our progress is mixed. As with many other MOOC developers, our course enrollment numbers are far smaller than what was common in the first years of the MOOC phenom; we have thousands rather than tens of thousands of registrants and hundreds rather than thousands of people who complete our courses. Like other MOOC providers, we find that our most committed learners have terrific learning experiences. Our learners report that our courses make a substantial difference in their professional practice and provide both the scaffolding and inspiration for them to successfully launch reform initiatives in their local contexts and to share what they have learned with colleagues. That's the good news. The bad news is that, heartbreakingly, inequalities continue to haunt us. While we serve teachers from all kinds of schools, our learners are disproportionately likely to come from independent or suburban schools serving affluent students. Perhaps we aren't offering the right courses or marketing in the right way to recruit learners serving the most vulnerable learners, or perhaps educators in well-resourced schools simply have more time and professional development support to take our courses. Social inequality is a tenacious feature of educational systems.[37]

The Troubling Recent History of Instructor-Guided Learning at Scale in K-12

Thus far in this chapter, I have focused on higher education and lifelong learning because K-12 institutions have mostly avoided instructor-guided, large-scale learning environments. My intuition is that K-12 educators (and parents and school boards) recognize the inherently social nature of learning as well as the limits of young people's self-regulated learning skills, so school systems rarely adopt technology-based systems like MOOCs that try to entirely bypass teacher-student relationships.

Where K–12 systems have adopted models that look like MOOCs, the results have generally been disastrous, particularly for students in poverty-impacted communities. Two places where self-paced online learning have found their way into K–12 education have been virtual schools and credit-recovery programs for students at risk of failing to graduate. Full-time virtual schools offer an option for students who cannot or choose not to attend traditional schools. They have served a subset of learners reasonably well—the very ill, the bullied, athletes, artists, and homeschooling families that want a more structured curriculum. On average, however, learning results from virtual schools are quite poor—often worse than the weakest results from the most struggling traditional schools—and they are least effective at serving learners most impacted by poverty. Online credit recovery programs typically take students who have recently failed in a traditional classroom and try to have them pass a course independently online, and these also have a very poor track record. The most effective self-paced online courses in K–12 are those providing advanced learning experiences to successful secondary-school students, such as those in rural areas where access to advanced courses may be limited. For the oldest, most successful students who have already developed the kind of self-regulated learning skills that self-paced online learning requires, instructor-guided online learning environments might be a valuable resource. Overall, though, K–12 educators should use caution in putting students, especially those who have struggled academically, in self-paced online learning environments.[38]

Two more common models used in K–12 schools have been adaptive tutoring programs, which I discuss at length in the next chapter, and online platforms that have some opportunities for self-paced learning but are intended as a learning resource within classrooms with typical teacher-student ratios. Probably the most well-known of these latter offerings is the Summit Learning Platform, developed by a charter school network in northern California. Like a MOOC, Summit Learning is an LMS with learning content for typical middle and high school courses. Unlike MOOCs though, students are not expected to progress entirely on their own. Students are meant to spend part of their school day independently clicking through lessons, but the system has a variety of checkpoints and reports that are meant to encourage students to connect with their teachers for coaching, small group lessons, projects, and so forth. The platform has been used very successfully within the Summit charter schools to foster more independent learning by students. As Summit has exported the platform around the country, the results have been more mixed, and research remains nascent and inconclusive; some schools report that teachers and students are very happy with the program, and some implementations have been disasters, with family protests and student walkouts. My hunch is that when schools with strong student-teacher relationships, coaching, and mentorship use Summit Learning like a textbook, as one resource among many, then it becomes an age-appropriate way to start fostering independent learning. In schools where educators use Summit Learning like a MOOC to be completed independently, they generate an additional point of evidence that for learning to be successful, most young people (and most adults, too) require robust social supports from teachers and peers.[39]

The Future of MOOCs and Instructor-Guided Learning at Scale

My bumper-sticker summary of the MOOC enterprise is that "MOOCs are good for helping people pursue a second or third degree." In the years ahead, I predict that MOOC efforts and investment will be targeted at learners seeking a master's degree or a professional certificate, mostly in technical fields such as computing or accounting. Rather than becoming on-ramps into higher education for populations at the margins, MOOC providers will create opportunities for learners who already have self-regulated learning skills and stable financial situations to pursue additional instructor-guided, self-paced online learning.

Another way to summarize the MOOC phenomenon is to return to the construct of the iron triangle of cost, access, and quality. When MOOC providers tried to lift the access barriers of cost by recording lectures and replacing teachers with autograders and discussion forums, their new systems enacted a new tacit barrier: the requirement for MOOC learners to have preexisting, well-developed, self-regulated learning skills. Since most people develop these skills through an apprenticeship in formal education, the evidence to date suggests that cost savings and quality learning will probably accrue primarily to already-affluent, already-educated professional learners. Most learners require support and human contact that are unavailable in MOOCs, and provisioning that human support would raise costs and erase the financial "benefit" of automating faculty labor. The triangle is called "iron" for a reason.[40]

Other futures for MOOCs are certainly possible. For MOOCs to fulfill the original mission of broadening access to higher education, perhaps the best MOOC designers will be faculty not from elite universities but from the public universities with the strongest track records of advancing social mobility—the very best instructors for Introduction to Biology might be at University of California, Irvine, or in the City University of New York system rather than in the Ivy League. Deep research insight and practitioner wisdom is also available from institutions like the Open University that have been offering distance education for decades. In 2013, Patrick McAndrew and Eileen Scanlon published advice for the MOOC enterprise in *Science* magazine that would still be worth heeding today: the MOOCs that are most likely to substantially advance our understanding of effective online learning will require interdisciplinary teams tinkering over multiple years and committed to research and continuous improvement.[41] For MOOCs to serve populations beyond the already educated, there will need to be substantial support for the social elements of learning—coaching, advising, peer support, and so forth. All of these efforts will require seeing MOOCs not as a technological solution to a complex social problem, but as one element of a comprehensive solution. A daunting challenge to be sure, but one commensurate with the vast global hunger for access to education.

2

ALGORITHM-GUIDED LEARNING AT SCALE

Adaptive Tutors and Computer-Assisted Instruction

ON EVERY CONTENT PAGE of an edX MOOC there are two buttons: "Next" and "Previous." The MOOC's instructional-design staff organizes course content into a linear sequence of pages, and every learner—novice or expert, confused or confident—who clicks the "Next" button will be moved to the following page in that sequence. It's one-size-fits-all learning at a massive scale. This chapter examines an alternative to instructor pacing: large-scale learning environments where the sequencing of content is determined by algorithmic assignment rather than by instructor designation. In algorithm-guided learning, the next action in a sequence is determined by a student's performance on a previous action rather than by a preset pathway defined by instructors. The tools in this genre go by many names; I'll call them adaptive tutors or computer-assisted instruction (CAI).

Earlier, I introduced Khan Academy, a free online resource with instructional materials in many subjects. Khan Academy is best known for its online explainer videos, but in K–12 schools, the majority of student time using Khan Academy is spent on math practice problems. Teachers assign (or students choose) a domain for study, such as "evaluating expressions with one variable," and then students are presented with a series of problems. These problems are instantly recognizable to anyone who has ever completed a worksheet. A mathematical expression is in the center of the screen, and below is an answer box for numerical answers (some questions have multiple-choice answers or allow for marking points on a Cartesian plane). There are links to video explainers and hints for each problem, and then there is a "Check Answer" button. When users get an answer right, there are pop-ups with stars, bings, and firework animations. When users get an answer wrong, they can try again, get hints, or move on. When students get problems right, the system assigns harder problems from the same domain, and when students get problems wrong, the system assigns easier problems. When students get enough problems correct, the system encourages students to move on to a new domain. Students who log into a user profile can also be assigned practice problems from older material to promote retention through retrieval practice, and teachers who register their classes can track student performance.

Imagine you are a K–12 school principal, and parents, faculty, and school board members are reading stories in *Time, Wired,* and *Forbes* about how Khan Academy is poised to change the world. Clayton Christensen has declared these new technologies to be a "disruptive innovation," a disjunction between an inferior past and a better future. Adopting adaptive tutors across a grade, a department, or an entire school would constitute a major initiative, requiring investing in hardware, scheduling computer lab or laptop cart times, selecting software, training teachers, communicating with parents and family, and tinkering with many other elements in the complex ecology of a school. As a principal, if you chose to invest your energy in this initiative, the opportunity cost would be all of the other initiatives that you chose not to take up.[1] You'd also want to be confident that introducing adaptive tutors would actually improve learning outcomes, especially for the students who are struggling the most. How do you decide whether implementing adaptive tutors is the best possible bet for your students and community?

School leaders facing these kinds of decisions about technology-based innovations should ask four sets of questions. The first order of business is to understand the basics of how the technology works as a learning tool: What is the pedagogical model? What are the fundamental principles of the underlying technology? Some educational technologists pushing their product may try to convince you that their technology is new, complex, and hard to understand. Demystifying the technology is the first step to understanding how it may or may not work for your students in your school.

The second task is to investigate how similar technologies have been integrated into schools elsewhere. Some of these questions should be about nuts and bolts: How much do teachers and students actually use the technology after it has been purchased? What kinds of changes in schedule, curriculum, physical plant, and other school elements must be adopted to make the new technology-mediated practices work?

After understanding how the technology works and how it might be integrated into schools, a third step is to investigate what the accumulated research evidence says about which kinds of schools and students are most likely to benefit from a new approach. Do these tools benefit learners on average? How do impacts differ between high- and low-achieving students, or between more-affluent and less-affluent students? In MOOCs, answering these questions was challenging because the research on large-scale, self-paced online learning has been relatively sparse. By contrast, there are dozens of high-quality studies that examine how adaptive tutors affect learner outcomes in the K–12 context that can inform a principal's judgment.

These first three questions are about average effects: What do we know about how the technology has been implemented across many kinds of schools? The final task for the principal (or school board member, or superintendent, or department head) is to consider all this history and evidence in the light of one particular, idiosyncratic school: yours. What are the unique features of your school, your faculty, your students, your community that might abet or thwart efforts to make a technology adoption of adaptive tutors a success?

If the evidence base for adaptive tutors suggested that they substantially benefited all students in all subjects in all contexts, this would be an easy question to answer (full speed ahead!). Unfortunately, as I will describe below, the track record of algorithm-guided technologies is not nearly so clear. Some evidence from some contexts suggests that they can be moderately helpful in some subjects, but many implementations of these technologies have shown null or even negative effects. This unevenness comes from a variety of sources. Schools are complex places, and factors like technology availability or teachers' willingness to adopt new practices play a role in determining the efficacy of the initiative. Furthermore, adaptive-tutoring technologies are well developed only in a few subject areas, including math and early reading, so a push toward adaptive learning can only benefit this limited subset of the curriculum. And students from different backgrounds have different experiences and outcomes with new technologies. All this complexity and nuance means that for a principal to answer the most important question—Will adaptive tutors help my students in my school?—the best place to start is by investigating the origins of CAI and understanding the pedagogy, technical underpinnings, and values of this approach.

Computer-Based Instruction, Sixty Years in the Making

In most K–12 schools, the day is organized around class periods of fixed length, and each class period is assigned to a single topic. On a given day, a student will spend forty-seven minutes learning to factor polynomials, whether the student needs 17 minutes or 107 minutes to learn the topic. For those seeking to maximize individual student learning, the inefficiencies here are stark: some students spend the majority of class bored and not learning anything new, and others leave class without having mastered the requisite material that will be necessary for learning in subsequent lessons.

One solution is to tutor every child so that all children receive the amount and type of instruction best suited for their intellectual development. In a now famous 1984 research paper, "The 2 Sigma Problem," Benjamin Bloom published results from two doctoral dissertations comparing students who were randomly assigned to learn in one of three conditions: a traditional classroom setting, a one-on-one tutoring condition, or a third condition called "mastery learning," in which students received additional instruction and practice on concepts that they struggled with. Bloom argued that the students in the one-on-one tutoring condition performed two standard deviations (2 sigma) better on a unit post-test than students in the classroom condition. If a typical student in the classroom condition would be at the fiftieth percentile, then a typical student in the tutoring treatment would be at the ninety-eighth percentile. Thus, Bloom and his colleagues used the full machinery of modern social science to argue what medieval lords knew: that tutoring, while expensive, worked quite well. Bloom's article became a call to action to design educational approaches that could achieve the kinds of gains that could be achieved with one-on-one tutoring. One of Bloom's suggestions was to explore "whether particular computer courses enable sizable proportions of students to attain the 2-sigma achievement effect."[2]

By the time Bloom published this suggestion in 1984, computer scientists and researchers had been working on this challenge for over two decades. Since the very first days of computer technologies, computer scientists have sought to use computers as individualized tutors for students. In 1968, R. C. Atkinson and H. A. Wilson wrote in *Science* that "ten years ago the use of computers as an instructional device was only an idea being considered by a handful of scientists and educators. Today that idea has become a reality."[3]

Among the first computer-based teaching systems was the Programmed Logic for Automatic Teaching Operations, or PLATO, developed in 1960 at the University of Illinois Urbana-Champaign. In 1967, with the development of the TUTOR programming language, PLATO formalized several innovations essential to the future of CAI, including automated assessment and branching.[4]

Problems in TUTOR included a minimum of a question and a correct answer, but the language also allowed for complex answer banks and different feedback for right and wrong answers. In the 1969 guide to the language, one of the first examples presents a student with a picture of the *Mona Lisa* and then asks the student to name the artist. The correct answer, "Leonardo da Vinci," produces the response, "Your answer tells me that you are a true Renaissance man." The incomplete answer "Leonardo" produces the prompt, "The complete name is Leonardo da Vinci." A blank entry provokes a hint: "HINT—MONA LISA—HINT." Any of the correct answers drives students to a subsequent unit in the lesson sequence, on the artist Rubens, but the incorrect answer "Michelangelo" takes students to MREVIEW, a review unit.

Here we see some of the crucial features of CAI. Lesson sequences were organized around a series of instructional units that both presented content and tested student recall or understanding. Students were given different feedback based on their responses, and the system was designed such that when students provided incorrect answers, they could be given different learning experiences to remediate different kinds of problems. These systems required that curriculum authors manually sequence each problem and learning experience, telling the computer how to address wrong answers, what feedback to give, and which problems were easier or harder.

In the five decades following the initial development of the TUTOR programming language, there were two critical advances that brought adaptive-tutoring systems to the forefront of education reform debate and dialogue in the twenty-first century. The first innovation was statistical. Starting in the 1970s, psychometricians (statisticians who study educational testing) developed an approach called *item response theory* to create a mathematical model of the relative difficulty of a question, problem, or test item. These quantitative representations of learning experiences paved the way for computers to automatically generate testing and learning sequences that could adapt to the performance of individual students rather than having to manually program branches as in the TUTOR example above. Nearly all contemporary adaptive-tutoring systems use variations on this forty-year-old statistical toolkit.

The second innovation was rhetorical. In the late 2000s, education reformers developed an interlocking pair of narratives about "personalized learning" and "disruptive innovation" that explained why and how Bloom's vision of computerized tutors for every child could be brought into reality. The most ambitious blueprints to put personalized learning at the center of students' school experience called for a dramatic reorganization of schooling institutions. Students would spend less time in face-to-face, whole-class instruction and more time working individually with adaptive learning software. Teachers might spend more time coaching individual students or working with small groups, and supervision of students working on software could be done by paraprofessionals. These models called for new schedules, new teaching roles, and new learning spaces. Very few schools adopted these personalized learning blueprints in any substantial way, and the predictions of transformation based on the theory of disruptive innovation proved incorrect, but these new rhetorical devices help explain why adaptive tutors experienced a surge of interest in the 2000s.[5]

Technical Foundations for Algorithm-Guided Learning at Scale: Item Response Theory

Few edtech evangelists of the twenty-first century can match Jose Ferreira for bravado and exaggeration in describing new educational technologies. Ferreira wanted educators and investors to believe that algorithm-guided learning technologies were unfathomably complicated. (Contrary to Ferreira's assertions, the important elements of nearly every education technology are, with a little bit of study and research, comprehensible.)

Ferreira founded Knewton, a company that tried to offer "adaptive learning as a service." Most publishers and start-ups offering adaptive learning have implemented their own algorithmic-based systems in their own platforms. Knewton offered to do this technical development for publishers. Publishers could generate textbooks and assessment banks, and then Knewton would handle turning those assessments into CAI systems.

Ferreira described his technology in magical terms: "We think of it like a robot tutor in the sky that can semi-read your mind and figure out what your strengths and weaknesses are, down to the percentile." The robot tutor in the sky was powered by data; Ferreira claimed that Knewton collected 5 to 10 million data points per student per day. "We literally have more data about our students than any company has about anybody else about anything," Ferreira said. "And it's not even close."[6]

These claims, however, were nonsense. If you have ever sat in a computer lab watching students—some engaged, some bored—click or type their way through an adaptive tutor, you will have seen quite clearly that students are not generating millions of useful data points as they answer a few dozen problems.[7] But Ferreira's was a particular kind of nonsense: an attempt to convince educators, investors, and other education stakeholders that Knewton's technologies were a disjunctive break with the past, a new order emerging. The truth was something much more mundane. While Ferreira made claims of unprecedented scale and complexity in Knewton promotional material, Knewton engineers were publishing blog posts with titles like "Understanding Student Performance with Item Response Theory." In one post, engineers declared, "At Knewton, we've found IRT models to be extremely helpful when trying to understand our students' abilities by examining their test performance." Lift up the hood of the magical robot tutor, and underneath was a forty-year-old technology powering the whole operation.[8]

In the 1970s, researchers at Education Testing Service developed a statistical toolkit called item response theory (IRT) that would eventually allow computer algorithms to generate customized sequences of problems and learning experiences for individual students. Item response theory was originally designed not for adaptive tutors but to solve a basic problem in test design. When testing large numbers of students, consumers of testing data (admissions offices, employers, policymakers) would like to be able to compare two students tested on the same material. Testing companies, however, would prefer not to test all students on the exact same material, since using identical test items and formats with different students in different places and times opens the door to cheating and malfeasance. Rather than giving students the exact same test, therefore, test makers would prefer to give students different tests that assess the same topics at the same level of difficulty, allowing results to be compared fairly. Doing so requires a model of the difficulty of each question on the tests. To understand how these models work, we'll need to do a bit of math (graphing logistic curves, to be precise).[9]

In IRT, every test question or problem—in psychometric parlance, an *item*—is modeled as an S-shaped curve called a logistic function. These S-curves start at the origin (0,0) in a Cartesian plane, start ascending slowly up and to the right, then ascend more quickly, and then ascend more slowly as they approach an asymptote, making them look like a stretched out "S." Logistic curves always go up and always follow these S-shaped patterns because of the way that they are mathematically defined ($f(x) = \dfrac{L}{1 + e^{(-k(x - x_0))}}$ for those inclined to remember their algebra).

In these models, the x axis represents the ability of a student in a particular domain (for example, recognizing Chinese characters or multiplying single-digit numbers), and the y axis represents the probability that a student at a given level of ability will get an item correct. On an S-curve, values of y—probability of getting an answer correct—are low at low levels of student ability (on the left side of the x axis) and are high at high levels of student ability (on the right side of the x axis). Psychometricians summarize the difficulty of any item by describing the level of student ability where the S-curve crosses the point where 50 percent of students are predicted to get the item correct. When item developers make a new item, they have to guess to set the initial parameters of these S-curve models (how quickly they ascend up and down and how far to the right they stretch), but then these models can be dynamically updated as they are piloted and used in the field. If lots of students who are highly skilled in a domain (as measured by other items) answer an item incorrectly, then its difficulty can be revised upward.

Those are the basics of item response theory, and even if your memory of logistics curves is a little fuzzy, your takeaway should be that IRT does nothing more than create a mathematical model (an S-curve) of the difficulty of an item. Test makers use these models to make equivalently difficult versions of the same test. For developers of computer-assisted instructional systems, IRT and its variants make it possible for a computer program to assign an appropriate item in a sequence based on the student's answers to the previous item (or a recent sequence of answers). Since computers have a model of the difficulty of each item in an item bank, when learners get an item right, the system can assign a slightly harder item, and when learners get an item wrong, the system can assign an easier item. Instead of humans manually creating branching instructional activities, as with the early TUTOR programming language examples, computers can algorithmically generate instructional sequences and continuously improve them based on student responses.[10]

These algorithm-guided large-scale learning technologies are decades old. Knewton, then, was not a magical new technology; rather, it offered one business innovation (adaptive learning as a back-end service rather than a product feature) on top of a very well-established set of learning technologies. My hope is that seeing the basic functioning and long history of a complex technology like adaptive tutors will help education stakeholders understand that new technologies are both comprehensible and historically rooted. If we can situate a new technology in its history, we can make predictions about how that new technology will function when integrated into the complex ecology of schools.

In education technology, extreme claims are usually the sign of a charlatan rather than an impending breakthrough. Knewton failed. Ferreira left Knewton in 2016, and soon after, the company hired a former publishing executive as its CEO and pivoted to publishing its own textbooks with adaptive practice problems. In 2019, the company was sold to publisher Wiley in a fire sale. Like Udacity, which became a provider of technical certificate programs, and Coursera, which became an online program manager, Knewton began with dramatic claims about transforming teaching and learning, raised vast venture funds, and within a few years pursued well-trodden pathways to financial sustainability that fit easily into existing educational systems.[11]

Even if Knewton wasn't effective as a provider of learning experiences, it was for a time extremely effective in deploying narratives about change to raise incredible sums of venture capital funding (a process that technology commentator Maciej Cegłowski calls "investor storytime"). These narratives about how technology can transform archaic, traditional educational systems were central to the surge of venture and philanthropic investments in adaptive tutors in the first two decades of the twenty-first century.[12]

Rhetoric of Transformation: Personalized Learning and Disruptive Innovation

In 2010, references to "personalized learning" began appearing at education conferences and in trade magazines. Computers had been in schools in various forms for decades by this point, but suddenly, the narrative of personalized learning was everywhere. For CAI enthusiasts, personalization meant that each child would be able to spend part or all of her day proceeding through technology-mediated learning experiences at her own pace. Students would sit at computer terminals using software that algorithmically optimized student pathways through a set of standardized curriculum material. Teachers would be available for coaching and small group instruction, particularly when software flagged individual students or groups as requiring additional supports.[13]

One challenge that the CAI enthusiasts had in advancing their vision was that it was fairly easy to characterize extreme versions of the model as dystopian: children wearing headphones sitting in cubicles staring at screens all day long. So CAI advocates sometimes argued that CAI approaches could save classroom time for more project-based learning. In the early years of Khan Academy, Salman Khan suggested that mathematics education could be transformed in a series of steps: (1) schools would adopt Khan Academy's free math resources; (2) each student could then pursue a personalized mathematics learning trajectory that allowed him or her to proceed at his or her own pace; and (3) with all the classroom time saved through personalized CAI, collaborative activities in math could focus on rich, real-world, project-based learning exercises. The idea was that if students learned the facts and basics of mathematics faster with technology, then they would have more time to do interesting projects and team-based work. As Khan said in 2019, "If Khan Academy can start taking on some of the foundational practice and instruction, it should hopefully liberate the teachers and class time to do more higher-order tasks."[14]

This argument has deep roots among CAI advocates; historian Audrey Watters found a variation of this argument made in 1959 by Simon Ramo, who like Khan was a businessman (vice president of the firm that developed the intercontinental ballistic missile) turned education technology advocate. As Ramo wrote in "A New Technique in Education," his 1959 CAI manifesto, "The whole objective of everything that I will describe is to raise the teacher to a higher level in his contribution to the teaching process and to remove from his duties the kind of effort which does not use the teacher's skill to the fullest."[15] Thus, the rhetoric of personalized learning made two grand claims: that adaptive tutors would be more efficient at teaching students mastery of key concepts and that this efficiency would enable teachers to carry out rich project-based instruction.

If personalized learning provided the vision for what schools could look like, the theory of disruptive innovation provided a blueprint for how technology innovations would inevitably lead to school change. In 2008, Clayton Christensen, Curtis Johnson, and Michael Horn published a book called *Disrupting Class* that argued that online education and CAI represented a new kind of disruptive innovation in education. The theory of disruptive innovation argues that, periodically, innovations come along that may be low quality in some dimensions but offer low cost and novel features. The Sony Walkman's sound quality was much worse than contemporary hi-fi systems, but it was relatively cheap and you could walk around with it; it appealed particularly to "non-consumers," people who were unlikely to buy expensive hi-fi systems, like those of us who were teens and tweens in the 1980s. Christensen and colleagues argued that online education was one such disruptive innovation that would eventually revolutionize education in the same way that the Walkman or iTunes revolutionized music and media.[16]

In *Disrupting Class,* the authors made three predictions about how online learning would reshape K–12 education. They predicted that by 2019, half of all secondary courses would be mostly or entirely online, that the cost of providing these courses would be about a third the cost of traditional classes, and that the quality of these online courses would be higher. Disruption, the theorists argued, often catches established stakeholders unaware, because early in their existence, disruptive innovations are obviously deficient in certain dimensions—like sound quality in a Walkman or the quality of the learning experience in online schools. But disruptive innovations are supposed to improve rapidly in both established dimensions and novel ones, so Christensen and colleagues argued that as online learning was rapidly adopted, it would quickly prove superior to existing educational models.

Christensen and colleagues argued that these disruptive processes could be predicted with precision. They claimed that adoption of disruptive innovations historically followed an S-shaped logistic curve, and a feature of logistic curves is that when plotted against log-transformed x and y axes, the S-curve becomes a linear straight line. If early adoption patterns followed this log-transformed linear model precisely—and the *Disrupting Class* authors argued that data on online course adoption showed that it did—then a new technology could be definitively identified as disruptive, and the timing of its adoption could be predicted with some precision. Their models showed that the adaptive online learning curve would pass the midpoint of adoption by 2019, at which point, 50 percent of all secondary school courses in the United States would be conducted through customized, personalized online software. In this model of disruption, schools could choose to be early adopters or late adopters, but progress and change were inevitable.

Personalized Learning: An Unrequited Disruption

Theories of personalized learning and disruptive innovation offer models of how schools might be dramatically transformed by algorithm-guided learning technologies—though one is challenged to find any school in which this grand vision of transformation actually occurred. It was something of a Rube Goldberg plan; to get better and deeper project-based learning, schools should buy computers, buy CAI software, train teachers on their use, reallocate time to individualized computer-based instruction, and then, when all of that was working, use additional time for projects. Schools are complex places, and they are not typically successful at implementing multipart schemes to improve learning. It is not surprising, then, that CAI did not remake education in the way predicted by true CAI enthusiasts.

Furthermore, the theory of disruptive innovation, the guiding force behind the bold predictions in *Disrupting Class,* has come under substantial critique. In 2014, Harvard historian Jill Lepore presented one of the most damning appraisals of the theory. In a piece published in the *New Yorker,* Lepore argued that the theory was based on idiosyncratically selected case studies of individual industries and circumstances, weak foundations on which to build new theories. Disruption theory evangelists disregard case studies showing contrary examples, and theorists observe disruption in hindsight but struggle to accurately use the theory to predict future changes (an unfortunate quality for a business management theory). Lepore

showed that many of the companies presented as laggardly dino-
saurs in Christensen's original tome, *The Innovator's Dilemma,* are
happily dominating their industries decades later. Both Lepore and
Audrey Watters have observed that disruption theory appears to
draw as much on millenarian narratives of struggle and redemp-
tion as it does from empirical evidence: the death of old worlds
trapped in old ways, reformed and reborn by the revelation of new
technologies.[17]

In the field of online learning, there is no evidence that the core
predictions from *Disrupting Class* have come to pass by 2020. The
data on online course enrollment by secondary school students are
incomplete, but no data suggest that secondary schools are even
close to provisioning 50 percent of their courses through adaptive
online offerings. In 2018, there were about 57 million children in US
pre-K–12 schools (40 million in pre-K–8, and 17 million in high
school), and only 430,000 students enrolled in fully online or
blended schools—about 0.75 percent. No evidence suggests that traditional US high schools have made substantial adoptions of online or blended offerings that would allow 50 percent of all courses
to be taken in online or blended forms.

Nor is there evidence that online education has become one-third
less expensive to provision than traditional education. In my home
state of Massachusetts, I sat for six years on the state's Digital
Learning Advisory Council to provide policy guidance on the state's
two K–12 virtual schools. In 2010, the state required school districts
to pay a tuition of $6,700 for each student who chose to attend one
of these virtual schools, which was about two-thirds of the state's
formula for per-pupil expenditures ($10,774). In 2018, the two virtual
schools requested a funding increase, and the state set the new
funding at $8,265, which was the state formula less estimated costs
for operating buildings. Rather than reducing costs as virtual
schools in Massachusetts expanded enrollment, virtual school
leaders argued that virtual schooling should cost about the same

as traditional education. Limited research exists in other states, but it does not appear that good virtual schooling can be provisioned for one-third the cost of traditional schooling. And as was noted at the end of Chapter 1 on instructor-paced learning at scale, learning outcomes for fully online schools are generally dismal. As we shall see in the rest of this chapter, the evidence on adaptive tutors implemented within K–12 schools is complex and somewhat more promising, but mainly in certain areas of mathematics instruction.[18]

Adaptive Tutors in K–12 Schools: Mathematics and Early Reading

Grand visions of disruption and transformation did not come to pass, but adaptive tutors have found two more modest niches in K–12 schools: providing supplemental practice for mathematics and for early reading. A confluence of factors is responsible for the limited role of adaptive tutors in schools, including the costs of computing infrastructure and mixed evidence of efficacy. Probably the most important limit, however, is technological. For adaptive tutors to assign a sequence of problems and learning resources to students, the system has to measure the performance of students regularly and automatically. The core technology of adaptive tutors is an IRT-powered assignment algorithm paired with an autograder. As we observed in Chapter 1 on MOOCs and will explore further in Chapter 7 on assessment technologies, the state of the art in autograders is quite limited. Autograders work reasonably well in mathematics, where quantitative answers can be computationally evaluated. In a few domains of early reading, they can be useful as well—testing students' ability to match sounds with letters (phonics), identifying basic vocabulary, or doing simple translations when learning a foreign language. Reading instructors sometimes discuss a transition, which happens in about the third grade, from learning to read—learning how to decode the sounds and meaning of text—to reading to learn—using reading to advance content knowledge. Generally speaking, the autograders of adaptive tutors have some applications in learning to read, but very limited applications in reading to learn. When educators need to evaluate whether students can reason based on the evidence provided in a text, autograders typically cannot effectively evaluate the quality of student reasoning.

These two subject domains of mathematics and early reading also overlap with a substantial portion of the standardized testing infrastructure in the United States. As high-stakes testing has spread throughout the United States since the 1990s, educational publishers have invested more in developing resources for tested subjects than non-tested subjects. The reasoning goes something like this: because schools are more likely to purchase products and services related to tested subjects like reading and math, and because autograding technologies work best in reading and math, publishers have generally focused on creating adaptive tutors in reading and math. (As we shall see in Chapter 7 on assessments, this alignment is not coincidental but instead part of a powerful feedback loop; standardized test developers have access to the same autograding technology as educational publishers, so our testing infrastructure evaluates domains like reading and math where autograders work best; then schools emphasize those subjects, publishers create products for those subjects, policymakers evaluate schools on those subjects, and the system becomes mutually reinforcing.)

Do Adaptive Tutors Improve Student Learning?

Adaptive learning tools for reading and mathematics have been researched extensively over the last thirty years, and the results are mixed at best. Two groups of researchers have conducted most of this research. The first group are the computer scientists, learning scientists, and CAI researchers who developed these systems. A second group are economists of education, who are typically interested in the return on investment for different educational interventions. The interest of CAI researchers is obvious: they want to know if their innovations improve student learning. To the credit of the CAI community, many CAI products have been regularly scrutinized through studies in which the CAI software companies help with implementation of the software and teacher training, but independent third-party organizations conduct the research evaluation. An easy way to tell if an edtech developer is serious about improving learning and not just hoping to extract dollars from the education system is to see how they participate in research studies with a real chance of showing that their products do not work. Economists of education are often interested in innovations that have the potential to substantially change educational practice at large scales, and they are interested in labor issues; computers that can do some of the work of teachers tick both boxes.

Over the past thirty years, there have been hundreds of studies about adaptive tutors in K–12 schools, allowing researchers to conduct meta-analyses (research studies that investigate trends across multiple studies). Through the early 2010s, the general consensus of economists and other education policy experts was that CAI should not be considered a reliable approach for improving student learning in math or reading. This conclusion was based on evidence from numerous large-scale randomized controlled field trials conducted in the 1990s and early 2000s; such trials are the best research methods we have to determine whether or not a pedagogical approach improves learning in typical school settings (as opposed to in research labs or special cases). Some of these studies showed a positive effect, some a null effect (no impact), and some a negative effect. The meta-analyses of these field trials suggest that on average, adaptive reading tutors do not lead to better reading test scores than traditional instruction. Meta-analytic findings about math CAI approaches have been more mixed; some meta-analyses found average null results and others found modestly positive effects for math CAI. In one meta-analysis, researchers argued that adaptive math tutors overall had a small positive effect on students but that they benefited students from the general population more than low-achieving math students. They warned that "computerized learning might contribute to the achievement gap between students with different achievement levels and aptitudes." This study provides some evidence of the edtech Matthew effect that will be discussed in Chapter 6.[19]

Even within studies that show an average effect of zero, there can still be considerable variation in how adaptive tutors effect change in individual schools or classrooms. An average effect of zero can happen when nobody's learning changes, or it can happen when some students experience large positive effects and some experience large negative effects, which cancel each other out. In his doctoral research, Eric Taylor, now on the faculty at the Harvard Graduate School of Education, articulated a version of this argument. He observed in a meta-analysis that the average learning gains of classrooms using CAI and classrooms not using CAI were about the same. But among teachers using CAI, the variance of learning gains from teacher to teacher was lower than the variance among teachers not using CAI. Put another way, the difference in learning outcomes from classroom to classroom for teachers not using CAI is rather large: some classes do very well, some very poorly. When teachers use CAI, the difference between the classes that do well and the classes that do poorly is smaller. Why should this be?[20]

Nearly all CAI implementations follow some kind of blended model, where human educators teach class for part of the time (usually a few days a week), and students work individually with computers during the other part of the time. In contrast, the traditional model of math instruction involves teacher-led whole-group instruction followed by individual practice problems without feedback.

Taylor argued that for the weakest teachers in the system, replacing one or two days a week of their instruction with individual time on computers improved outcomes for students—that time on computers was a boon for students who had the weakest teachers. By contrast, for the strongest teachers in the system, replacing part of their instruction led to worse outcomes; for their students, the time on computers took away from valuable time with a proficient instructor. This one study shouldn't be considered dispositive, but it provides an intriguing hypothesis for the effects of CAI on instruction and some real puzzles for implementation, which we'll come to soon.

Two Recent Studies of Adaptive Math Tutors with Positive Results

Two of the largest experimental field trials of adaptive tutors, Cognitive Tutor and ASSISTments, have occurred since the meta-analyses of the early 2010s, and these two studies showed much better outcomes for student learning than would have been predicted based on the history of CAI in schools. Both studies were conducted by reputable third-party researchers funded by the federal government, and they showed substantial positive effects for CAI in math classrooms.

In 2014, the RAND corporation released a study investigating the use of Carnegie Learning's Cognitive Tutor: Algebra in seventy-three high schools and seventy-four middle schools in seven US states. Cognitive Tutor emerged from three decades of research at Carnegie Mellon University, and it is among the most widely adopted CAI systems and among the most closely researched. In the RAND study, a large number of schools agreed to adopt Cognitive Tutor: Algebra, and then half of those schools were randomly assigned to get the CAI software and professional development support; the other half continued with business as usual. Carnegie Learning encourages teachers to spend three days a week doing regular whole-class instruction in which the pace of the class roughly matches the pace of a typical algebra class. Then, two days a week, students use the Cognitive Tutor: Algebra program for individualized practice; in these sessions, students are supposed to work through the material at their own pace. Thus, in a five-day week, students receive both in-person, group instruction and supplemental personalized computer practice provided by intelligent tutors.[21]

John Pane lead the RAND team evaluating test score data from the experiment. He and his colleagues found no effect of CAI in the first year of implementation in a new school, which they characterize as an "innovator's dip." They argued that it takes schools about a year to figure out how to productively integrate new tools into their math teaching routines. In the second year, they saw positive, statistically significant improvements in learning outcomes among ninth graders using the program (they saw more modest, positive, not statistically significant effects among eighth graders).

Describing learning gains in education research is a tricky business, and the shorthand references that researchers and policymakers use can often be confusing. The most common measure of an intervention's effect on learning is called the effect size, which is the average change in assessed outcomes in standard deviation units. Using a standard deviation unit allows comparisons across different interventions with different tests, different scales, and so forth. In the RAND study of Cognitive Tutor: Algebra, in the control condition without any CAI technology, the average student gain between pre- and post-tests after a year of learning was about 0.2 standard deviations. In the experimental condition, researchers found a 0.2 effect size in the second year of the study, meaning that on average, those students experienced a 0.4 standard deviation gain from pre-test to post-test. We could think of the 0.2 standard deviation growth in the control group as the baseline amount of learning that typically occurs in an algebra classroom, so getting an additional effect size of 0.2 standard deviations of test score gains from

CAI meant that students in the treatment group were seeing twice as much learning gains as a typical student. (Another way to frame the magnitude of the effect is that students in the fiftieth percentile in the control group would be, on average, in the fifty-eighth percentile if assigned to the treatment group.)

As may be apparent from the previous paragraph, effect sizes and standard deviations are difficult to parse, so researchers have tried using months or years of learning as a measure—taking a standard measure of average learning gains and translating that to one year, or nine months, of learning; in the case of the RAND study, 0.2 standard deviation represents a "year of learning." Since an additional effect size of 0.2 standard deviation, then, represents an "additional year of learning," the Carnegie Learning website claimed that Cognitive Tutor: Algebra doubled students' learning. One important clarification is that no one is claiming that students learned two years of material in one year. Rather, students showed performance gains in Algebra I post-tests as if they had studied for eighteen months in a traditional control setting instead of nine months, assuming a consistent rate of learning per month. Students assigned to Cognitive Tutors learned the Algebra I curriculum twice as well, as measured by standardized tests, as typical students, but they did not learn Algebra I and an additional year of math.[22]

These average effect sizes mask the great variation in effectiveness across schools. In some middle schools, students assigned to use Cognitive Tutor saw gains even greater than the 0.2 standard deviation average, and some saw gains that were much smaller. After the RAND study, Carnegie Learning researchers looked more deeply into the data to try to explain this variation, and they found that learning outcomes were better in schools where teachers most fully allowed students to proceed on practice problems at their own pace, even if that meant that sometimes, different students were working on problems from very different places in the curriculum.

In experimental studies, one concept that researchers study is "fidelity": do teachers actually use the pedagogical innovation in the intended ways? One of the core intentions of Cognitive Tutor is that while using the software, students should advance only as they demonstrate mastery so that students don't miss foundational ideas early on. This means that students should be working on different lessons at different times. Since Cognitive Tutor logs student activity, researchers can tell whether students in the same class are mostly working in lockstep or whether teachers are actually letting students work on a topic until they achieve mastery. In a 2016 follow up to the RAND study, Steve Ritter from Carnegie Learning presented evidence that how teachers used Carnegie Learning mattered a great deal for student learning outcomes. Ritter's research team looked at how much adaptive mastery learning teachers actually allowed in their classes, and they found that some teachers assigned work in Carnegie Learning in such a way that it wasn't really personalized—these teachers required students to work on problem sets related to the topics being taught at that moment to the whole class. By contrast, other teachers allowed students to work at their own pace, even if this meant that some students were still doing practice problems on topics that might have been covered in class weeks earlier. Ritter's team found that overall learning gains were higher in the classes where students were allowed more opportunities to move at their own pace; in other words, the teachers who used Carnegie Learning as intended had more learning gains in their classrooms than did the teachers who kept their students moving in lockstep. That suggests that more professional development and coaching for teachers implementing Cognitive Tutors might be able to improve outcomes further if all teachers could be convinced to let students work on practice problems at their own pace.[23]

In 2016, the contract research group SRI International evaluated a major field trial of a similar CAI system called ASSISTments. ASSISTments was created by Neil and Cristina Heffernan, both former middle school math teachers. Neil did his dissertation at Carnegie Mellon with Ken Koedinger, who was instrumental in the development of Cognitive Tutor. The Heffernans took ASSISTments in a slightly different direction than Cognitive Tutors. Cognitive Tutor: Algebra was designed to replace part of routine class activity; students would spend three days a week on in-person group instruction and two days a week on computers using Cognitive Tutor: Algebra. ASSISTments, by contrast, is mostly a homework helper: students do teacher-assigned homework problems at night, get immediate feedback about whether they are right or wrong, and have the option to do some additional "skill-builders" that incorporate some adaptive elements of CAI.[24]

The program was rolled out in middle schools across Maine, where a statewide laptop initiative ensured universal access for middle school students. Teachers received professional development from the ASSISTments team for using the freely accessible ASSISTments system. The research team estimated that students would use ASSISTments three or four nights a week for about ten minutes a night, although data later showed that students used ASSISTments somewhat less than that. Most student work was probably on non-adaptive teacher-assigned homework problems rather than the skill practice, so the intervention probably wasn't really testing adaptive learning environments—for the most part, kids were doing the same textbook problems they would have been doing, except the problems were online. The main levers of learning were probably two-fold: students got immediate feedback on problems in the evening, and teachers got a simple report each morning that showed which problems students struggled with, allowing them to tailor their morning homework review in class to the most challenging problems and issues.

Like the RAND / Cognitive Tutor study, the SRI team found that students in the treatment condition assigned to use ASSISTments learned more on average and did about 0.2 standard deviations better on pre- and post-test gains, which was about 75 percent more than the control group. They also found that most of the gains were among low-achieving math learners, so the intervention played a role in closing achievement gaps.

In comparing the ASSISTments study with the Cognitive Tutor: Algebra study, one difference that leaps out is how much simpler ASSISTments is. Cognitive Tutor: Algebra is a full CAI adaptive learning solution, while ASSISTments is more of an online homework helper. Cognitive Tutor: Algebra requires major changes in classroom practice, which reduces teacher contact time with students, increases in-classroom computer usage, and creates the opportunity for individual pacing. By contrast, as used in the Maine study, ASSISTments just lets kids see the answers to their problems and lets their teachers get more information about how students are doing. Cognitive Tutor rearranges math teaching; ASSISTments gains some efficiencies in homework and review. In the two experimental studies, the effects of both interventions were about the same. This suggests that all the complex machinery of the full CAI system may be unnecessary, and a lightweight online homework helper could perhaps be just as good as a complex adaptive tutor.

For policymakers or school leaders trying to decide what role computers should play in teaching mathematics, these two recent studies can help advance our understanding of the value of CAI. New studies do not replace previous studies; rather, they help stakeholders in math and computer-assisted education regularly update our understanding of the state of the art. One view of this research is that two large, well-conducted, randomized field experiments should revise our consensus to have a more positive outlook on intelligent tutors in math. This pair of experiments with Cognitive Tutor: Algebra and ASSISTments suggests that researchers, developers, and educators have developed an understanding of computer-assisted instruction that allows teachers using this software to consistently get moderate learning gains from incorporating these tools. If this were the case, we should expect future studies and implementations to show similar gains from CAI systems, perhaps even with modest improvements over time as developers continuously improve these systems. In this view, even though the older consensus was that CAI systems in math did not significantly improve learning, these new studies suggest that the field is maturing.

A more cautious view would be that over the last three decades, there have always been occasional studies that show positive results, but these are regularly "balanced out" by other studies that showed negative or null results. For instance, in early 2019, Teachers College at Columbia University released results from a study of Teach to One, another computer adaptive learning system developed originally in the New York City Public Schools. While not a randomized field trial, this study showed that schools adopting Teach to One did not improve on state test scores. No single research study perfectly captures the "true effect" of an education approach, as our measures are always affected by errors in measurement, sampling variation, and other exigencies of research. Perhaps in the Carnegie Learning and ASSISTments studies, these errors nudged the results in the positive direction; it could be that the next two big CAI assessments will have negative effects, and the two after that will be null, and as a field, we will realize that the evaluation that economists had in the mid-2010s probably holds into the future.[25]

My own view is that these recent positive results represent a maturing of the field, and in the future, we should expect these kinds of consistent, replicable gains for adaptive tutors in math. That said, I am constantly trying to look at new studies and new evidence, and I try to revise my thinking as more studies come out. I hope that the case study above of adaptive tutors provides a model for how people interested in education technology can steadily revise their thinking on a topic—looking for meta-analyses or studies that provide a consensus view of a field, and then gradually updating their thinking as new studies emerge.

So What Should a Department Head Do?
Synthesizing Research in Computer-Assisted Instruction

Let's put ourselves back in the shoes of a K–12 principal considering whether it's worth pursuing adaptive tutors as a way to improve student performance in a school. We understand a bit more about how these tools work; they are not magical robot tutors in the sky, but rather are software programs with a long history of designers and researchers tinkering toward incremental improvement. They have not found a wide purchase in the K–12 curriculum, but they have been used in early elementary reading and throughout the math curriculum. On average, studies of adaptive tutors in early reading have not shown positive impacts on learning. A school looking to be on the cutting edge of innovation might be willing to try some newly developed approach, but elementary schools looking for reforms with a strong track record of research should probably turn to other approaches to support early reading.

In a sense, then, the decision to explore adaptive tutors in K–12 schools probably belongs primarily to the math department head, as math is the only domain where adaptive tutors have consistently shown some evidence of efficacy, especially in a few recent studies. In the ideal world, a math department head looking to improve teaching and learning in her district would take all of these studies and perspectives into account before identifying whether CAI would be a good fit for her math teachers, and if so, what specific products might work well. Randomized control trials are good tools for figuring out if interventions work on average. But no school district is average; every context is unique. If schools have already made big investments in technology, as the middle schools in Maine did with their laptop program, then the costs to schools of implementing CAI are much lower than the costs of buying new machines just for math. If math teachers in a district are generally quite strong, then Eric Taylor's research suggests that adaptive tutors might not be the best tool for getting further improvements, or maybe that a complementary system like ASSISTments would be more promising than a supplementary system like Carnegie Learning. By contrast, in a system where math teachers are generally not as strong—maybe a district with frequent teacher turnover and many new teachers—computer-assisted instruction may be a more compelling path forward.

Some schools may have teachers of varying quality but with a high willingness to try new approaches. A school district with math teachers willing to dive into a new program may have better results with Carnegie Learning than a district with teachers who aren't as willing to change their teaching practices. Steve Ritter's research suggests that Carnegie Learning works best with teachers who are most willing to let the tutors personalize student practice on the days devoted to computer-based instruction.

One of the wonderful and challenging things about schools is that they can always be improved; teaching and learning are so immensely complex that there is always room for tinkering and improvement. There is no evidence that computer-based instruction regularly outperforms traditional instruction or that CAI leads to dramatic transformation of math learning. The best way to understand CAI is as one possible tool among many for improving mathematics education. There are other options too, of course: investment in human tutors to provide more support for the students struggling the most; professional development for teachers in rich mathematical discourse or a deeper understanding of fundamental math content; new software that facilitates new kinds of visualization in mathematics, like Geometer's Sketchped or the Desmos graphing calculator. For some schools, CAI might be the right tool to improve math instruction, and in other schools, one of these other approaches might be a better fit, based on the strengths, weaknesses, and interests of the teachers in a given school or district.

This argument about the utility of intelligent tutors should feel familiar, as it is structurally similar to the case made in the previous chapter in regard to MOOCs. Both technologies are useful but not transformative. They have particular niches in which they appear to work well (math education for CAI, professional education for MOOCs) and other niches in which evidence suggests that they are much less useful (reading education for CAI, remedial or entry-level higher education for MOOCs). Both technologies raise serious concerns about issues of inequality, though some studies of adaptive tutors suggest ways that they might benefit struggling students. Instead of transforming educational systems, they are best understood as technologies that can offer limited but meaningful value in particular parts of our existing education systems. With ongoing research and tinkering, I suspect that technologies and implementation models for adaptive tutors will continue to incrementally improve, and perhaps over time, the weight of evidence will shift to support more widespread adoption and implementation. Technology evangelists who claim that a new generation of adaptive tutors can reshape the arc of human development should be treated with suspicion.

3

PEER-GUIDED LEARNING AT SCALE

Networked Learning Communities

WHEN THE rhetoric of "personalized learning" seized the education world starting in 2010, I was struck by the diverse constituencies advocating for technology-mediated personalization. The enthusiasm for personalized learning cut across many of the typical partisan divides in the politics of education reform. From pedagogical progressives to free-market reformers, people who agreed about nothing else—charter schools, unions, school boards, direct instruction, national standards—agreed that personalization was (1) going to be enabled by technology and (2) going to improve student learning.

The consensus about the great potential of personalized learning depended on a stark disagreement about what the term actually meant.[1] For the advocates of adaptive tutors and blended learning whom we met in Chapter 2, personalization meant that each individual child would be able to spend part or all of her day proceeding through technology-mediated learning experiences at her own pace. For other educators, it wasn't the *pace* that should be personalized; it was the *content* and *learning experience*. For these educators—usually aligned with John Dewey's vision of apprenticeship models of education—personalization meant that students would be able to leverage online networks to explore their own interests. Students would identify passions, join online learning communities, study topics of their choosing, and create performances and artifacts of their learning that could be shared online. Learning in schools would look more like the experience of the Rainbow Loomers whom we met in the Introduction.

These twin visions of personalization—personalization as algorithmically optimizing a student's pathway through established, traditional curriculum and personalization as students choosing topics for study and communities for participation—are not only very different, they are in some sense irreconcilable. It is only possible for adaptive tutors to algorithmically optimize student pathways through content if educators define all of that content in advance and limit assessment to those domains in which computational assessment is tractable. If learners are to be empowered to choose their own topics of study and demonstrate their understanding through different kinds of assessment, then online networks that can support diverse investigations become more essential than adaptive tutors that can accelerate learners through pre-defined content.

Behind these two perspectives on personalization, there is another important distinction in how these camps view the notion of "scale." For most systems of instructor-guided and algorithm-guided learning at scale, the tutorial is considered the ideal mode of learning, and the goal is to bring the best possible tutorial experience to as many learners as possible. And since human tutors are too expensive, the model uses technology to create something as close to the tutorial ideal as possible. The massive scale of human-learning needs is a problem in this model; scale is a hurdle to be overcome through technology.

An alternative vision sees scale not as a hurdle, but as a crucial resource for creating powerful learning experiences. Scale means knitting together a community of learners from across the networked world, leveraging their interests, talents, and inclinations to teach and share. In this chapter, we will focus on examples from the peer-guided genre of learning at scale, where learning designers and instructional leaders are intentional about weaving networked learning environments into formal educational institutions. In the peer-guided genre of learning at scale, a learner's progress through an experience is decided not by an instructor or an algorithm but by the learners themselves, who navigate a network of learning experiences generated by a community of peers and curated by a set of designers and instructional leaders.

Whereas much that happens in MOOCs and adaptive tutors feels very familiar to anyone who has spent time in traditional schools and colleges, many designs in the peer-guided genre of learning at scale can appear novel or foreign to both learners and educators. One place to begin exploring the opportunities and challenges presented by this new approach is with the original learning experiences that called themselves MOOCs but differed in form and philosophy from the instructor-guided MOOCs discussed in Chapter 1. These connectivist MOOCs, or cMOOCs, formed primarily in Canada several years before Thrun and Norvig's Introduction to Artificial Intelligence course started the MOOC phenomenon in elite higher education.

Connectivism and Peer Learning

The term *massive open online course* was coined in 2008 by David Cormier, an instructional technologist on Prince Edward Island in Canada, to describe a new kind of online course that a handful of educational technologists were experimenting with. These early

MOOCs had a few thousand participants whose primary learning activity was engaging in conversations over social media, and they differed dramatically from what Coursera and edX would create four years later. One of the first MOOCs was called Connectivism and Connected Knowledge, taught in 2008, and known by its social media hashtag #CCK08. It was offered for credit to twenty-four students at Manitoba University, but through its open design, over 2,200 students participated in the course in some way.[2]

The form of the CCK08 learning experience was influenced heavily by its subject matter, the epistemology of connectivism. Two Canadian instructional technologists, George Siemens and Stephen Downes, were the principal architects of the theory, which argues that knowledge exists in networks. At the biological level, this means that knowledge exists in the networked structure of the brain; at the sociological level, knowledge exists within communities of people and practitioners. This epistemological position on the nature of knowledge—it primarily exists in networks—led naturally to a pedagogical position: the way to increase knowledge is to generate richer, denser networks. In this model, the best learning happens when learners connect with other people and resources that support ongoing inquiry.[3]

In the original connectivist MOOCs, the home base for a course was a publicly accessible site on the open web—no logins, no paywalls. This home base offered shared content, guidelines, and instructions for students. Instructors encouraged students to create their own online web presence, typically by creating individual blogs and social media accounts. Learners came to the home base to find shared texts (reading assignments) and prompts for discussion and interaction, and then they responded to those prompts on their individual blogs and social media accounts that were networked with other students on social media. To organize this cacophony of activity, instructors developed techniques that came to be called syndication.[4]

One of the simplest syndication techniques was using a course hashtag. Students could write a blogpost on their own blog and then tweet the link using the #CCK08 hashtag so that other people following the course could find it. More sophisticated syndication techniques used RSS, or real simple syndication, which was one of the gems of the open web that has been marginalized by the growth of walled-garden platforms like Facebook. Stephen Downes developed an RSS software toolkit called gRSShopper, which allowed students to register their individual blogs and other content sources, and then gRSShopper would make a copy of each submission and aggregate it elsewhere in a variety of forms. gRSShopper automatically published a daily digest of all submissions, and it also allowed the instructors to easily curate a few highlights from each week in a course.[5]

While instructors played an important role in shaping the direction, membership, and cadence of activity within these communities, the learning experience of each individual student in the course was dramatically shaped by the student's peer network. Siemens and Downes argued that it was the discussions and connections in the network, rather than the instructor-selected content in the home base, that defined the learning experience. Stephen Downes wrote that the "content is a MacGuffin," the narrative trick in a movie that brings people together. For an educator, this is a provocative stance: that the content of a course is a kind of trick designed to bring people together into conversation, and it is through this conversation—rather than through direct instruction—that the learning happens.[6]

The primary learning activities in the Connectivism and Connected Knowledge course were reading and commenting on other people's thoughts via blog posts, Twitter threads, and other forms of social media, and then responding with a student's own posts and perspectives. Among the most important learning tasks were connecting with other people—adding new people to follow on Twitter, bookmarking blogs, and adding others' RSS feeds. Successful learners used technology to create a learning community.

To those steeped in pedagogical theory, the approach of Siemens and Downes had much in common with what Jean Lave and Etienne Wenger called "situated learning." Lave and Wegner studied vocational communities and how apprentices in those communities developed their expertise. They argued that a central part of apprenticeship was a mode of interaction called "legitimate peripheral participation." Legitimate peripheral participation is when a novice hangs out on the edge of a community of experts, looking for opportunities to move from the edge toward the middle—a kid hangs around the auto repair shop, watching the mechanics at work, until one day, a mechanic asks him to hold a bolt in place for a minute, and the next week he's asked to actually tighten the bolt, then he's hired a few hours a week, and from there, the journey commences.

Stephen Downes argued that what makes someone a physicist is only in part her knowledge of the facts and formulas of physics. Even more important to becoming a physicist is having colleagues who are physicists, knowing the current debates in physics, and becoming inculcated in a physics community. Situated learning and connectivism are pedagogical approaches that are attentive to the social and cultural dimensions of learning. In particular, they encourage designs that let people move from the periphery to the core of a learning experience or learning community. In the twenty-first century, those communities are often defined by their online networked connections. The technological scaffolding of connectivism— blog posts, Twitter hashtags, and other open web technology practices—were novel and attuned to a moment when social networking was transforming society, but as with so many things in education and education technology, it built upon ideas and practices that had come before.[7]

Building the Infrastructure for Peer Learning

In the connectivist vision for peer-guided learning at scale, learners need to develop a variety of online learning skills as a precursor to learning about particular topics or subjects. Learners need to be able to set up blogs and social media accounts, use social networking features such as following accounts or feeds, and navigate a decentralized web of resources and people. Engaging in these processes just to access the learning experience is much more complex than figuring out how to click "Next" in a MOOC or how to submit an answer in an adaptive tutor and wait for the next problem to appear. Just getting started in a cMOOC required that learners develop a whole set of new skills for participating in online learning. While most cMOOCs addressed these needs through online tutorials or peer mentoring sessions, a few places experimented with building institutional infrastructure to help students develop these skills.

The most ambitious efforts to have students develop the technical fluency needed to participate in connectivist-inspired learning communities were centered at the University of Mary Washington, where a team of innovative instructional technologists tried to reimagine digital learning infrastructure in higher education. One of the leaders of this effort was Jim Groom, who in 2008 defined the term *edupunk* to describe a way of relating to education technology that rejected corporate solutions, especially learning management systems, and promoted student ownership of the means of technological production. In 2010, Groom helped develop the online course Digital Storytelling, or DS106, a computer science course with a goal of helping students develop skills related to media production, web development, and storytelling online. Like the Canadian cMOOCs, DS106 developed an open online component that let other universities participate in the course (parallel sessions have been offered at the University of Michigan, Kansas State, and several other colleges) and individual learners from the web join in.[8]

As in other connectivist, peer-guided learning experiences, the home page of DS106 serves as a guide, a syllabus, and an aggregator, syndicating the feeds of blogs, Flickr, YouTube, and other accounts from learners around the world. There is a DS106 online radio station and a livestream video station for media projects. Perhaps the most distinctive feature of the course is the Daily Create—a challenge to make media in twenty minutes or less every day. The Daily Creates are inspired by materials out of the Assignment Bank, a repository of media creation prompts ("Make a video where you tell the stories of the keys on your keychain"). These assignments have been submitted over nearly a decade by instructors, enrolled students, and passersby. Through these kinds of assignments, students developed the skills in media production, web hosting, and social networking to be able to participate in peer-guided large-scale learning communities. If CCK08 was a cMOOC about the ideas animating cMOOCs, then DS106 was a cMOOC about the technical skills required to participate in cMOOCs.[9]

Having every student who was enrolled in DS106 create his or her own blog through a commercial provider was a logistical barrier to student participation, so Groom and colleagues developed their own blog-hosting solution for the school. This eventually turned into a Domain of One's Own, a project to give every freshman at University of Mary Washington his or her own server space and online presence. Much in the same way that learning management systems provided institutional infrastructure for teacher-directed instructionist learning, the Domain of One's Own project attempted to create an institutional infrastructure for connectivist learning. Other universities took an interest in the Domain of One's Own approach, and Groom left the University of Mary Washington to start Reclaim Hosting. To reclaim universities' web presence from learning management systems and to reclaim the web from centralized commercial interests more broadly, Reclaim Hosting offered a turnkey solution for universities to create their own Domain of One's Own projects. A number of universities—University of Oklahoma, Drew University, Brigham Young University, and others—tested using Reclaim Hosting to make a student-controlled online space a central part of their information technology infrastructure.[10]

Groom and colleagues realized that implementing their student-centered, peer-guided vision would require not just making a new site or app, but also developing an entirely new technology infrastructure for supporting higher education. Few universities to date have taken this path, but Reclaim Hosting maintains an alternate, edupunk, indieweb approach that, like a global seed vault, stores possibilities for alternative futures.[11]

What Happened to cMOOCs

For those who had the technical prowess to generate and navigate content on the open web and the time to invest in navigating these communities, the connectivist MOOCs were powerful learning experiences. Participants explored new ideas, developed new technical skills, and perhaps most importantly, developed a set of relationships and connections that in some cases long outlived their original course communities. One could head onto Twitter a decade after CCK08 and still find participants occasionally posting on the #CCK08 hashtag. But despite the passion that cMOOCs evoked among enthusiasts, they never expanded much further than a few hothouses of fertile experimentation.

For a time, it looked like both connectivist MOOCs and instructionist MOOCs might coexist side by side in an online learning ecosystem, and commentators came up with the terms cMOOCs and xMOOCs to distinguish the Canadian open web experiences from the increasingly paywalled, linear learning experiences offered primarily by elite universities. Researchers conducted comparative studies of both approaches, and the xMOOC-mania of 2012 gave rise to a small surge of renewed interest in and attention to cMOOCs. In 2012, as a response to public attention on instructionist MOOCs, a pair of women's studies professors, Anne Balsamo and Alexandra Juhasz, came together to create a distributed open collaborative course called FemTechNet around feminist dialogues in technology. The course was designed much like CCK08 or DS106, with a series of online resources to support small local "nodal" classes facilitated by local instructors with ideas and feedback permeating back to the core. If Downes and Siemens framed their project as pedagogical, FemTechNet was more explicitly political, contesting not just the instructionist pedagogy of xMOOCs but also their hegemonic model, where elite universities sent their digital emissaries to the far corners of the world to instruct rather than to listen and share. In these efforts, cMOOCs were not just an alternative to xMOOCs but a critique of them.[12]

Connectivist MOOCs blossomed at a peculiar historical moment in the history of the web, in the pivot point between a dramatic increase in the number of people creating content online and the capture of all that activity by a handful of proprietary platforms. The peer-guided cMOOCs were made possible by a series of new technologies called Web 2.0—WYSIWYG ("what you see is what you get") web editors that let people create web content without HTML or CSS, and hosting solutions for blogs and websites that let people upload images and other files without using file transfer protocol (FTP) services. In 2008, when CCK08 started, people on the web created their own blogs through Blogger and Wordpress, hosted and shared their pictures on Flikr, and read through news and blog feeds through Google Reader. In the years that followed, the largest technology companies were successful at integrating all of those different features into their "walled-garden" platforms. People could share thoughts, host images, and scroll through a news feed all in one place on Facebook, LinkedIn, or Snapchat. Advocates of the indieweb have lamented the concentration of power within a few platforms, and the loss of the richness that emerged from the multiple, distributed voices on the open web. But for most users, the integrated experience of posting ideas, connecting with people, and reading content in a single, tidy, walled garden was simpler and more compelling than the additional efforts required to maintain and participate in the open web.

The simpler, centralized, linear approach won out among MOOCs as well. In the same way that Facebook came to define what it meant to "go online," the edX and Coursera xMOOC cemented what it meant to be a MOOC in the public consciousness. Courses and platforms adopting the xMOOC model accumulated the overwhelming majority of registrations in large-scale learning experiences. Learners consistently found cMOOCs confusing and difficult to navigate, like wandering through a corn maze rather than the tended linear paths of xMOOCs There are still a few cMOOCs offered every year, mostly to other educators, but the connectivst experiment in higher education increasingly appears to be the road not taken, or perhaps a road to be reclaimed.[13]

While peer-guided approaches to learning at scale have generally foundered in schools, there is one striking exception: the Scratch programming language and online community that has been translated into over sixty languages and widely adopted by schools and systems around the world.

The Scratch Community and Peer Learning in K–12

Scratch is a block-based programming language, which means that rather than learning to write software code through syntax (print:"Hello World"), people learn to write code by snapping together digital blocks, each of which represents a function, variable, or other programming element. Scratch was developed by Mitch Resnick, Natalie Rusk, and their team at the Lifelong Kindergarten lab at MIT. Scratch has integrated graphics editing, and when combined with the programming language, it is a powerful platform for making animations, games, and other visually appealing programs.[14]

From the beginning, Scratch was imagined as a creative learning community of users, called Scratchers. Each Scratch program contributed by a user is automatically made available for inspection and remixing—starting a new project with a copy of another project—by anyone else on the site. In his recent book, *Lifelong Kindergarten,* Mitch Resnick describes the Scratch platform as the intersection of four alliterative learning dimensions: projects, passion, peers, and play. There are a few tutorials on the site and some exemplar projects created by staff, but the instructional approach of Scratch leans heavily on learners sharing examples of their projects with the community. The home page hosts a collection of curated examples, sometimes from project staff and sometimes from community members, along with a few algorithmically curated sets of projects based on what's currently being "loved" by the community or remixed. Every project page includes space for the author to post instructions, notes, and credits, along with a comment thread where other Scratchers can offer feedback, ask questions, and interact with the project author. Scratchers also communicate about their projects in the very active forums, where they ask for suggestions, share tips and tricks, and discuss projects with the community as a whole.[15]

For Resnick and the Scratch team, the whole point of the learning environment is to empower young people to explore their passions through creativity and design. There is no right way to program in Scratch or right pathway to learning how to program, so the site generally stays away from the kinds of linear instruction provided by MOOCs or adaptive tutoring systems. Resnick and his collaborators were influenced by the ideas of Seymour Papert and Cynthia Solomon, who codeveloped the Logo programming language that many of us from Generation X used when we were in elementary school. Papert argued that programming environments for young people should offer "low floors and high ceilings"; it should be easy to get started programming in the environment, but still possible to create sophisticated programs. To this, Resnick adds the idea of wide walls; community members should be able to create a wide variety of projects, based on their interests and passions, with different themes and purposes.[16]

Learning in the Scratch community looks much like learning in the connectivist MOOCs. Scratchers use the features of the platform to develop their own identity, make connections with people and resources, and develop their skills along the lines of their interests. The learning environment supports a wide variety of activities and levels of participation. While tens of millions of registered users have made over 40 million projects on the Scratch platform (as of 2019), many of these learners pass through the system relatively quickly, lurking on a few projects or starting one or a few simple ones. A small percentage of Scratchers get seriously into creating, remixing, and commenting on projects, and a very small number of users become leaders in the community, creating tutorials, moderating forums, editing the wiki, curating collections, and so forth. People choose how they want to participate, and they do so to varying degrees.[17]

Just as connectivism provides a useful framework for explaining the learning designs in cMOOCs and higher education, the theory of connected learning, developed by cultural anthropologist Mizuko Ito and colleagues, provides a lens for understanding networked learning among younger learners. Connected learning is interest-driven and peer-supported, but crucially, it also provides opportunities for academic connections; connected learning is realized "when a young person is able to pursue a personal interest or passion with the support of friends and caring adults, and is in turn able to link this learning and interest to academic achievement, career success or civic engagement."[18] Realizing connected learning in the Scratch community means letting kids develop new skills to create projects that reflect their interests, but also supporting young people in seeing how creating animations and games or learning how to program can connect to other academic pursuits in school.

In a 2014 TEDx talk, Resnick tells the story of a boy who was using Scratch to create a video game. Seeing that the boy would need to include mathematical variables in his program if he were to realize his vision, Resnick explained how to encode variables in Scratch programming blocks. Resnick described the moment when the concept of a variable clicked for the boy: "He reached his hand out to me, and he said, 'Thank you, thank you, thank you.' And what went through my mind was, 'How often is it that teachers are thanked by their students for teaching them variables?'" By placing the concept of variables in the context of a meaningful project, Resnick and Scratch helped the boy connect his interests in gaming with at least one crucial algebraic concept.[19]

Scratch was developed out of Resnick and Rusk's work in Computer Clubhouses, a network of afterschool programs around the world for exploring computational creativity, and in the early years, Scratch was primarily used by individual kids and informal learning programs. More recently, Scratch adoption has taken off in K–12 schools as a way of introducing computing and computer programming, but not always in the ways that the Scratch team had intended. As Resnick noted, "Over the past decade, we've found that it's much easier to spread the technology of Scratch than the educational ideas underlying it." In Resnick's TEDx story, a boy starts a project connected to his own interest in video games, and when he encounters a particular challenge, Resnick steps in with some just-in-time learning to help the boy develop the skills and knowledge needed to advance the project. By contrast, Resnick and his colleagues in the Lifelong Kindergarten lab have countless stories of schools where teachers introduce students to the Scratch programming language through teacher-structured activities rather than through open-ended exploration. It is very common for teachers introducing Scratch to create their own model program and then ask students to create a replication of that model, sometimes even by requiring that students reproduce step by step a project that a teacher projects on a screen. Many of the core expectations of schools—that students produce their work independently, that all students complete a project in a similar amount of time, that all students study topics regardless of their interest level— conspire against a pedagogy that seeks to empower students as leaders of their own creativity and learning.[20]

Comparing Peer-Guided with Instructor-Guided and Algorithm-Guided Learning Environments: Shared Visions of Mastery and Different Approaches to Get There

Having examined all three of the learning-at-scale genres of instructor-guided, algorithm-guided, and peer-guided large-scale learning environments, we are now better equipped to compare them.

People with very different pedagogical proclivities often have surprisingly similar views about the end goals of learning. When sociologist Jal Mehta of Harvard University and educator Sarah Fine of High Tech High Graduate School of Education studied dozens of highly lauded high schools in the United States that approached instruction quite differently, they found that many of them pursued a similar vision of "deeper learning," a set of interrelated competencies that include traditional disciplinary knowledge as well as the skills of communication, collaboration, problem solving, and self-regulation. Mehta and Fine characterize deeper learning as the intersection between three important learning outcomes: mastery, identity, and creativity. When students experience deeper learning, they develop mastery of deep content knowledge in a domain. They also experience a shift in identity where the learning activity is a part of who they are rather than something that they do—the shift from "learning to swim" to "being a swimmer." They also have opportunities to create novel, authentic, interesting new projects and performances with their new skills and knowledge.[21]

Sal Khan of Khan Academy and Mitch Resnick and Natalie Rusk of Scratch would all agree that students should learn math in order to create wonderful things in the world. I suspect they would agree that great mathematicians and great computer programmers have a deep understanding of content knowledge in the domain, develop an identity around their practice, and show true mastery not by replicating what has been done before but by creating things that are new. But if they do not differ in ends, they differ dramatically in how they believe learners should make progress toward these ends.

Traditional instructionist educators believe that content mastery is a necessary precursor to shifts in identity and opportunities for creativity. They rightly observe that people who do the most novel and important creative work in a field tend to have extensive mastery of the domain knowledge in that field, so they start their teaching by focusing on knowledge mastery and hope that content mastery will provoke shifts in identity and that mastery can then lead to creative output. By contrast, social constructivists observe that most motivation for learning comes from opportunities to be creative. As people play with Scratch, they become Scratchers, and the opportunities for creativity unlock their passion for learning about programming and mathematics to make ever more intricate programs and creations.

In Khan Academy, the proper first step toward deeper learning is learning mathematical procedures and facts that might eventually lead to doing interesting collaborative projects. In Scratch, the first step in that journey is getting people to play with tools for computational creativity that will inspire learners to understand how variables and other mathematical concepts can enrich their creations. I think there is room for both models in our education systems. But given that our formal educational systems are overwhelmingly organized around the mastery-first models, I'm enthusiastic about approaches that create more opportunity for creativity-first and identity-first learning in schools and colleges.

Different Goals Lead to Different Research Approaches across Genres of Learning at Scale

The divergent pedagogical beliefs of traditionalists and progressives about idealized pathways to learning lead to differences in how each camp conducts research about their large-scale learning environments.

The research concerning the efficacy of adaptive tutors that we explored in Chapter 2 had a set of shared assumptions, and those shared assumptions were part of what made meta-analyses and comparisons across multiple studies possible. Adaptive-tutor research assumed that instructors and designers identified a body of content knowledge that students should learn, and that teachers and the system as a whole should be judged on the basis of how much progress all learners made toward content mastery. Usually, progress toward that goal was measured by the change in the average proficiency of learners before an intervention (such as the adoption of adaptive tutors in classrooms) and the average proficiency afterward. This research assumed that the goal of education is for every student to make progress toward mastery and that the bell-shaped distribution of student competence, measured in effect sizes, should shift to the right over time.

These assumptions about essential features of a learning environment are not shared by the researchers in Resnick's Lifelong Kindergarten group or by the designers of connectivist MOOCs. If educators take seriously the idea that learning ought to be driven by the interests of students, then when students decide that Scratch is not really interesting to them but that something else is, then it's no loss to the Scratch designers to see those students move on to other things. For supporters of peer-supported, interest-driven learning, the concerns are less about whether an entire class of learners is developing new capacities in one subject, but rather whether the subset of learners who are really interested in and devoted to a learning experience can steadily improve their skills and that the environment can successfully invite in new community members who share their interests.[22]

Part of the challenge of measuring peer-driven learning is that in many of these learning environments, goals are determined by individual students and the networked community, not by teachers or evaluators. If, as Downes says, the content is a MacGuffin, then what would be reasonable measures of learning in that environment? If a participant in #CCK08 knows little or nothing about connectivism but has built a network of new peers and colleagues, is that a successful course? These problems plague other learning-at-scale environments as well—for instance, some xMOOC students are more interested in learning and practicing English than the particulars of course content—but the challenges posed by the multiple aims and goals of learners in peer-guided large-scale learning environments make summarizing their effectiveness particularly challenging.

Because the goals of a peer-guided educational environment are different from those of an instructionist one, so too are the research methods used to evaluate them. Researchers in the Lifelong Kindergarten lab have largely studied the Scratch community through intensive qualitative research—thick descriptions of the lives and practices of individual Scratchers. Much of this research tends to focus on individuals who have powerful learning experiences online and share that learning with others. In a sense, the purpose of Scratch is to create the conditions for these deeply invested learners to thrive, while also allowing other learners at the periphery to participate at less intense levels. Having a learner leave the Scratch community or pass through with only a light touch isn't necessarily a loss or a concern.[23]

The goals and research methods for the different types of learning environments then interact with the pedagogies and instructional designs of developers in mutually reinforcing ways. The outlook shapes the questions that designers and researchers ask, the methods to conduct research, and the answers to research questions—and the answers to those questions then feed back into the iterative design of these large-scale learning systems.

A group of advocates for the merits of traditional instruction wrote one of my favorite papers on education, provocatively titled "Why Minimal Guidance during Instruction Does Not Work: An Analysis of the Failure of Constructivist, Discovery, Problem-based, Experiential, and Inquiry Teaching." They argue that over and over again, experimental studies that contrast traditional methods of direct instruction with minimally guided, open-ended learning demonstrate that for a wide variety of learning outcomes, direct instruction works better. They draw on a set of ideas from cognitive science called cognitive load theory to explain why this is the case. Put simply, people have a limited working memory, and when learners allocate that working memory to solving a problem, they often are not permanently encoding learning about the patterns and practices that let them solve that type of problem. It is more efficient and effective to have an instructor demonstrate through worked examples how to solve an individual problem and less efficient and effective to have students try to discover solutions and patterns from problems without much instruction.[24]

It is crucial to understand, however, what these authors mean by "successful learning." For these critics of minimally guided, peer-led instruction, a learning environment that works is one that helps shift a bell-curve-shaped distribution of learners toward higher levels of mastery; indeed, the statistical models they use to test their interventions require as an assumption that there is a measurable skill that is normally distributed across the population of learners. That is one useful definition of a learning intervention that "works," but it's not the only one. The Scratch learning community is a powerful refutation of the argument that minimally guided instruction does not work. Scratch does everything wrong according to the advocates for traditional instruction—there is almost no direct instruction, there are very few formal assessment mechanisms, there is no assigned sequence of learning activities, there is no attention given to managing learner cognitive load, there are no experimental tests of interventions, and nearly every change to the Scratch platform is evaluated on the basis of qualitative case studies and user observations rather than randomized control trials. And yet Resnick and his team have built one of the most widely adopted engines of creative learning in the world.

When something "works" for Resnick and the Lifelong Kindergarten team, it allows individuals to explore their passions, publish authentic performances of understanding to the world, and develop deep mastery. They have tuned the Scratch learning environment to allow for widespread participation, but they have also ensured that accommodating widespread participation doesn't place undue restrictions on the individual pathways of the most devoted learners. As a result, Scratch "works" brilliantly, in the sense that millions of students are introduced to block-based programming through the system, and a subset of those young people develop remarkably deep understandings of block-based programming, creative digital expression, and computational thinking through the system.

I have a vigorous commitment to methodological pluralism; I think both of these approaches to learning are necessary and can lead to great outcomes for learners. Our society needs instructional systems that address both kinds of aims. We need our entire population to have fundamental skills in reading, writing, numeracy, civics, science literacy, and communication; in these domains, we need to take the entire distribution of learners and help them move toward mastery. We also need learning environments that let young people discover their interests and explore them deeply, much more deeply than might be allowed if the environment were equally concerned with bringing along the unenthusiastic with the enthusiastic. We need learning environments that shift whole distributions to the right, and we need learning environments that enable deep learning for a self-selected few.

That said, one of the challenges in understanding peer-guided learning environments is that the research defies easy summarization. For peer-guided learning environments, we know that some learners become deeply immersed in these learning environments and can develop very high levels of proficiency, but we have less understanding of what learning looks like across the whole distribution of people who engage.

Teaching Hate on the Open Web

Pedagogies come bundled with philosophies and moralities. For instance, advocates of instructionist approaches tend to emphasize that learning is difficult and results from struggle; advocates of progressive pedagogies tend to emphasize that learning is natural and easy. Seymour Papert argued that just as people learned the French language naturally from living in France, so too the Logo programming language could become a "Mathland" where people naturally and easily learn math. In Jean-Jacques Rousseau's novel *Emile, or On Education,* the protagonist's education emphasizes exploration and observation in the natural world over formal study, and Rousseau associates this naturalistic approach with preparation for a more democratic society that would transcend the feudal and monarchical structures of eighteenth-century Europe. An assumption that cuts through these older ideas and contemporary approaches to peer-guided learning is that if young people are given the opportunity to explore their interests and passions, then they will generally choose interests and passions that are enriching and interesting.

Throughout this chapter and this book, I've celebrated peer-guided learning at scale, not as the best learning methodology for all learning, but as an approach to empowering learners that provides an important counterbalance to the instructionism that dominates schools, colleges, and formal learning institutions. I have also celebrated the peer-led, informal learning that happens among Rainbow Loomers and enthusiasts of all kinds. Part of my enthusiasm for peer-guided learning at scale is rooted in a general optimism about learning and humanity that Papert and Rousseau shared: given the freedom and resources to learn, people will generally choose to learn about worthwhile things.

Unfortunately, peer-guided learning environments can be used to recruit people into dark and hateful ideologies in much the same way that people can learn Rainbow Loom or digital storytelling. In 2018, there was a terrible incident where a man in his mid-twenties rented a van and proceeded to drive it down a busy Toronto sidewalk, killing ten and injuring fifteen. As police and others explored the online history of the murderer, they found that he had participated in an online community of men that call themselves incels, or involuntary celibates. These are men who gather on subreddits and the troll-filled message board of 4chan to lament their inability to persuade women to have sexual relationships with them. Incels promulgate a worldview of male radicalization according to which all men are owed sex from women, but women only provide these opportunities to men from certain social strata. The ideology is a mixture of resentment and madness, and periodically it explodes into violence. The Toronto van murder was inspired by a similar incel mass murder in California some years earlier.[25]

Even the introduction here of the term *incel* in explaining this particular murder is in itself a potentially dangerous act. The word *incel* functions as a potential aggregator for male radicalization in the same way that "starburst bracelet" might operate for a Rainbow Loom enthusiast or "#CCK08" works for a cMOOC enthusiast: it is a search term that can bring people into a broader online community interested in educating new members. In an October 2018 talk by danah boyd, founder of Data and Society, boyd excoriated members of the media for broadcasting the term *incel* in the wake of the Montreal murder:[26]

> I understand that the term "incel" was provocative and would excite your readers to learn more, but were those of you who propagated this term intending to open a portal to hell? What made amplifying this term newsworthy? You could've conveyed the same information without giving people a search term that served as a recruiting vehicle for those propagating toxic masculinity. Choosing not to amplify hateful recruiting terms is not censorship. You wouldn't give your readers a phone number to join the KKK, so why give them a digital calling card?

When boyd accuses journalists of helping their readers "learn more" about incels, it is useful to realize that incels and other advocates of male radicalism have built a sophisticated online learning environment on the open web—hidden in plain sight—that has much in common with connectivist-inspired learning environments: it is a distributed network of people and resources that seek to invite new members to join them in a community in which they will learn new ideas, knowledge, and skills. Those seeking to inculcate new—primarily young—men into male radicalism post a range of materials online, from mainstream critiques of political correctness to targeted social campaigns like Gamergate to extremist forums, and these communities strategically guide people along these paths toward extremism.[27]

There is mounting evidence that some of the architectural features of online networks can, unfortunately, be more powerful in amplifying extremist messages than more moderate messages. The video-hosting platform YouTube illustrates this phenomenon best, but the features of the YouTube recommendation engine can be seen in other algorithmic recommendation engines as well. In 2018, sociologist Zeynep Tufekci observed that in a variety of situations, after a viewer watches a YouTube video, YouTube will recommend another video with content more intense, extreme, and disturbing than the last. After watching videos in support of Donald Trump, she observed recommendations for videos about white supremacy or Holocaust denial. After watching Bernie Sanders videos, she got recommendations for videos claiming that 9/11 was an inside government job. Watch videos about vegetarianism, and you'll get recommendations for veganism. Watch videos about jogging, and you'll get recommendations for videos about ultramarathons. As Tufekci argues, "It seems you are never 'hard core' enough for YouTube's recommendation engine."[28]

Of course, in learning, "getting more hard core" is often quite wonderful, as when a Rainbow Loomer graduates from a simple design to a more complex one. When a casual watcher of Rainbow Loom videos starts posting comments and then making her own videos, we can celebrate the process of legitimate peripheral participation, moving from the periphery of a community to a core. Online educators and policymakers, however, must come to understand that the bad guys have learned these educational techniques as well. Anti-vaccine conspiracy theorists understand that videos with open-ended questions about vaccine safety can draw in new "anti-vaccine learners" and that those videos, comment threads, and recommendations can be used to move people toward more hard-core anti-government conspiracies.

The proliferation of online communities organized around hate groups or the kinds of conspiracies that Richard Hofstadter called the "paranoid style in American politics" reveals one of the virtues of the centralized learning experiences provided by publishers of adaptive tutoring systems or university providers of MOOCs. These traditional institutions provide an editorial filter. This filter is imperfect, and elite educational consensus can countenance truly terrible ideas (such as the dark history of segregated schooling). For all these flaws, though, it would be virtually impossible for Coursera to host a MOOC that indoctrinated learners in explicitly white nationalist ideology or for Carnegie Learning to produce an intelligent tutor on the physics of a flat earth. And if they did, there are various watchdogs and other methods to police such transgressions. When Walter Lewin, a physics professor whose extraordinarily popular lectures were available online, was found to have sexually harassed women in online course contexts, his lectures and MITx courses were removed.[29]

In the introduction to this book, I argued that new technologies make this the greatest time in history to be a learner. In this chapter, I have enthusiastically endorsed approaches to peer-guided learning that give learners agency and help them learn to navigate online networks of peers and resources to develop new skills and knowledge. But participating in vast network of online learning resources doesn't guarantee that people will inevitably learn ideas and skills that will bring about better individuals and a better society. Our technologies and learning resources are shaped by the broader culture, and political battles about whether we have a culture of dignity, respect, and inclusion or a culture of divisiveness and tribalism will determine whether or not our extraordinary infrastructures for learning will, in fact, lead to a better, more just world.

The Puzzle of Peer Learning in Schools

Participation in open-web, peer-guided learning environments is ubiquitous. People all over the world have hopped online to learn how to use a certain block in Minecraft, how to debug a software problem, how to cook an apple pie, or how to crochet a dragon out of rubber bands. Quantifying the exact scope of this learning is difficult, but when millions of people have created Scratch accounts and YouTube videos like "How to Make a Rainbow Loom Starburst Bracelet" have tens of millions of views and hundreds of comments, it seems clear that the global community of online learners is massive.

One of the complexities of peer-guided learning environments is that participants can find them both completely intuitive and utterly baffling. With instructor-guided and algorithm-guided learning environments, students find it easy to use the system but may not always be motivated to do so. People get bored going through xMOOCs and cognitive tutors, and they quit, but it's less common that they are so confused that they don't know how to participate. By contrast, many cMOOC participants find these networked learning environments overwhelming, and students "getting stuck"—not knowing what to do next to advance their learning— is a common challenge in classrooms adopting Scratch. One of the signature design challenges of peer-guided learning environments is to figure out how to make them more accessible to novices without turning them into instructor-led learning environments.[30]

Peering into these kinds of mysteries reminds us that learning and teaching remain, after millennia of practice and study, unfathomably complex. Somehow, millions of people around the world find ways to teach and learn with one another online without any formal training and sometimes without any organization, and yet when designers try to create these kinds of environments with intention, they encounter substantial challenges with motivation and comprehension. It's frustrating how far we are from understanding how best to create online learning communities where people support one another's learning in powerful ways, but inspiring to see how despite our limited understanding, people make progress anyway.

And all of the challenges of designing powerful, accessible, and equitable large-scale learning environments are magnified by the additional challenge of integrating these environments in formal education systems. Schools and colleges are tasked with doing more than just helping individual people learn whatever they want. Formal education systems mandate that all students learn certain fundamentals, whether or not they have an intrinsic inclination to do so. Teachers evaluate learners in part to provide feedback, but also so that learners can be ranked, sorted, and tracked into different parts of the educational system. While there may be opportunities for collaboration and peer learning, students in schools are expected to tackle many of their most consequential assessments alone so that their individual competency can be measured. These expectations for teaching, assessing, ranking, and sorting individuals create an inhospitable institutional climate for peer-guided learning environments to take root.

Forward-looking schools, therefore, face a challenging dilemma. Peer-guided networked learning environments will be central to how people, young and old, learn across their lifetimes. In some professions, participation in these kinds of networks will be essential to professional advancement. For instance, computer programming languages advance so quickly that it is almost impossible to be a successful computer programmer without participating in networked learning communities, such as Stack Overflow, where people ask and answer questions about specific programming languages or coding approaches.[31] Formal education systems need to teach students how to engage with and learn in this type of open, large-scale, peer-guided network. But the learning practices in these environments grate against some of the key commitments of formal educational systems; they mix like oil and water. A few schools will respond to these challenges by dramatically changing their practices to more closely match the patterns of learning that happen outside of schools, and some schools will simply ignore the changes happening beyond their classroom walls. The most adaptive approach in the near-term is probably for creative educators to find more spaces where peer-guided large-scale learning can be woven into the periphery of schools—in electives, extracurriculars, and untested subjects—so that learners can have some practice in navigating these new networks with a community of local peers and mentors to support them.

4

TESTING THE GENRES
OF LEARNING AT SCALE

Learning Games

OVER THE LAST FORTY YEARS, the growth of digital games has profoundly changed the landscape of entertainment in the networked world. Some of my earliest childhood memories are of computer gaming: batting balls with handheld wheel controllers in *Pong* on an Apple II+, blasting space aliens in *Zaxxon* on a Commodore 64, and typing "go north" to venture into the unknown in the *Zork* text adventures. In my 1980s childhood, video gaming was a niche hobby marketed primarily to young boys, but the gaming industry now rivals film and television in size, scope, and cultural significance. People of all ages, all genders, and all walks of life play billions of hours of games every year.[1]

Games offer a nice microcosm of learning at scale and a good place to recap the major themes from Part I of this book. In the early 2010s, games and "gamification"—the process of adding game elements to learning technologies—experienced a surge of interest against the backdrop of the widespread growth of gaming. Futurists imagined a more playful future for schools, and technology developers created new educational games and, in some cases, promised dramatic results. From 2012 to 2014, the *Horizon Report*—a publication from education futurists—predicted that "games and gamifications" were "two to three years" away from generating considerable impact in formal education. Some interesting experiments, which I will discuss in this chapter, proved to be popular and effective in a few niches within the ecology of human development, but overall, the learning game movement remains another unrequited disruption.[2]

Games are indisputably great engines of learning: ask a passionate *Pokémon* player about the virtues of Charizard versus Pikachu or the strategies for deploying these monsters in imaginary battles, and you can unleash a torrent of factual knowledge, strategic thinking, and hard-won wisdom from hours of experience. Many modern games are immensely complex, and developers deploy a variety of features for helping players learn that complexity. They gradually and dynamically adjust difficulty, adding levels, new elements, and new challenges in response to player success and development, which keeps players at the sweet spot between what a learner knows how to do without help and what a learner can't yet do, the liminal space that psychologist Lev Vygotsky called the zone of proximal development. Games provide a narrative world of meaning, consequence, and relevance to motivate and engage players. Hinting systems, online wikis, video tutorials, and discussion boards provide as-needed resources for just-in-time learning as players seek to improve. Through these kinds of strategies, gamers are unquestionably learning and getting better at the game. The core question of learning games is one of transfer: Do people who develop new skills, knowledge, and proficiencies within a game world flexibly deploy those new insights back in the humdrum of everyday life?[3]

Learning Games and the Problem of Transfer

While many educational technologists make claims about product benefits that far exceed the evidence, very few developers manage to venture so far into the realm of falsehood that they attract the attention of the Federal Trade Commission. The developers of Lumosity, then, hold a special place of ignominy in the history of the 2010s edtech hype cycle for earning a $2 million fine from the FTC for false advertising.[4]

Lumosity develops "brain training games." They take cognitive tests of mental capacities like working memory and divided attention, and they turn these tests into mini-games. Lumosity advertised to users that practicing these games would lead to more generalized benefits "in every aspect of life," including improvements in school work, age-related cognitive decline, and brain injuries. If a person played a game that helped them improve their working memory in a puzzle, for example, then Lumosity claimed that their performance would improve on a wide range of real-world tasks that require working memory. In 2016, the FTC found no evidence to support these claims, and psychology researchers conducting experimental evaluations of these programs also found no evidence of these general benefits.[5]

In psychological terms, the Lumosity advertisers were making a claim about the concept of "transfer," the idea that what people learn in one situation (such as a game) can be applied to novel situations (such as in day-to-day life). One of the first psychologists to study transfer was Edward Thorndike, the pioneering education scientist whom we met briefly in Chapter 1. In the early twentieth century (and long before), educators and curriculum developers claimed that the rigorous study of Greek and Latin built up "mental muscles" that, once strengthened, could be productively used for tackling other cognitive problems. Transfer emerged as a critique of this line of reasoning. Thorndike observed that when learners developed new knowledge or skills, they were far more likely to be able to apply those skills in novel contexts if the new context had many similarities—Thorndike called them "identical elements"—to the original learning context. Situations that are only slightly novel are known as near transfer; if you learn to drive in a sedan and then hop into a station wagon, you are practicing near transfer. Learning contexts that are substantially different from the original are known as far transfer, like learning to drive a car and then trying to fly a helicopter, or learning Latin and then trying to do math, or playing puzzles on your phone and then being a better thinker in everyday life.[6]

While Lumosity's claims were sufficiently specific and incorrect to merit regulatory attention, claims about the general cognitive benefits of games and pastimes are quite common. For example, many people believe that chess experts develop generalizable strategic thinking skills. A recent meta-analysis examined studies of chess training, music training, and working-memory training, and found little compelling evidence that any of these three practices improved people's general cognitive performance. It turns out that chess expertise primarily depends upon an encyclopedic knowledge of common chess moves and board positions; if you show chess board positions that come from actual, realistic chess situations to both masters and novices, masters are much more likely to be able to recreate those situations from memory. If you show chess masters and novices board positions that are nearly impossible to occur in actual chess games, then masters have little advantage in recreating the nonsense boards. The knowledge of common board positions is essential to getting better at chess, but this knowledge is mostly useless when trying to play other games or conduct other strategic tasks. Similarly, the research from Luminosity shows that people who play working-memory games indeed get better at other working-memory games (near transfer), but getting better at these working-memory games does not help with other kinds of cognitive tasks (far transfer).[7]

The implications of this feature of human development are quite significant and quite challenging for educators. As a society, we hope that schools can teach domain-independent, broadly useful skills like critical thinking, collaboration, and communication, but it turns out that most skills are actually quite domain specific—thinking critically about a chess move requires different knowledge and skills than thinking critically about the interpretation of a novel. This also proves to be a substantial challenge for the field of educational games. Part of what makes games fun and engaging is immersing people in an alternate world, but theories of transfer suggest that the more distance between those alternate worlds and our own, the less likely it is that learners will be able to deploy game-world learning in the real world.

So if far transfer doesn't work, are educational games worth pursuing? Learning games, like adaptive tutors, have been used long enough in schools and other settings that a track record of research exists about their effectiveness. One of the best ways to evaluate a class of learning experiences is to look not just at an individual study but at collections of studies, or meta-analyses. In a meta-analysis, researchers collect a set of published research studies—usually experimental and quasi-experimental designs that draw comparisons between an intervention group and a control group—and draw comparisons across a whole set of findings. Two major meta-analyses of classroom use of games were published in 2013 and 2016, and they both pointed in the same direction. Across the studies, students who participated in game-based learning experiences had modestly better learning outcomes on measures of knowledge and intrapersonal domains like intellectual openness, work ethic, and contentiousness. Playing games over multiple sessions was more effective than one-time games, and when basic versions of a game were compared with versions with more advanced and theoretically informed features, the more advanced games led to better results. Yet even experiments using games with simple mechanics—limited narrative, goals targeting lower-order thinking skills, basic content exercises with badges, stars, and points layered on top—showed modestly better outcomes than control conditions without games. Of course, what happens on average won't perfectly predict what will happen in any particular classroom or school, but these kinds of studies provide some useful guidelines for reasonable expectations. Using learning games as part of teaching can probably lead to modest improvement in student learning and motivation. Enthusiasts promising a dramatic transforming of schooling and learning through games and gamification should be regarded with skepticism.[8]

The research on learning games isn't overwhelmingly negative or positive, and the effects of individual games vary. But by using the concept of transfer and applying the genres of educational technology at scale that we have learned over the first part of this book, we can imagine how individual games might interact with school systems. Think back to the last educational game that you played. Who designed the order of your activities and experiences in the game world? Did you move from one set piece to another, and was the order of set pieces determined by the designers? Did your actions or answers in one part of the game trigger algorithmic decisions that determined what happened next? Did engagements with peers shape your playing experience? Most learning games fit reasonably well into one of the three genres of instructor-guided, algorithm-guided, and peer-guided learning at scale. Placing games in those genres helps throw into relief where any given game might provide targeted benefits to some learners. Other strategies introduced throughout the last three chapters—asking "What's really new here?," reviewing published evidence of effectiveness, and finding the alignments or misalignments between learning technologies and existing educational systems—can all prove useful in reviewing learning games and imagining how they might support learning in different parts of the education landscape, even if we can be confident that they won't profoundly transform schools.

Instructor-Guided Learning Games: *Math Blaster* and Chocolate-Covered Broccoli

Most learning games are simple to classify, and most are instructor-guided experiences. For many in my generation, *Math Blaster* was the first learning game they encountered. The on-screen playing field was arranged roughly like *Space Invaders* with aliens from the top of the screen descending upon a village below while the player shoots laser beams at the aliens. In this case, however, the lasers are inexplicably powered by math problems, and the game stops periodically to have students answer a question, where the variables in the questions are randomized but basically arranged in predesignated sequences. As students complete the sequence, they get to do harder problems. My nine-year-old daughter has a math app from school called XtraMath where the conceit is different—she's racing against a "teacher" to provide math facts (for problems like "12 minus 9"), but the mechanism for XtraMath and *Math Blaster* are basically the same: solve simple math problems, get points, solve harder math problems, get more points. These instructor-guided games exist on a walled-garden platform or inside a software package or app, assess student performance and progress through pattern-matching autograders, and draw pedagogical inspiration from pail fillers rather than flame kindlers.

Game researcher Brenda Laurel developed the vivid analogy of "chocolate-covered broccoli" to describe these kinds of games. The core activity in *Math Blaster* or XtraMath is no different from the core activity on a worksheet: solve arithmetic problems. Since many students experience worksheets as dreadfully boring, game designers add a layer of points, stars, beeps, and other rewards on top of drill-and-practice activities. Underneath this layer of external rewards and incentives are very traditional math activities. The process of pouring behaviorist chocolate over instructionist broccoli is often described as "gamification," and these practices have a broad foothold in schools. Gamification can be found as elements in learning software, like the points and badges awarded in Khan Academy. Platforms such as Kahoot allow teachers to author their own content within a gaming platform, turning typical classroom routines such as quizzes and review sessions into classroom game shows.[9]

These approaches to gamification fit relatively easily into traditional school settings by making minimal changes to what David Tyack and Larry Cuban call the "grammar" of schooling, or the unquestioned processes, beliefs, and assumptions deeply embedded in the educational system.[10] As we've discussed in previous chapters, the grammar of schooling tends toward Thorndike's pedagogical philosophy, in which students learn through organized, direct instruction, and their learning can be measured. Gamified learning exercises are simple to use and short to play, making them easy to assign in class in lieu of similar kinds of activities. They take worksheet problems and add game elements to them. One purpose of doing worksheet problems is practicing for the kinds of classroom and standardized tests that serve as gatekeepers to advancement in the education system. In that regard, learning games have the advantage of aiming to bridge a problem of near transfer, using games about problems found on math tests to help people do better on math tests.

Algorithm-Guided Learning Games: Duolingo

Relatively few learning games have managed to become breakout hits beyond the classroom, but one of the most successful efforts in recent years is the gamified language-learning app Duolingo.

A game-like, algorithm-guided, adaptive tutor for language learning, Duolingo was cofounded by Luis von Ahn, a computer scientist at Carnegie Mellon and the inventor of the CAPTCHA crowdsourcing system. Most Duolingo activities are some form of translation or recognition activity, where students earn points, complete progress bars, and earn badges for translating text between the target and native language in speech and writing. As of 2018, over 300 million people had signed up for an account with Duolingo, making it one of the largest platforms for independent learning in the world. One of the distinctive features of Duolingo is that it includes adaptive features that allow for personalized spaced repetition. These adaptive features offer some interesting targeted benefits for learners, but as with other algorithm-guided large-scale learning technologies, limitations of autograding are an important constraint on the overall utility of these kinds of tools.[11]

Going back nearly a century, psychologists have recognized that people remember things better when they practice recalling them over a long period of time rather than through cramming. If you have a choice between studying for an hour one day before a test or studying for twenty minutes each of the three days before a test, the spaced practice is almost universally better. These systems can be improved further if the studying experience focuses most on the facts or topics that a learner remembers least well. When studying language facts on flash cards, learners should spend little time on the flash cards they always get right (despite the emotional rewards of doing so) and nearly all their time on flash cards that they always get wrong. The benefits of spaced repetition are some of the oldest and most well-established findings from cognitive psychology with obvious implications for learning, but they are very rarely implemented in actual classrooms.[12]

Your Spanish teacher probably could not implement personalized space repetition in your class because it is very logistically complicated—an instructor has to identify word definitions or other language facts (like verb conjugations) that each student has not mastered, provide opportunities to practice these facts alongside introducing new content, and then slowly withdraw facts from practice as students demonstrate mastery. Tossing a few vocabulary words from week two on the week-six test is not too difficult for an instructor, but personalizing practice tests for dozens of students on the basis of their individual progress and mastery is nearly impossible for a typical teacher to organize. Computers, however, can implement these complex, personalized schemes of spaced repetition for each student. The results are promising, at least for the introductory parts of learning a language. In 2012, independent researchers found that Duolingo users who spent an average of thirty-four hours on Duolingo learning Spanish would learn material roughly equivalent to the first semester of college Spanish.[13]

An interesting feature of a language-learning curriculum is that midway through a typical course progression, the cognitive complexity of the learning sharply increases. In introductory Spanish, students are memorizing the Spanish word for *cat* and how to conjugate the verb *to have*. In advanced Spanish, students are reading and interpreting Cervantes. Autograders are much more useful for the former kinds of tasks with well-defined correct answers than for the latter kinds of interpretive tasks, so it is unlikely that Duolingo's usefulness in learning introductory language concepts will extend to more advanced language acquisition skills. The assessments in Duolingo can evaluate whether a person has defined or translated a word or short phrase correctly; they cannot evaluate a student's arguments for the impact of *Don Quixote* on Spanish literature and culture. Language-learning games may be a great way for people to start learning a language, but for the foreseeable future, developing real fluency will require engagements with native speakers and culture that are not possible through an autograded app.

Peer-Guided Learning Games: *Vanished* and *Minecraft*

If the chocolate-covered broccoli approach is to slather gamification elements on top of traditional schooling activities, then the alternative is to search within content areas to find fun and playful elements that already exist. In this approach to developing learning games, the fun isn't getting to shoot aliens after doing some math, the fun is doing the math.

My colleagues in the MIT Education Arcade develop what they call "resonant games," games that try to immerse players, individually and in communities, into activities that are personally engaging and provide rich insights into academic content. If most learning games align best with the instructionist, banking model of education—filling students with content and testing their recall—then the Education Arcade's resonant games tend to look more like the flame-kindling, apprenticeship model of learning, where the game world immerses players in some kind of cognitive apprenticeship.[14]

For instance, the game *Vanished* doesn't quiz people on science facts, but rather immerses players as members of a community of scientists trying to understand the fate of a lifeless planet. Developed by researchers and designers at the Education Arcade in partnership with the Smithsonian Institution, *Vanished* was a massive multiplayer puzzle experience played out on the open web—a kind of online escape room for thousands of people at once. In the game narrative, scientists from the future send messages back in time to warn humanity about a forthcoming asteroid-induced apocalypse. They communicate to the players through a series of puzzles and mini-games hidden throughout the web and at physical museums. Some of the puzzles required large-scale collaboration; each user randomly received one of ninety-nine codes that needed to be assembled to solve a puzzle. Players could purchase documents with points that they earned throughout the game, and some documents were so expensive that players could buy them only while pooling points. Over 6,000 player accounts were registered in the game, and over 650 were active toward the end.

While not explicitly influenced by connectivism, the game has much in common with connectivism-inspired pedagogies—participants in the game form networks, communicate with one another, share resources and solutions. Players both learn about a topic (in this case, climate change that renders humanity incapable of responding to the asteroid threat) and develop a shared identity as scientists. The story provided an opportunity for players to learn about a range of scientific content areas, from unit conversion to forensic anthropology, but perhaps more importantly, it gave participants the opportunity to develop their identities as scientists. As one player wrote as part of an evaluation of the game, "I really feel like a future scientist now. Imagine, when we all have famous jobs at research centers across the world, someone will discover how we all as kids worked on a game." *Vanished* shares a series of common challenges with other peer-guided learning experiences: attrition limited the number of learners who benefited from the full experience, participant experiences were idiosyncratic and learning outcomes uneven, and a long-term, unfamiliar learning experience was challenging to integrate into traditional classroom practices. For those who invested deeply in the experience, however, the game provided a uniquely powerful learning experience that was not just about science but also about what it is like to be a scientist.[15]

MINECRAFT

Math Blaster, Vanished, and Duolingo represent efforts to create games or gamified experiences designed for educational purposes, but another approach to learning games is to find commercial games that have both widespread appeal and the potential to foster powerful learning experiences. Rather than making and marketing new games, what if educators could take existing games and use them for teaching and learning academic content? In 2020, *Minecraft* and *Minecraft: Education Edition* represent one of the most ambitious efforts along those lines.

Minecraft is one of the world's largest learning communities—millions of young and young at heart around the world play, build, and explore in the *Minecraft* world. *Minecraft* is an open-world game made up of square blocks of various kinds—dirt, stone, sand, water, lava, iron, gold, diamond—that can be mined with tools and then recombined to make Lego-block-like creations in the game world. Resources that drop from different blocks can be combined to create a wide variety of items, from new tools, weapons, and armor to decorative elements like doors and carpets. It is among the most popular games of all time, with over 180 million copies sold. *Minecraft* worlds can be set up as multiplayer servers so people can enter the same world and play, build, share, and collaborate.[16]

The scope of the learning community on *Minecraft* is extraordinary in its breadth. Like many recent games, *Minecraft* is highly complex but ships without any kind of manual. Through in-game experimentation and examination of game files, users essentially have cocreated the manual themselves on sites like the Gamepedia Minecraft wiki. That wiki is maintained by over three hundred active contributors and has over four thousand articles on topics that range from the original staff of the Swedish game developer Mojang to the probability distributions of finding diamonds at various depths in the game world. There are countless YouTube accounts devoted to demonstrating features in *Minecraft,* including genuine global celebrities such as Joseph Garrett, also known as Stampylonghead, whose YouTube channel has 9 million subscribers and whose *How to Minecraft* introductory series has tens of millions of views. Twitch has hundreds of active streamers playing *Minecraft* at any given time; Reddit has a subreddit with photos of incredible creations and gifs of funny moments. Any one of these content distribution channels is an endless rabbit hole of narrative and creativity.[17]

All of these digital learning resources form a dense, complex, and intricate peer learning network, with resources to guide players from their first actions in the *Minecraft* world to the complex management of resources necessary to visit the far reaches of the game world or to create massive built environments atop the randomly generated game world. There is an easily recognizable peer-guided learning-at-scale network that teaches people about *Minecraft*, but to what extent can the game itself be used for learning both within and outside of formal education systems?

Given that *Minecraft* has consumed billions of hours of youth time over the last decade and is increasingly being seen in the classroom, there is surprisingly little research about the experience of playing *Minecraft* and what benefits it might accrue. Studying these kinds of informal learning environments is profoundly difficult. When students come to school, we have particular goals for them, we give them assessments, and we combine these assessments with observations of classroom processes to understand what learning is taking place. Tracking the learning that happens across tens of millions of households as kids play informally is much, much harder.

Researchers who study play and informal learning can point to a variety of behaviors in *Minecraft* that could potentially lead to positive outcomes for young people. Games encourage discovery and perseverance, requiring self-regulation in single-player settings and communication and collaboration in multiplayer settings. Game designer and researcher Katie Salen suggests a list of *Minecraft* related skills: teamwork, strategic communication, asking for help, persistence, recovery from failure, negotiation, planning, time management, decision-making, and spatial awareness. This is the optimist's view of transfer, that time invested in learning these skills in a game like *Minecraft* will translate into domain-independent skills. Teamwork skills developed through collaboratively building a castle in *Minecraft* might prove useful when building teams in a workplace or civic setting.[18]

A more pessimistic view built upon the research on transfer is that people who spend a lot of time playing *Minecraft* will primarily learn about playing *Minecraft*. If people who invest considerable time mastering chess do not appear to be developing domain-independent strategic thinking skills, then it is not clear that people playing *Minecraft* are necessarily developing any particular domain-independent architectural or design skills, or any of the other skills developed in *Minecraft*.

My own view is that there probably are some domain-independent problem-solving skills that players develop in *Minecraft*. For instance, players might develop the intuition that if they get stuck on a task, there is likely to be a community of teachers and learners online who have documented solutions to similar tasks or would be willing to engage in online dialogue about how to solve the problem. As the last chapter on peer-guided learning at scale suggests, that is an enormously useful disposition to adopt in a networked world, because in nearly any domain of human endeavor, there are people online willing to help. That said, there are particular skills and facts required to take advantage of each of those distinct networks of learning. To figure out how to do something in *Minecraft*, a player must understand the mechanics of the game, the vocabulary of the game, the most common repositories of reliable knowledge, and the norms of information dissemination and online discourse. One has to learn similar things to figure out how to write a particular function and debug a program in JavaScript, but in another domain: the mechanics and syntax of the JavaScript language, the vocabulary of its functions and primitives, the common repositories of reliable knowledge, how to search within Stack Overflow, and how to ask new questions within community norms. The domain-independent skills, a disposition to seek out peer-guided online learning networks, and an understanding of their common structures are a little bit helpful in many different circumstances; extensive content knowledge in a domain, like memorizing common board positions in chess, is essential to mastery in a local context and not very useful elsewhere. These distinctions do not reduce the value of the broader disposition of online help-seeking and participation in online networks, but that disposition alone will not bridge the chasm of far transfer. Domain-independent skills are slightly useful in lots of different domains but not deeply useful in any particular domain.

Recognizing the popularity and potential for learning in *Minecraft*, some classroom educators have explored making tighter connections between *Minecraft* play and classroom learning. At Carnegie Mellon University, materials science professor B. Reeja Jayan used *Minecraft* to teach the basics of material science to engineers by having students build models of atoms and molecules out of digital blocks. The *Minecraft* universe includes a substance called "redstone" that can be used to create circuits within the game, and educators have developed a variety of tasks for learning the basics of physics, electrical engineering, and computer science. In a kind of learning-at-scale special crossover episode, faculty at UC San Diego have created a MOOC about teaching coding in *Minecraft*.[19]

The open-world design of *Minecraft* is terrific for play and exploration but imperfectly suited for targeted content learning that happens in schools. In an effort to add more classroom-friendly features, in 2011, TeacherGaming released *MinecraftEDU*, a version of *Minecraft* developed with specific modifications to aid teachers in using *Minecraft* in their classrooms. The modifications made certain logistical tasks easier, such as registering students and assigning them to a world. It also allowed educators to create specific worlds with specific tasks, constraints, and game rules so that teachers could give students a more instructor-guided experience within the open-world platform. In the 2010s, both *Minecraft* and *MinecraftEDU* were bought by Microsoft, which released a *Minecraft: Education Edition* that provides new ways for instructors to control the game world and a set of turnkey lesson plans and game worlds that teachers can use for teaching academic content ranging from biodiversity and extinction to Boolean logic in circuits.

In a sense, these modifications run counter to some of the fundamental principles of *Minecraft*. For most players, *Minecraft* is fun because they can do whatever they want: building structures, inventing arbitrary challenges (harvesting enough diamonds to build a full set of armor), or just exploring to see if there are any llamas around the next corner. The *Minecraft: Education Edition* projects constrain some of this creativity; in order to teach specific content, they ask students to do what teachers want them to do. In the worst cases, the imposition on the freedom of *Minecraft* will spoil the fun, and the high time-cost for instructors setting up these worlds won't be worth the modest gains in engagement. In the best cases, these additional scaffolds will form a productive hybrid of open-world play and teacher-guided problem-based learning. Little rigorous research exists as yet about *Minecraft* in education, but I would predict findings similar to what researchers have discovered with other approaches to learning at scale that fit uncomfortably in the constraints of formal schools: a handful of really extraordinary applications in a few institutions but no widespread adoption across many schools.

Hybridity and Learning-at-Scale Genres:
The Logical Journey of the Zoombinis

A worked example is a teaching strategy where an instructor explains, step by step, how he or she would solve a type of problem. In this chapter, I have tried to offer a worked example of a classification exercise that takes a type of large-scale learning technology, in this case educational games, and situates that technology within the learning-at-scale taxonomy to demonstrate what patterns emerge.

Throughout the chapter, I provided several examples of games that fit well in the three learning-at-scale genres: *Math Blaster* as an example of an instructor-guided learning experience; Duolingo as an adaptive, algorithm-guided learning app; and *Vanished* and *Minecraft* as peer-guided large-scale learning communities. Placing games in these categories provides a way to quickly frame some of their strengths and weaknesses; if you can see that Duolingo is an adaptive tutor, then you can review what you know about the history of adaptive tutors and make some good guesses about its strength and limitations. That history can also reveal ways in which a new product is distinct; we've had decades of adaptive tutors, but few have been as widely adopted by individuals outside of formal learning environments as Duolingo. Something about the design of Duolingo—its gamified elements, the subject matter of language learning, a mobile-first platform—led to a wider adoption than might have been otherwise expected. Designers can tinker with these standout aspects of a particular approach and consider which of them might be applicable to other technologies within that same genre or beyond.

Not all learning-at-scale approaches fit neatly within the three genres that I have proposed, and hybridity is a promising site for sources of innovation. In finding novel combinations of elements within a game or other new technology, we might be able to take inspiration in devising new approaches to learning at scale. One example of a learning game that demonstrates this kind of hybridity is *The Logical Journey of the Zoombinis,* one of the all-time great mathematics games, developed by Scot Osterweil.

In the game, players have a small band of Zoombinis, which are basically little blue heads with feet, who are on a journey across a series of landscapes to find a new homeland after being enslaved by the evil Bloats. Each Zoombini has four distinct characteristics—eyes, nose, hair, and feet—and each of these characteristics has five options (for instance, wide eyes, one eye, sleepy eyes, glasses, and sunglasses) for a total of 625 unique Zoombinis. The player must bring bands of these Zoombinis through a series of puzzles in which the puzzles are responsive to the characteristics of the Zoombinis. For instance, in the Allergic Cliffs level, there are two bridges, and each bridge has a set of allergies to certain Zoombini characteristics— like wide eyes or green noses; although the player is given no instructions about these particular bridges, and it is left to the player to discover their properties. If the player tries to move a Zoombini with an allergen across the bridge, the bridge will sneeze and blow the Zoombini back. The game is designed to help players explore ideas about logic, pattern recognition, and combinatorics.[20]

To classify the game, we can start by asking who controls the pace and pathway of the learning. As a single-player game, there is no peer element, but the game has a blend of features that support both algorithm-guided and instructor-guided elements. Within a puzzle, there is no "Next" or "Previous" button; players try a series of steps, moves, and combinations, and the game levels react to player choices. When players complete a puzzle level, they are exposed to a branching structure to choose the next puzzle that splits autonomy between designers and players. The results are somewhere between a fully sequenced system like a MOOC and a fully adaptive system. While the visual skin of *Zoombinis* and edX are quite different, they share a set of sequenced learning activities evaluated by autograders.

The Logical Journey of the Zoombinis defies easy categorization in the learning-at-scale schema that I have proposed, but the genres help us to situate the gameplay and learning relative to other learning experiences. Pedagogically, the game is an open-ended immersion into logical thinking exercises, with a strong emphasis on inquiry. Levels have no written instructions, and there are no demonstrations or worked examples; rather, players need to discover the rules of each puzzle through visual contextual clues, trial and error, and logic. Despite wildly different appearances, the technological infrastructure of the game has important commonalities with MOOCs, as a walled garden with an automated assessment system. The pacing and gated objectives have more in common with MOOCs or adaptive tutors than with Scratch or the Rainbow Loom community. Despite these similarities to MOOCs and intelligent tutors, the pedagogy behind the game is more about apprenticeship and play than instruction; it has a closer philosophical kinship with Seymour Papert's Logo programming language than with Salman Khan's practice problems.

Zoombinis is a learning experience that cuts against the grains of the patterns that I have described in the past chapters, and it can provide inspiration for new avenues of development. What might it look like to have an automated assessment system in the Scratch platform that maintained the values of playfulness and apprenticeship? What might it look like to have the ideas of playfulness and apprenticeship embedded into an intelligent tutor or an xMOOC? Tinkering with hybridity offer potential ways of offsetting the limitation of one learning-at-scale genre with the strengths from another.

From Learning-at-Scale Genres to As-Yet-Intractable Dilemmas

In Part I of this book, I highlighted the differences among large-scale learning environments to define three genres, and in the next four chapters I turn to a set of similarities. In some respect, the technology innovations that I've described over the past four chapters are astonishing: free online courses in nearly any subject from anatomy to zoology, a repository of free online videos that cover the entire mathematics curriculum, adaptive tutors that personalize practice for individual students, peer communities where learners gather to study computational creativity or online learning, and games for learning languages or building worlds. As these innovations were introduced, particularly in the late 2000s and early 2010s, they were accompanied by dramatic predictions about how these tools might pave the way for fundamental transformations of educational systems. Yet for all the adoption of large-scale learning technologies in informal learning environments and formal institutions, fundamental transformations have been elusive. New learning-at-scale technologies have proven limited but useful supplements to traditional education systems, rather than levers for fundamentally remaking those systems. Why?

Across very different kinds of large-scale learning systems—inspired by Dewey or Thorndike, found behind paywalls or on the open web, guided by instructors, algorithms, or peer communities—certain dilemmas emerge over and over again. The *curse of the familiar* starts from the observation that technologies that look like typical elements in schools—like the practice problems on Khan Academy—scale much more easily than things that look very different from anything that has come before, like the open-ended programming environment on Scratch. Schools are complex institutions finely tuned to a kind of homeostasis. And if old ideas are easier to adopt than truly novel, and potentially much more powerful, approaches, how then can schools change and evolve to meet the challenges of the future? From MOOCs to adaptive tutors to Scratch, evidence suggests that an *edtech Matthew effect* is quite common: that new technologies disproportionately benefit learners with the financial, social, and technical capital to take advantage of new innovations. How might we design learning technologies that ameliorate rather than exacerbate opportunity gaps? I have described technologies as unevenly useful across different subject domains, and one of the core sources of unevenness is assessment technologies. These technologies work much better in domains where problem solving is structured and routine; the *trap of routine assessment* is that the places where automated assessment works best may overlap closely with the domains where automation and robotics are most likely to replace human work. Throughout each of these first four chapters, I have observed that one of the characteristics of the best learning technology systems is that they are subject to constant research, iteration, and refinement. This kind of research might be greatly aided by the vast stores of data collected by online learning environments, and yet these data also include deeply personal information about people's lives and learning experiences—how they learn, where they succeed and fail, how they rank compared to others, their interests and beliefs. Navigating this tension requires addressing the *toxic power of data and experiments* and weighing the privacy risks with the research benefits of data collection. Across very different technologies, pedagogies, and designs, all learning-at-scale initiatives are forced to confront these common challenges that take up the second half of this book.

II

DILEMMAS IN

LEARNING AT SCALE

5

THE CURSE OF THE FAMILIAR

Rip Van Winkle and Skeuomorphism

AN OLD JOKE and over-used keynote riff among education innovators is that if Rip Van Winkle awoke today from his hundred-year nap, he would be befuddled by the new world. He might wander across town marveling at people's constant staring, swiping, and tapping into mobile phones. He might balk to see cars driving themselves and stores with automated checkout lines. And when he finally made his way into a school, Rip would heave a great sigh of relief that schools are just as he remembered (insert uproarious laughter here).

This joke overemphasizes the stability of schooling, but it contains an important kernel of truth: schools are conservative institutions in society. People tend to teach how they were taught, and new technologies are far more likely to be bent to fit into existing systems than they are to lead to major reorganizations.

When faced with integrating new technologies, most educators take an approach constrained by a combination of an anxiety about trying new things, a desire to make the best possible use of students' time, and the stress of the demanding workloads required just to keep classes running. It is only with support, professional learning opportunities, collaborative planning time, and other system-level resources that most educators can become comfortable enough to try new approaches to teaching and learning with technology.

Even when teachers have adequate support for technology integration, research has shown that adoption of new technologies is a process that usually begins with using new technologies in old ways. In the 1980s, Judith Sandholtz and a team of researchers conducted the Apple Classrooms of Tomorrow project, an initiative to place cutting-edge personal computers like the Apple IIe and some of the first wired computer networks into K–12 classrooms. She found that teachers needed to proceed through a developmental trajectory of stages: entry, adoption, adaptation, appropriation, and invention. At early stages, teachers replicated existing practices with technology, and over time, teachers developed approaches to teaching and learning that would be impossible without the new technologies. When introduced to new technology, most teachers start at the early phases, and many do not progress much beyond that. This isn't necessarily a criticism, as great teaching can happen with or without technology, but it is an empirical observation. Developing the capacity to integrate new technologies in ways that lead to meaningful changes in teaching and learning takes time, opportunities for professional development, coaching, and peer support.[1]

Many learners approach education technology with the same conservativism that we find with teachers. While working for HarvardX in the first few years of MOOC development, I was struck by how common it was for a subset of learners to vociferously critique anything that didn't look like a "standard" MOOC. When microbiology professor David Cox created a MOOC with animations and simulations for learning about the human brain, learners dismissed it as non-serious compared to more lecture- and test-based MOOCs. In 2014, George Siemens led the development of an edX MOOC about learning analytics called Data Analytics and Learning, or DALMOOC, which attempted to include components of both instructionist and connectivist MOOCs. The edX portion of the MOOC had lecture videos and autograded items, and there was a parallel online community that functioned more like a cMOOC, with social features and more open-ended learning. In the edX forums, several learners railed against the cMOOC portion, even though it was optional. In a 2014 interview, Siemens explained, "If you take a MOOC today, you basically have the same structure as you had in 2011 when Coursera and edX were introduced—students have a certain set of expectations. They want that format, it seems." In three short years, learner expectations around xMOOCs had solidified around a conservative notion of what MOOCs should be.[2]

Designers of popular consumer technologies also often assume some conservativism in their users. One of the most widely recognized icons on a computer screen is the "trash" or "delete" icon, which often looks like a wastepaper basket. This is a classic example of a user-experience design strategy called skeuomorphism, which involves making digital tools look like their analog components. Early versions of Notes, Apple's iOS notebook app, were made to look like a leather-bound legal pad; the pages were yellow and had straight lines across them, and a leather image ran down the left edge. These markers of familiarity were included to help people imagine how they might use a new technology. But that imagination is constrained by the presence of visual markers of an older technology, and that constraint is imposed by design; the invitation from the leather-bound Notes app was to continue taking notes as you had in the past, not to imagine new ways that a digital notebook might lead to more interesting, useful, or effective habits of study or practice. Skeuomorphism gives users hints about what to do at the cost of limiting their imaginations about what new things might be possible with a new technology.[3]

Skeuomorphism is a useful metaphor for education technology; most new tools are designed to harken back to some kind of analog antecedent in typical classroom practice. Watch five seconds of a Khan Academy video, and you will know that you are watching a lecture. Peek at one of their problem sets, and you'll recognize the questions and response boxes as a digital worksheet. The stars and points and bing noises that accompany correct answers are as familiar as the gold star that your first grade teacher might have affixed to the top of a homework sheet.

One of the most widely used education technology products in the world is Quizlet, an app for creating decks of online flash cards for practice, testing, and sharing. Quizlet has over 50 million monthly users around the world and claims to engage 50 percent of all K–12 students in the United States (there are over 50 million students each year in US K–12 schools). If government leaders convened a panel of global experts to discuss the most urgent needs in our education system, it is hard to imagine that "a dearth of flash cards" would rise to the top of the list. Managing a global transition from index cards to digital flash cards is probably not the most compelling strategy for education reform. Quizlet may have successfully engaged half of American students with a single app, but there is no reason to believe that this technology adoption has led to substantial improvements in national learning. But digital flash cards offer some efficiency gains over paper flash cards, they fit neatly into existing educational systems, and they can be easily used and adopted by a wide range of teachers and learners.[4]

This, then, is one side of what I call the curse of the familiar. Easily adopted technologies will be those that replicate existing classroom practices, but digitizing what teachers and students already do is unlikely to lead to substantial improvements in schools. Whether students are testing themselves on 1 million, 1 billion, or 1 trillion Quizlet study sets per year, online flash cards are not going to profoundly change the experience of schooling and learning.

Bafflement or Banality, and the Flip Side of the Curse of the Familiar

The flip side of the curse of the familiar coin is that when edtech developers do create novel learning environments that offer the promise of substantially changing learners' experiences, many learners will find these environments confusing and teachers will find them difficult to adopt. I discussed this dynamic in several earlier chapters. Recall that when many learners encountered the connectivist MOOCs developed by Canadian educators, they were baffled by the decentralized structure, the new aggregation technologies, the freedoms afforded to learners, and the minimally specified ends of the exercise. From figuring out how to sign up and participate to making sense of the point of it all, learners had to put substantial effort into meta-learning about how to participate in a new learning environment. This was precisely the point of connectivist MOOCs, but it was also their stumbling block.

Efforts to adopt the Scratch programming environment in schools provide another example of the curse of the familiar. Developers and advocates hope that Scratch can generate opportunities for students and learners to develop computational creativity through a pedagogy that emphasizes projects, passion, partners, and play (recalling Scratch founder Mitch Resnick's description of the project in *Lifelong Kindergarten*). In the ideal use cases of Scratch, learners should have a high degree of autonomy in pursuing projects of interest, and as they develop personally relevant animations, games, programs, and resources, they'll encounter moments of difficulty or opportunities for learning. To respond to those challenges, Scratchers would ideally search their online and local communities, including teachers, to find learning resources. For some Scratchers—a large number but a relatively small proportion—Scratch provides precisely the motivation to pursue these investigative pathways. But for many students who open Scratch, the open-ended learning environment and possibilities for collaboration are confusing or overwhelming. It is not clear what to do with coding blocks or how they might work; it is not obvious how one might go from the blank canvas in Scratch to the sophisticated animations and games that experienced programmers create. Many people who sign up for Scratch start a project then quit soon after. As of 2019, Scratch had about 40 million registered users and about 40 million Scratch projects. The typical engagement with Scratch is a one-off.

The dilemma that Resnick and colleagues face as Scratch is widely adopted in schools is that a variety of typical school structures are inimical to the pedagogical philosophy behind Scratch. Scratch values remixing of projects so that new ideas can build upon and reimagine older ones, and schools typically insist on clear, individual provenance of work to allow for assigning grades to individual students. In schools, remixing is cheating. Scratch values open-ended exploration and discovery, but class periods have strict time limits, and teachers often ask students to complete particular milestones at particular time points in order to assign grades, credit, or other markers of compliance. Scratch is designed as the technology avatar and vehicle for constructionist pedagogy, and schools are often successful at neutering those elements of Scratch so that it can be implemented in learning environments emphasizing teacher control and student compliance with specific routines or instructions.[5]

Funding New Tech for Conservative Educational Systems

The curse of the familiar poses a two-sided dilemma: reproduce the ordinary and get adoption but not change, or attempt to do something different and either confuse your intended audience or have them take your novel approach and transform it into something conventional. Venture-backed education technology efforts over the last decade have overwhelmingly chosen the former.

Over the past ten years, the involvement of venture capital in education technology has grown substantially, with millions of dollars now invested annually in new startups from Boston to Beijing and a global landscape of edtech incubators, coworking spaces where startups can find comradery and networks of support. Venture capital firms purchase a portion of equity in new startups in exchange for an infusion of cash that startups can use for hiring and operations.

For venture-funded edtech startups, one of the core goals is to amass as many users as possible as quickly as possible. A growing install base attracts additional venture capital funding and is supposed to provide the basis of value that would attract an acquisition (where a larger edtech company purchases a smaller new entrant) or investors for an initial public offering. Often, growth is prioritized over revenue generation in startups on the theory that if a company can offer a service to a large enough group of consumers, then revenue generation will sort itself out down the road.

The way to grow as fast as possible is to create something that people are already familiar with. In 2018, education technology historian and critic Audrey Watters compiled a list of eleven edtech companies with the largest investments; seven of them were focused on tutoring for test prep. The other four companies developed administrative software for schools, intelligent tutors for K–8 math, and tutoring for music lessons and English language learning. Venture capital firms are structurally incentivized to be more concerned with getting a return on their investment than in supporting products that substantially improve education. The conservatism of educational systems and the conservativism of financial systems reinforce one another. It is perhaps no surprise that some of the most interesting education technology efforts emerge from universities—connectivist MOOCs from Canadian universities and Scratch from the MIT Media Lab—where there is an unusual combination of available funding, intellectual freedom, and long time horizons. If widespread adoption is conditional on familiarity, then it is hard to imagine truly novel approaches from teaching and learning emerging from funding structures that are concerned with maximizing adoption and return on investment.[6]

The Path through the Curse of the Familiar is Community

The curse of the familiar emerges from trying to use technology alone to change schooling. Schools, with their innate complexity and conservatism, domesticate new technologies into existing routines rather than being disrupted by new technologies. For anyone hoping to substantially change teaching and learning through technology, the most promising way of passing through these thickets is to prioritize systems change alongside technology adoption. And the most important stakeholders in educational change are teachers. What's needed to encourage the design, transmission, and adoption of new ideas is a large, thriving community of teachers who are committed to progressive pedagogical change and designers who are excited about seeing this community as partners.

Peer-to-peer connections among teachers are crucial to transmitting new ideas in schools. When K–12 teachers and faculty in higher education are surveyed or interviewed about the process of pedagogical change, they commonly respond that the number one influence over their pedagogy is other teachers. Principals, state requirements, and other factors can heavily influence what educators teach and their curriculum choices, but peers play the most powerful role in shaping how they teach. It is people that scale new pedagogical practices: educators engaging one another in conversations about teaching and learning, communities forming to understand and advocate for new ideas, and individuals and groups of individuals practicing the time-consuming, patience-testing work of changing institutional cultures and structures. Changing teacher behavior at scale requires nurturing widely distributed networks of peer learning among educators.[7]

Technology can help in this process, in the sense that new technologies can be provocative ways of starting new conversations. When schools adopt the Scratch programming language and online community into a computer science curriculum, an entry point is created for educators to discuss the many purposes of computing and how technologies can spark and support student creativity. Perhaps my main motivation for spending the last decade in education technology is that I have found educators to be genuinely more willing to engage in open discussions of pedagogy when encountering new technologies. But even if technology helps as a catalyst, it cannot replace the hard work of reshaping educational systems to take advantage of the potential of new technologies.

As we have seen in the first part of this book, technology evangelists often use the language of disruptive innovation to tell stories about how old systems will give way to new technologies. In reality, it is community, not technology, that offers the best chance of changing practice in schools. Two organizations are exemplars of groups trying to drive meaningful change in pedagogy through conversations about technology: the Lifelong Kindergarten group and their Scratch project and the developers of the Desmos online graphing calculator.

Scratch: Technology, Community, and Teacher Learning

While Scratch started primarily as a resource for after-school programs and for kids during their leisure time, the more recent growth of Scratch has been driven by school-based adoption. Mitch Resnick, Natalie Rusk, and their colleagues in the Lifelong Kindergarten lab are proud of the widespread adoption of Scratch, but that is not their only goal; they are constantly working to help educators not only to use Scratch, but also to embrace its under-lying ideas. In a sense, the adoption of Scratch in schools has out-paced the adoption of creative, constructionist pedagogy, and the Lifelong Kindergarten team is working to help bridge the gap.

One set of strategies that the Scratch team has pursued is to pro-vide more structure as teachers and students are introduced to Scratch. Seymour Papert, who codeveloped the Logo programming language that pre-dated Scratch, argued that good learning designs have low floors and high ceilings. They should be easy to start working with while allowing for more complex engagement over time. Resnick later added "wide walls" to the design specifications, noting that good learning designs allow for a wide variety of cre-ations that align with student interests. The Scratch team is cur-rently exploring the development of more "narrow foyers"—places with constraints and scaffolds that help people get into both the ideas and the operational nuts and bolts of Scratch. To create new entry points, the Scratch team created Microworlds, Scratch pro-gramming environments with a subset of programming blocks and prepopulated graphics organized around themes that con-nect with youth interests. For instance, one Microworld empha-sizes hip-hop; dance has a series of interesting connections with programming—including the concepts of synchronicity, parallelism, and order of operations—and can serve as a natural connection be-tween coding and urban arts. Other Microworlds include topics such as fashion, art, and comedy. After starting projects in the Mi-croworlds, Scratchers can activate the full set of blocks and "graduate" to more complex projects. The hope is that by reducing the initial complexity of Scratch and providing learners and educa-tors with interest-based entry points, educators will better under-stand how Scratch supports creative expression through code.[8]

Another approach from the Scratch team has been to develop decks of physical coding cards that show the range of projects that students can create—from games to stories to music to animations—and activity guides that again introduce students to diverse forms of expression in Scratch. The wide range of options is meant to guide educators toward seeing the potential of Scratch for individual expression—to push them away from homogenous, recipe-based projects for a whole class toward learning environments where students have the freedom to learn to code driven by their interests and a sense of play and exploration.[9]

While developing a computer programming language that can be used by children around the world is, on its own, a massive undertaking, the Lifelong Kindergarten lab is also invested in the massive undertaking of engaging educators around the world with these ideas. Even as the technical team at Scratch works to distribute the Scratch programming language as widely as possible, the outreach team is committed to building a community of educators and other fellow travelers invested in the ideas behind Scratch.

The Lifelong Kindergarten group has a variety of approaches to help educators better understand the ideas behind Scratch. At the annual Scratch conference, educators and Scratchers come to MIT to share ideas, connect with the Lifelong Kindergarten team, and build community. Each year on Scratch Day, teachers, librarians, after-school educators, young people, and other Scratchers around the world host their own local Scratch-related events and meetups. In 2018, there were over 1,200 registered Scratch Day events of all sizes around the world. The Scratch team recommended that these events include a welcoming ceremony, workshops for learning, "festive activities," and times for people to share their experiences and celebrate the day. Resnick and his team engage educators online as well. The group has taught various iterations of Learning Creative Learning, an open online course that introduces educators to the ideas behind Scratch while engaging in projects with Scratch and related technologies from the group. In tandem with the release of Scratch 3.0 in early 2019, the lab launched a series of other online efforts aimed at educators, including Scratch in Practice, a more modular approach to online learning with resources organized around monthly themes. The site includes educator stories and examples, "Minute with Mitch" videos to share bite-sized ideas behind Scratch, "Natalie's Notes"—blog posts with ideas for educational approaches—featured resources, and a curated Twitter feed of student ideas. Another experimental way to connect with educators is WeScratch, where Scratchers gather to work in small video conference rooms online to collaborate on projects or just do parallel programming with other Scratchers online.[10]

Another team at Harvard, ScratchEd, led by Resnick's former student Karen Brennan, also works directly with educators to help them implement Scratch in classrooms in ways that are aligned with the project's pedagogical foundations. Brennan and her team have led online courses like Getting Unstuck, a twenty-one-day email-based course during which participants received daily creative challenges, not unlike the Daily Create in DS106. ScratchEd organizes Scratch meetups, regular gatherings of Scratch educators throughout the year, where participants are encouraged to learn about Scratch through engaging in peer-led, open-ended learning experiences that immerse participants in the pedagogical foundations of Scratch so educators can create similar experiences for their own students.[11]

These efforts at tinkering with community building have not yet broken the curse of the familiar. Scratch has millions of students around the world logging in from schools, and the ScratchEd meetups have, in 2020, a little over 3,500 members. To be sure, these educators likely have influence over a wider circle of peers and colleagues, but they still represent only a fraction of the educators engaging students with Scratch. Scaling dissemination is far easier than scaling community, but educators change their practice in response to new ideas from peers, not through encounters with new technology alone. If the Scratch team is successful in encouraging the adoption of constructionist learning practices in schools, their success will come not just by building the right technological features in the Scratch platform, but by building communities of educators who can help their peers understand the pedagogical foundations underneath that technology.

Desmos: Designing with and for Community

Another of my favorite examples of community building comes from Desmos, a platform for teaching and visualizing mathematics. Desmos has its roots as an online graphing calculator project meant to replace the nearly ubiquitous Texas Instrument TI-84 calculators that are used in advanced math classes. The idea behind Desmos is that since many students have access to phones, tablets, laptops, and other mobile devices, they would no longer need to purchase a separate, single-function calculator if they could use an online graphing calculator on their multifunction device. Desmos is able to make the calculator free for students and teachers by licensing it to publishers and testing companies for use in their commercial projects. Pearson, College Board, and other companies pay Desmos for institutional uses, and Desmos can give away individual and classrooms uses of the technology for free. Over time, Desmos has developed beyond just mimicking the functions of a calculator to become a platform where students and teachers can build and share visualizations of mathematical models.[12]

Desmos's chief academic officer is a former high school math teacher named Dan Meyer, who has built an extraordinary career as a math education researcher, designer, and teacher educator. Meyer's vision of high-quality mathematics instruction has a strong emphasis on mathematical modeling, and he argues that much of the work that students do in math class should be organized around social and creative problem solving as a framework for developing conceptual understanding and procedural fluency.

Meyer first became well known in the mathematics education community for what he calls "three-act" math problems. In a three-act math problem, students watch a short video with some kind of interaction in a world; one of the original examples was a video with one of those octagonal tanks that are often seen in a geometry textbook (but almost never in the real world) being filled with water from a hose. The videos are simultaneously banal and somewhat mesmerizing. Dan recounts how in many classes, at some point, a student will say, "Man, how long is it going to take to fill it up?" and Dan can respond, "I'm so glad you asked!" The video begs a question, and once students find the question, then Dan provides more information. In the second act of the task, Dan presents the video again with slightly more detail: a timer and a few measurements, so that students have enough information to produce a set of mathematical models predicting when the tank will be filled. In the third act, the video runs again to the very end with a timer so students can see how their models line up with reality. The approach makes mathematical modeling, rather than just procedural computation, central to math classrooms. Desmos is one tool for creating graphical representations that support these kinds of modeling activities.[13]

Meyer has presented to math teachers in all fifty states, and he has written extensively about mathematical modeling and student agency in problem solving and how Desmos supports those ideas. He has worked relentlessly to simplify his pedagogical principles so that they can be shared and adopted. His talks and workshops provide a rationale for his approach, explain the limits of typical instruction, and demonstrate concretely how changes in teaching materials can spark new kinds of participation and mathematical thinking from students, especially those who are not typically active in math classes. In a keynote address, he might take a typical math problem from a textbook and show how it can be modified in slide presentation software to make it more open-ended and amendable to modeling, discussion, and discovery. Through traveling, speaking, and actively participating in math educator communities on blogs and Twitter, Meyer has nurtured a community of math educators excited about incorporating these kinds of modeling approaches into their teaching.

In late 2016, Meyer made an unusual announcement on the Desmos blog. Five years after its founding, Desmos was adding two features: the ability to incorporate short videos in instructional materials and multiple-choice items. Meyer wrote, "These are the *first* features lots of companies add to their online activity platforms, so we wanted to explain why we waited so long."[14]

Meyer offered two reasons for the wait. One reason was that the Desmos team had an intuition that their earliest users would define the development of their product and its use and reputation. Desmos was attentive to the idea that in order to have a technology project that changed teaching, it had to scale through a community with a shared set of values about what good teaching looked like. Much as Scratch saw teacher meetups, after-school computer clubhouses and programs, and teacher online communities as central to their efforts to spread and scale, Meyer saw teacher networks, such as the state-level branches of the National Council for Teachers of Mathematics and online communities like the #iteachmath hashtag on Twitter, as essential to the spread of the ideas of modeling, discovery, and participation that are integral to the vision behind Desmos.

The second reason was that delaying the release of these features allowed Desmos to develop them in ways that aligned with the pedagogical goals of the company and community. For instance, Desmos's multiple-choice-item creator requires by default that students have to explain their answer when they select one, and it also displays (when possible) three answers from other students to the same question. Meyer describes these features as "consistent with our interest in connecting students and their thinking together."[15]

This combination of cultivation of community alongside deliberate development of technology is the tightrope that developers will need to walk to create technologies that can support meaningful changes in classroom practice. The impact of new technologies should not be measured by conventional metrics for the scale of an adoption: the number of user accounts, minutes of activity, or total clicks in log data. Instead, scale needs to be measured in terms of the communities of people that are engaged in sustained exploration of how technologies can lead to meaningful changes in practice. These technologies will not, in and of themselves, change institutional structures and practices. But communities of committed educators might.

Building New Technologies While Engaging Complex Systems

For designers of educational technology like Desmos and Scratch to bring their visions to life, they must address the full complexity of educational institutions. They have to engage communities of practicing teachers, teacher educators in colleges and universities, and the material conditions of learning environments. Education technologists need to consider how teachers and learners access devices and software, how time is used in learning environments, how new technologies are embedded into assessment systems (whether that be how to adopt Desmos to high-stakes math tests or block-based programming languages to advanced placement computer science tests), and how state and district policies address math and computer science teaching and learning. It is a tall order for a technology company or research group to address these complex factors, but the nature of their engagement with the public is that they do not have to do this work alone. By thinking of educators and learners as partners and stakeholders, technologists empower allies in policy positions, district leadership, testing companies, higher education, teacher training, and other places to consider how different elements of a complex system might be tinkered with to be more amenable to the pedagogical visions espoused by Desmos and Scratch.

Stimulating change in conservative, complex systems is not easy. If Desmos and Scratch continue to be widely adopted in schools, I'd wager that it would be in precious few of these implementations that Mitch Resnick, Natalie Rusk, or Dan Meyer would say upon walking into a classroom, "Yes! This is what I think the teaching and learning with these technologies should look like!" In far more places, I suspect, their observation would be, "It looks like some of the teaching and learning we'd hoped for is happening here, but there are still too many ways where the technology is being bent to conform to an existing, conservative pedagogical structure." Education historian Larry Cuban refers to this pattern as teachers "hugging the middle" of the pedagogical poles of pail filling and flame kindling. In his half-century of research on classroom practices, he has found that when pedagogical progressives encourage teachers to substantially reform their practices, it is much more common for teachers to adopt bits and pieces of new approaches, while maintaining consistent attachment to the kinds of routines that have dominated the grammar of schooling over the past two centuries.[16]

David Cohen and Jal Mehta describe this dynamic in a 2017 paper titled "Why Reform Sometimes Succeeds: Understanding the Conditions That Produce Reforms That Last." Cohen and Mehta examine several of the major curriculum reform efforts over the last century, including the Sputnik-inspired efforts in STEM and social science in the 1950s and 60s and the efforts to reform math education as part of the standards-based reform movement beginning in earnest in the 1990s. Both movements critiqued the emphasis on memorization and procedure in American classrooms and pressed for more inquiry-oriented, student-centered instruction. In both cases, reforms took hold firmly in a handful of places with committed teams of educators, and ripples of influence could be found throughout the American system. For instance, in math education reforms, researchers found more evidence of instruction focused on making meaning of mathematics over just procedural learning, but this meaning was typically conveyed through teacher-centered instruction—pail filling on the kinds of things that students might have discovered through flame kindling if teachers only had the time.[17]

Cohen and Mehta argue that more substantial and durable changes can occur in "niches" within the ecology of educational systems. Certain forms of ambitious instruction can be found in Waldorf and Montessori schools and certain charter-school networks operating outside the public district-based education system. Other forms thrive in International Baccalaureate or Advanced Placement classrooms operating within, but somewhat cordoned off from, the public education system.

These historical perspectives offer a somewhat grim choice for ambitious reformers: thrive in small places (perhaps over populated with the affluent and privileged) or allow watered-down ideas to spread widely. If large-scale learning technologies offer a path through this Scylla and Charybdis of school change, it will be in offering technologies that can balance a set of competing priorities. They need to provide easy entry points—narrow foyers—that allow busy educators to adopt them, while affording the opportunity for educators to grow beyond their initial experiences. Quizlet has a narrow foyer, but there is nowhere to go beyond it. For a tool to break the curse of the familiar, the design of the experience needs to function as a vector for new pedagogical ideas. The experience of using the technology needs to remind or nudge or compel teachers and students to look beyond the familiar routines of the grammar of schooling and imagine new possibilities. The technology also needs to make complex teaching and learning practices easier to implement; it needs to be simpler and less time consuming for teachers to attempt ambitious instruction. And all of these technological changes need to be accompanied by equally difficult efforts to build networked communities of educators who can evangelize new ideas and practices and offer supports to novices attempting to shift their practice.[18]

The curse of the familiar will have a tight hold over education technology around the globe in the decades ahead. Those who break the curse will be tinkering not just with technology, but with ways of nurturing communities of innovative educators working on re-forming systems while adopting new technologies. I view this problem as immensely difficult to solve but one worth working on nonetheless. Education technology is a good field for those who see themselves as patient optimists.

6

THE EDTECH MATTHEW EFFECT

FOR MANY YEARS, educators, designers, and policymakers have hoped that free and low-cost online technologies could bridge the chasm of opportunity that separates more and less affluent students. This dream has proven elusive.[1]

When I was a graduate student, I visited a classroom in rural New Hampshire where an ambitious young teacher was planning to have her students build collaborative presentations on wikis—websites that allow for multiple authors to publish together online. The technology in the lesson required a linked chain of resources: internet networks came into the building through cables to a wireless router broadcasting in her room; the students had laptops that had been successfully charged the night before and were receiving the wireless signal; the teacher had a computer plugged into a projector; the screen on the wall came down to receive the image (teachers reading this will shudder to remember those flimsy screens that wouldn't stay down); and the teacher took the power cord from the projector and went to plug it into the wall to show students what to do from her computer. As she pushed the plug into the outlet, the outlet rocked out of position and fell back behind the drywall, unrecoverable. After a few moments of fishing behind the insulation, the teacher gave up on using the projector and shifted to plan B, rather miraculously making the lesson work without a demonstration.

Since that visit, I've often thought of the delicacy of that chain of resources—power, broadband, wireless signal, equipment, bulbs, chargers—that allows people to learn from technology in their classrooms, schools, dorms, and homes. Affluent communities—neighborhoods, families, schools, and institutions—have more resources devoted to building and maintaining this delicate chain to take advantage of free, online learning tools and apps. Sociologists call this kind of phenomenon a Matthew effect, named for a verse in the biblical Gospel of Matthew: "For whoever has will be given more, and they will have an abundance. Whoever does not have, even what they have will be taken away from them."[2] The edtech Matthew effect posits that this pattern is quite common in the field of education technology and learning at scale: new resources—even free, online resources—are more likely to benefit already affluent learners with access to networked technology and access to networks of people who know how to take advantage of free online resources.

As we shall see, despite robust evidence for the prevalence of the edtech Matthew effect, edtech funders, developers, and enthusiasts continue to be animated by three linked myths about technology's potential to democratize learning. Working toward a more equitable future for education technology requires rejecting these myths and confronting the realities that could guide us toward more productive development, policy, and practice.

The first myth is that technology disrupts systems of inequality. For all the hope and hype that technology might enable major organizational changes in educational systems, the reality is that technology reproduces inequalities embedded in systems. New apps, software, and devices are put in the service of existing structures and systems, rather than rearranging them.

The second myth is that free and open technologies will democratize education. The rich data that can be collected from new digital platforms allow closer investigation than ever before about how learners from different life circumstances access and use new learning technologies. The research from these investigations makes the reality clear: new technologies, even free ones, disproportionately benefit already-advantaged students. In a sense, the digital divide is more of a digital fault line, and each new innovation opens chasms of opportunity between our most and least affluent students.

The third myth is that digital divides can be closed by expanding access to technology. Helping learners access functioning, modern computers with reliable broadband connections is only one step toward digital parity. Social and cultural forms of exclusion are as powerful, and often much harder to understand and address, than challenges of technology access. Turning the potential of education technology toward the benefit of the students who are furthest from opportunity will require reckoning with the social and cultural contexts in which marginalized students live and the very different contexts in which most new technology applications and services are developed.

The accumulated evidence disproves these myths and makes clear that education technology will never simplistically close digital divides. No matter how many transistors we squeeze into a square millimeter, no matter how many bits are passing wirelessly over our heads, the hard parts of reducing educational inequality will remain hard.

Edtech Equity Myth No. 1: Technology disrupts systems of inequality. Reality: Technology reproduces the inequality embedded in systems.

From the earliest days of signals technologies, inventors and evangelists have promised that new technologies would provide more equitable learning experiences for young people. In his 1984 book *Teachers and Machines,* Larry Cuban shows an image from the 1930s of children huddled around a giant radio transceiver with the caption, "With Radio, the Underprivileged School Becomes the Privileged One." Cuban chronicles developments in film, radio, television, and early efforts to place personal computers in classrooms, and he observes how each generation of technology advocates promised a radical reconfiguration of teaching and learning. Cuban found a handful of bold, interesting experiments, but for the most part, they primarily reproduce the patterns, behaviors, and inequalities that already exist within schools.[3]

One of the most unfortunate and inequitable practices in schools is the separation of students into learning experiences of very different quality. In her classic study *Keeping Track,* Jeannie Oakes documents how students in honors and college preparatory courses engage with rich content, solve complex problems, and communicate their understanding in diverse ways. In the same schools, students in basic and remedial courses encounter a simplified curriculum, solve less interesting problems, and find fewer opportunities for creative and intellectual expression. Assignment into these tracks correlates with race and class; affluent majority students are most likely to find themselves in the most challenging and meaningful learning environments, while students from low-income families or racial minorities are more likely to be placed in classrooms that limit their growth and potential.[4]

For the past thirty years, education technology researchers have collected evidence showing that similar patterns of diverging educational quality emerge in the implementation of digital learning technologies. At the turn of the twenty-first century, sociologist Paul Attewell proposed that educators think of these patterns as two digital divides. The first digital divide is the divide of access: students from low-income or marginalized backgrounds typically have less access to new technologies than more affluent students. But even more important is the second digital divide of usage: students from low-income or marginalized backgrounds are more likely to use technology for routine drill and practice with limited adult support, while more affluent students use technology for more creative activities with greater mentorship from teachers, parents, and adults.[5]

In the 1990s, Harold Wenglinsky at the Educational Testing Service analyzed test scores and survey data from the 1996 National Assessment of Educational Progress (NAEP). Students were asked about patterns of technology usage in their math classrooms, and Wenglinsky found that low-income, non-white children used technology primarily in math class for drill and practice, while affluent white children were more likely to use technology for graphing, problem solving, and other higher-order exercises. Wenglinsky argued that "poor, urban, and rural students were less likely to be exposed to higher-order uses than non-poor and suburban students."[6] The same survey questions were used again in the 2009 and 2011 NAEP tests with basically identical results: the most promising uses of educational technology were mostly available to already-advantaged students. Qualitative researchers have found similar patterns through close observations of schools and families. For his dissertation, Matthew Rafalow conducted an ethnographic study of three high schools in southern California that all had the same levels of technology access but served different populations of students. One of his study sites was a majority white school in an affluent neighborhood, where teachers and educators described creative and playful uses of technology—even playing games like *Minecraft*—as a valuable part of student development. By contrast, in the two schools Rafalow visited serving middle- and lower-income students, educators described these uses of technology as irrelevant or disruptive, and their technology use focused on more basic skills. In affluent schools, kids who played around with computers were hackers, and teachers saw their play as preparing for careers in technology; in schools serving low-income families, kids who played around with computers were treated as slackers.[7]

For the most part, new technologies don't rearrange practices in schools. They reinforce them.

Myth No. 2: Free and open technologies promote equality. Reality: Free things benefit those with the means to take advantage of them.

In recent years, technology advocates have used the phrase "democratizing education" to describe the potential for new technologies to reduce inequality. *Democratize* is a slippery word, and it's usually used to describe making something more fair, more equitable, or more just, without describing exactly how these goals might be achieved. One theory of change is that because affluent learners and families already can afford high-quality learning experiences, if new technologies are made free or more easily accessible, then less affluent learners will get access to what the affluent already have.

One of the virtues of new large-scale learning technologies is that they generate data sources that can be used to delve deeper into how technologies are used differently by students from different backgrounds. In the last ten years, I've worked on two major studies about the second digital divide of usage. In the late 2000s, I studied how teachers and students used social media and peer production tools such as blogs and wikis. At the time, there was a real optimism that these tools would be as transformative in education as they had been in journalism, business, social relationships, and information management. Wikis and blogs could create new opportunities for students to collaborate with peers across the classroom or around the world, and they could provide new means for students' digital expression. Before the arrival of these web-based collaboration tools, collaborative computing projects would require a major investment in computers, networks, and specialized software (like Hypercard). The hope was that with computers more accessible and the software free or low cost, these opportunities for rich digital learning would be much more widely available, especially for low-income students.[8]

Starting in 2009, I looked at data from hundreds of thousands of wikis used in K–12 education settings. Each wiki recorded every change made by every user, and in many wikis, we could examine the content created on the site, identify the school where the wiki was created, and use data from the National Center for Education Statistics to learn more about the demographics of the schools creating the wikis. We found that wikis were more likely to be created in schools serving affluent neighborhoods, and the wikis created in those affluent schools were used for longer periods of time with greater opportunities for student involvement. Wikis created in schools serving low-income families were more likely to be used for teacher-centered content delivery, and they fell into disuse more quickly.[9]

To try to understand these patterns, I started visiting wiki-using teachers around the country, which is how I found myself in the New Hampshire classroom with the dodgy power outlets. I saw a phenomenon similar to what Attewell observed in the 1990s: in more affluent schools, more resources were devoted to the maintenance of technology networks, which could then be used more easily and more reliably. Teachers had more access to planning time and professional development, and because they had fewer pressures from standardized testing, they could take more pedagogical risks and try new things like wikis. Teachers in affluent neighborhoods could count on more access to technology resources in homes, which made them more comfortable assigning complex projects that might require online homework. While the wiki cloud software was free for teachers to use, the maintenance of technological systems and expertise was expensive.

After the passing surge of interest in integrating social media and peer production in education, MOOCs became the next participant in the edtech hype cycle, with advocates again declaring that free online courses would democratize education. As I discussed in Chapter 1, when my colleague John Hansen and I connected MOOC registration and participation data from edX with demographic data from the US census, we found that people living in more affluent neighborhoods were more likely to sign up for edX MOOCs. Moreover, markers of socioeconomic status—like having a parent with a college degree or living in a more affluent neighborhood—were positively correlated with course completion. MOOCs opened a door of opportunity, and although there are remarkable stories of learners from very difficult circumstances who took advantages of these new opportunities, the majority of people who walk through that door of opportunity are already educated and already affluent.[10]

Learners in affluent neighborhoods are better able to take advantage of new education technology, even when those technologies are free. The research record becomes increasingly clear with each passing year: we should expect that most education technology initiatives—including those made available for free online—will disproportionately benefit the affluent.

Myth No. 3: Expanding access will bridge digital divides. Reality: Social and cultural barriers are the chief obstacles to equitable participation.

While financial and technical barriers are real and important, social and cultural exclusions are often the thornier obstacles to educational equity. These social and cultural barriers are harder to discern, require more nuance to address, and vary substantially across different communities and contexts.

The "digital divide" is too simple a metaphor to characterize educational inequality. I prefer the image of a digital fault line; inequalities emerge and disappear as tectonic shifts from new technologies change the social landscape. As new technologies arrive and as older technologies become obsolete, the shape of the digital fault line constantly changes. In the 1980s and 1990s, the digital divide in education referred primarily to the differences in student-computer ratios between more and less affluent schools or to gaps in home desktop computer ownership. As more schools began to acquire computers, the most pronounced digital gaps have shifted toward broadband access rather than device ownership. For a short time, when mobile internet first became accessible, youth of color actually led adoption, since it was a better value for many families than home broadband subscriptions. As mobile phones have become increasingly sophisticated, however, gaps in mobile broadband adoption have emerged. In their study of the broadband subsidy program Connect2Compete, Vikki Katz and her colleagues found that policy decisions often showed a profound misunderstanding of the populations that they were trying to serve. The subsidy program assumed that families were completely disconnected and would welcome even a single ethernet connection. In reality, most families were already online and needed to reliably connect multiple devices via Wi-Fi in order to meet the needs of the entire family for school, work, community engagement, and leisure. The subsidy program was trying to close a gap in the digital fault line that had already mostly closed while ignoring the one that had opened right next to it.[11]

The easiest gaps to measure along the digital fault line are gaps of access—who has access to how many computers or mobile devices with what kinds of broadband speeds. But the more challenging obstacles are those that are social and cultural in nature. Katz and colleagues documented that in the Connect2Compete program, uptake across low-income communities differed by levels of community trust. In one case study where community trust in schools and municipalities was high, the program was more effective in helping families get access to new resources. In their case study site in Arizona, however, uptake was much less, because many immigrant families were concerned about using school-issued laptops out of fear of state surveillance. Matt Rafalow's three-school case study, discussed above, reveals how even when technology is held constant across different schools, teachers can celebrate technology usage by privileged students while questioning it among other students.

Large-scale quantitative research also sheds some light on these challenges at a global scale. One robust finding from MOOC research is that a person's country of residence can be a strong predictor of course completion. Using the Human Development Index (HDI), a measure of a country's affluence, education, and general well-being developed by the United Nations Development Program, research shows that MOOC learners from countries with low HDI measures are significantly less likely to complete courses than learners from countries with high HDI scores, a kind of global achievement gap in MOOCs. Obstacles that online learners in developing countries face that contribute to this gap might include unstable internet and electricity, structural poverty, and many other challenges.[12]

My colleague René Kizilcec theorized that learners from less developed countries might face an obstacle called social identity threat. Social identity threat occurs when learners use cognitive resources attending to concerns about stereotypes or feelings of exclusion rather than to learning. We cannot say definitively what causes these feelings in online courses, but triggers could include the elite branding of universities offering MOOCs, the predominantly white American and European faculty who offer these courses, the English language usernames in the forums, and other markers that feel excluding to minority participants. Feelings of social identity threat can lead to negative recursive cycles: when people start a class, they may feel like an outsider. This feeling of exclusion might lead to their not doing as well in the first week as they might have, which makes them more attuned to things that would make them feel like outsiders, which makes them do less well in the course, and so on. In other words, Kizilcec hypothesized that some of the challenges that learners from developing countries might face would be psychological in nature, in addition to the structural and economic barriers that learners from developing countries might face in trying to participate in online courses.[13]

To test this hypothesis, Kizilcec, myself, and a team of colleagues from Harvard, MIT, and Stanford randomly included an intervention that addressed social identity threat in the pre-course surveys of more than 250 MOOCs. In this simple intervention, learners were asked to read a list of values and identify two or three that were most important to them. They then wrote a short note about why taking an online class aligned with those values. The intervention was designed to deepen the connection between a learner's sense of purpose and his or her participation in a class, and in theory, it served as a kind of "inoculation" to the negative feedback cycle induced by social identity threat. The writing exercise addressed feelings of exclusion by having learners themselves write new narratives about inclusion. Learners in the control group received the standard survey without the intervention. We found that the intervention worked in courses where students from more affluent countries earned certificates at much higher rates than students from developing countries. In these courses, students from medium- and low-HDI countries who were randomly assigned to the intervention were more likely to complete courses than students in the control condition. In other words, where a "global achievement gap" existed, the intervention closed a portion of that global achievement gap. While MOOC students from less developed countries may still face challenges from infrastructure quality and access, our study suggests that at least some of the differences seen in educational attainment in MOOCs might result from feelings of exclusion.[14]

This idea that social and cultural exclusions could be as powerful as economic and technological obstacles can seem very counterintuitive. When Kizilcec and I first submitted an earlier paper about our interventions to *Science,* the paper was rejected without explanation and without having been sent out for review (a process called desk rejection, not uncommon for a prominent journal). One anonymous editor had written in his comments, "Not clear to me that this 'fear that they could be judged in light of negative stereotypes about their nation' is more of a hurdle than, say, irregular power supply, intermittent internet, gender, lack of tailoring of materials to local contexts/cultures, etc." The central premise of our paper was that our experiment only affected learners' psychological state; students from low-HDI countries in the treatment condition faced identical challenges with technology and access as students from low-HDI countries in the control condition. The experiences of students in the experiments differed only in terms of access to one short exercise designed to provide psychological support. Even in the face of experimental evidence that cultural exclusions matter, this one reviewer remained convinced of the importance of technical dimensions. The story does have a happy ending. After we reframed our writing to emphasize that the only factor we changed in learner experiences was a psychological one, the editors chose to accept the paper.[15]

One challenge in addressing cultural exclusions is the chasm of social status between edtech developers and advocates and the communities of learners that they are trying to serve. Sociologist Tressie McMillan Cottom argues that technologists often imagine their students as "roaming autodidacts," which she describes as "a self-motivated, able learner that is simultaneously embedded in technocratic futures *and* disembedded from place, culture, history, and markets."[16] If this description fits any group aptly, it might be the developers of education technology themselves—primarily white and Asian men coming from a handful of top-tier universities, at ease whether in Cambridge, Massachusetts, or Palo Alto, California, and part of the global elite that uses technology and affluence to transplant their culture and comforts wherever they go. Most people, however, live in a particular place, grounded in cultures and families that shape their interactions with learning experiences. It is astoundingly complex to create learning experiences that effectively scale to millions while responding productively to local differences, cultures, and contexts. It's even harder to do when the developers of technologies share a homogenous set of formative cultural and educational experiences, and the students they serve come from places both less privileged and more diverse.

Addressing the challenges of education technology and equity requires rejecting the myth that free online educational opportunities are in and of themselves democratizing. Instead, educators, developers, and policymakers must grapple with the extensive data that show us the reality: educational technology is implicated in perpetuating inequality. We now know enough about these dynamics that when the next wave of educational hype comes along, whether that is with virtual reality or artificial intelligence, we can step back and question who will be best served by new innovations.

Design Principles for Digital Equity

For all of the incredible opportunities for learning that may be generated by education technology, the hard parts of creating a more equitable future through education will remain hard. And for all these challenges, there are many educators, developers, and researchers who are experimenting with a variety of approaches that do have some traction in closing digital divides. The solution space in this domain is not nearly as well understood as the problem space: we can confidently describe how new technologies typically reproduce or expand educational inequalities, but as a field, we don't have a good handle on what kinds of approaches or strategies can reliably address new gaps along the digital fault line. There are a variety of intriguing cases, experiments, and initiatives but not enough by way of unifying theory or principles.

What the field needs is a set of "design principles for digital equity": guidelines that can be used by funders, venture capitalists, philanthropists, developers, educators, and policymakers to guide investment decisions, development strategies, policy, and practice around the equitable use of learning technologies. My colleague Mizuko Ito and I have taken a first stab at this set of design principles, and we've come up with four main themes: unite around shared purpose; align home, school, and community; connect to the interests and the identities of culturally diverse children and youth; and measure and target the needs of subgroups.[17]

First, designers should unite around shared purpose with learners and their communities. Equity-oriented efforts can bring developers, educators, and learners together with common purpose. When initiatives are codeveloped and cofacilitated with stakeholders, they are more likely to be attuned to important elements of social and cultural contexts, and teachers and learners are more likely to take ownership of these initiatives.

Second, designers should align home, school, and community. While affluent students often have tech-savvy parents and the latest technology at home, less well-resourced students cannot count on these supports. This disconnect can be exacerbated when developers and reformers focus all of their efforts at building technology literacy and capacity in schools. One fruitful strategy for reducing this gap is building the capacity of parents and mentors alongside that of young people. Intergenerational learning experiences can strengthen family ties while giving parents and children skills to explore new domains.

Third, educators should connect to the interest and identities of minority children and youth. Peer learning communities are exclusionary when they reflect a dominant culture in ways that create a hostile environment for outsiders, but they can also be harnessed to create safe affinity spaces for minority children and youth. Powerful learning experiences result when students have the opportunity to connect their interests from outside of school to learning opportunities in more academic contexts.

Finally, designers and researchers should measure and target the needs of subgroups. When developers and reformers understand the specific needs of the communities they serve, they can deploy targeted programs that give the greatest advantage to the neediest groups. These strategies might include addressing psychological threats, addressing specific costs that matter more to low-income groups, and targeting high-risk moments in students' learning trajectories.

Unite around Shared Purpose

People from different backgrounds and life circumstances can experience life very differently, and these experiences can lead to divergent ways of understanding the world. An affluent white computer science major from an elite college who goes to work in education technology may see the world quite differently from black and Latinx children who grow up in poverty-impacted neighborhoods. Uniting around shared purpose involves including diverse stakeholders in education technology initiatives. For her doctoral thesis, Betsy DiSalvo wanted to develop new pathways for African American boys into computer science, and she worked with a cohort of young men to create a program called the Glitch Game Testers. Glitch Game Testers became an after-school program where high school students worked on quality-assurance projects for computer game companies and were involved in shaping the trajectory of the initiative—choosing the name and logo, developing practices, and instigating more formal computer science education learning experiences. Including the young men in the design ensured that participants were engaged and that educational opportunities met the real needs of learners rather than the needs and circumstances that program leaders might have imagined.[18]

School-based student tech teams are another mechanism for uniting around shared purpose. The Verizon Innovative Learning

Schools program is in the midst of a ten-year initiative to provide tablet computers and three years of free 4G wireless access to more than five hundred Title I middle schools across the United States. One of the requirements of the program is that schools create a student tech team to codesign technology policy, help lead the program roll-out, and serve as advisors and troubleshooters throughout the program. Giving students co-ownership of the program increases engagement and reduces disciplinary issues.[19]

In addition to including student voices as key stakeholders in educational programs, venture capitalists and philanthropists can include more diversity in their funding and program teams and encourage developers and entrepreneurs to include people on their teams who share the backgrounds with those they are trying to serve. Edtech companies can do more development and testing in a variety of real-world contexts and include more teachers and families as paid advisors and consultants. Uniting around shared purpose empowers new voices for leadership in education and increases the chances that designers of new edtech products and programs will meet the needs of their target audiences.

Align Home, School, and Community

If it takes a village to raise a child, then edtech developers should consider how programs can build capacity among not just young people but their family members and caretakers as well. One promising approach for supporting educational equity for young people is creating new kinds of learning experiences for the adults around them. As we discussed in the chapter on peer-driven learning environments, Scratch is a block-based programming language and social community where young people can code up games, animations, and other programs. Qualitative interviews with Scratchers, especially from before the widespread use of Scratch in schools, revealed that many are from families in which one parent is a computer programmer or engineer or has some other connection to STEM and programming. When Scratchers grow up in families with computing expertise, their learning is supported and accelerated through that expertise. These kinds of advantages inspired Ricarose Roque, now at the University of Colorado Boulder, to do her doctoral work at the MIT Media Lab on a project called Family Creative Learning. Roque engaged parents and children in creative-technology workshops held at community-based organizations like Boys and Girls Clubs. Unlike in more traditional crafts such as knitting, parents and children have fewer intergenerational touch points when it comes to new technology, particularly among less tech-savvy parents. By hosting meals and conducting activities using Scratch and the Makey Makey invention kit within safe and welcoming spaces, the project builds capacity within families to support children's becoming digital creators. Some activities are done separately by youth and parents or guardians, and some activities are shared and done together. Kids and families build new skills, parents have new strategies for supporting young people's learning with creative technologies, and families have an experience that bonds and connects.[20]

Tech Goes Home is a similar project in the Boston Public Schools in which families can get access to a $50 laptop and discounted internet options. Parents of Boston Public School children take a fifteen-hour computer literacy course taught by a teacher in the child's school, and at the end of the course, they can buy their computer. The course isn't only about using technology for learning; it is also about helping parents use computers to find work and community opportunities and stay connected through social media, among other applications. Parents go home with a computer that everyone in the family can benefit from, and parents have new skills for guiding technology usage at home and a new relationship with a teacher inside their child's school. The program simultaneously improves computer access, parent and child technology literacy, home-school connections, and teacher relationships with communities, all by situating a program about technology access in a broader social context.[21]

LaunchCode is a program for adults based in St. Louis that originally began as an opportunity for community members to take an introductory programming MOOC together. Jim McKelvey, who cofounded the payment processing company Square, wanted to create more opportunities in his hometown of St. Louis, so he sponsored a community group to take HarvardX's CS50x course together. The initial demand was much greater than expected, and the program quickly moved from the local library to the Peabody Opera House to accommodate demand. CS50x is an extremely demanding course, and participants are very unlikely to finish without external support—Harvard's on-campus version of CS50 has a veritable army of teaching assistants available almost around the clock during the semester to support Harvard undergrads. LaunchCode provided some of these same supports to help participants successfully complete the MOOC, and then moved on to include additional support for employment and interview preparation, internships and apprenticeships, and other structures to help CS50x grads (and later, grads of their own Introduction to Computer Science course) move into careers in computer programming. The HarvardX MOOC provided a valuable learning resource for bootstrapping Launch-Code, and LaunchCode built a set of human supports around the experience. These wrap-around services mean that LaunchCode looks more like a community college than a MOOC, and scaling supportive communities to create pathways of opportunity is far more difficult that scaling and spreading a new MOOC learning management system. But for those concerned with issues of equity, blended approaches to addressing inequalities are far more likely to be successful than online-only efforts.[22]

Engage Diverse Student Interests

A third strategy for addressing inequalities with technology is to create entry points into learning experiences that connect to student interests. As discussed in Chapter 3, connected learning is a model advanced by Mizuko Ito and others that puts student interests at the center of learning design and builds connections between learning institutions so that interests that young people pursue at home and in after-school activities can have academic connections with school-based learning opportunities. Interest-based learning pathways start with student passions and showcase connections between their interests and academic subjects.[23]

In the Coding for All project, Scratch developers and designers are building new entry points into the Scratch community that target common interests of girls and students of color. The projects that have been historically popular and featured on the Scratch website include many with traditionally geeky themes around video games, anime, and related topics. These are enticing entry points for some young learners but discouraging for others. To create new entry points, the Scratch team is creating Microworlds that provide different ways into Scratch programming—including the Microworld mentioned in Chapter 5 that emphasizes hip-hop and others that feature such topics as fashion, art, and comedy—to help different young people connect their interests to coding.[24]

In Chicago, the Digital Youth Network's Digital Divas project creates culturally relevant STEM learning activities for middle school girls offered in after-school programs. Girls learn programming and engineering through e-textiles and other design projects. In these cases, designers are not only creating engaging new programs that build on student interests, but also working with community partners to ensure that they serve lower-income and minority students.[25]

There is no assurance that these kinds of approaches will work. There is perhaps no group of parents that is more successful at surrounding their children with interest-driven learning experiences than upper-class white families. An edtech culture that simply focuses on aligning technologies with student interests ("all student interests matter") will likely contribute to educational inequality, but a focus on connecting with the interests of learners alienated from schools or unable to access rich educational experiences could be a powerful bridge across digital fault lines.

Study and Address the Needs of Specific Subgroups

Finally, serving subgroups well requires actively studying them, addressing specific needs in particular communities, and deploying targeted programs that give the greatest advantage to the neediest groups. The research that I have conducted with René Kizilcec and colleagues addressing social identity threat in MOOCs followed this model; we studied variation in how students from different backgrounds performed differently in MOOCs, identified ways we might be able to support particular groups of learners who might need extra scaffolding, and experimentally tested different interventions, first in pilots and then in larger scale replications. Only by understanding how different subgroups experience learning at scale differently can we try to address some of the gaps in opportunity that emerge.

The issue of pricing reveals how similar product features can operate very differently in different social contexts. From 2013 to 2018 or so, most MOOCs were available for free (during this period, Udacity, Coursera, and eventually edX added a variety of paywalls to their products), and the evidence suggests that the bulk of benefits of MOOCs accrued to more affluent learners. But there are other online learning experiences that set prices at zero that do appear to disproportionately benefit the families furthest from opportunity. In particular, when the cost of an educational product is substantial for low-income families but trivial for affluent families, free goods may be particularly effective at closing gaps.

OpenStax develops free, peer-reviewed, openly licensed textbooks for introductory college courses. A substantial portion of all college enrollments in any given semester are in a relatively small number of introductory courses: algebra, biology, calculus, economics, psychology, and government, among a few others. The textbooks for these survey courses can cost more than $100, a substantial burden on students in community colleges and other settings who may be paying only a few hundred dollars per credit hour. OpenStax claims that by providing free alternatives, in the 2016–2018 school years, they saved students about $177 million in textbook costs. While students from all backgrounds may be benefiting from these resources, the families and students benefiting most are those for whom a $175 textbook represents a major financial hurdle.[26]

Similarly, Desmos has developed a free browser-based graphing calculator as a direct competitor to the Texas Instruments line of calculators, such as the TI-84+ that retails for over $100. The Desmos graphing calculator has substantially more functionality than a handheld calculator and represents a major improvement in terms of accessibility through integration with screen readers and other accessibility software. As with the cost of a textbook in the case of OpenStax, the $100 price tag for a TI calculator is modest for affluent families but a substantial burden for low-income schools and families—especially when many families already sacrifice to make more fully functional laptops, phones, and tablets available to their children.

Targeting subgroups can also mean understanding the barriers to access and progress that are unique to particular groups of people. In 2014, Ben Castleman and Lindsay Page defined a phenomenon that they called "summer melt." Castleman worked at the MET School in Providence, Rhode Island, an urban charter school that was unusually effective at supporting students in making it through high school and toward graduation with acceptances to colleges and universities. As MET staff tracked their graduates past high school, they discovered a shocking phenomenon: a surprising number—between 10 and 40 percent—of high school graduates who were accepted into college did not register for their first semester. This is a problem almost unimaginable to the parents of elite students, who can assume that college matriculation will naturally lead to attendance and graduation. In studies of three large urban districts, they discovered that schools that had successfully improved graduation rates and college acceptance rates were losing students in the transition to college.[27]

The bureaucratic hurdles that high school graduates faced throughout the summer in registering for classes and applying for financial aid were particularly mystifying for first-generation college students. Castleman and Page joined with foundations, schools, and other researchers in try to tackle this particular challenge, though their initial efforts have had mixed results. They launched a series of text-message-based interventions that reminded students of key dates and actions related to enrollment, registration, financial aid, and orientation. These interventions didn't address every challenge for every student, but they successfully raised college entry by several percentage points at very low cost. Unfortunately, these initial improvements in registration did not lead to improvements in graduation rates among students receiving the "summer melt" treatment; students who got a boost over the bureaucratic hurdles into college didn't necessarily persist all the way through. The ultimate success of Castleman and Page's research program will depend upon deeply understanding the needs and challenges of an important group of students and then identifying widely accessible technologies that could be used to support students' learning trajectories.[28]

Building a New Movement for Edtech and Equity

As a field, we understand the challenges of digital fault lines much better than we understand potential solutions. We have a substantial body of research that characterizes myths and realities about education technology and equity, but our understanding of solutions is a spottier collection of case studies. The field needs a surge of research into strategies for digital equity to guide new education technology efforts.

One way to approach this research effort would be to consider the full life cycle of an education technology product through a set of stages—bringing together a team, funding an idea, developing the technology, selling and marketing to schools and learners, implementing in schools or other environments, collecting feedback and data, and evaluating programs. Issues of equity can be addressed at each of these stages: Does the founding team have a diverse leadership that can bridge social gaps between technology developers and student communities? Will the funders hold grantees or entrepreneurs accountable for addressing equity goals? Are the learners who need the most support included as codesigners in the development process? Do data collection and evaluation practices investigate the needs, strengths, and opportunities of different subgroups?

To provide guidance at each of these stages, we need much more research about effective, equity-focused practice. The case studies we have of Tech Goes Home, Family Creative Learning, OpenStax, and other initiatives are a terrific start, but we need to develop a much richer understanding of the programs and strategies that are effectively addressing the needs of the learners farthest from opportunities. From additional case studies, we could identify practices worthy of more rigorous research and develop a set of design principles for digital equity that could guide the work of all the different stakeholders who have a hand in supporting learning through new technologies. The principles in this chapter offer a starting point for that work.

7

THE TRAP OF
ROUTINE ASSESSMENT

Routines for Computers, Unstructured Problem
Solving, and Complex Communication for People

AUTOGRADERS EXCEL AT assessing routine tasks. These are exactly the kinds of tasks that we no longer need humans to do.[1]

As personal computers were widely adopted in the workplace throughout the 1980s and 1990s, executives, policymakers, and researchers wondered what influence these new machines would have on human labor. An early hypothesis was that computers would complement high-wage workers and replace low-wage workers—computers would replace cashiers but not professionals like doctors. Computerization has certainly replaced human work in the labor market, but the story that has unfolded over the last forty years is much more complex than this simple prediction. Economists interested in education have investigated computerization not just to understand how labor and skill demands would change, but to better understand how these changes could and should impact education. Richard Murnane and Frank Levy have explored these issues for many years, and one story they use to help people understand automation is about airline check-in counters.[2]

Some of us remember checking in for an airplane flight with an actual human being. The conversations with these people were extremely structured. If you fly frequently, you can probably remember exactly how these conversations are supposed to go:

- Do you have a ticket?
- What is your final destination?
- Do you have identification?
- Do you have bags to check?
- Have your bags been in your possession since you packed them?
- Did anyone else help pack your bags?
- Here are your tickets and luggage receipts. Have a nice flight.

The people behind the counters were solidly middle-class workers. They joined unions, wore uniforms, and had decent salaries and benefits. And many of these jobs are gone. Today, few people check in first with a human being to get on an airplane.

The information needed to process these conversations was highly structured—a ticket is a number, a passenger name, a seat ID, and an origin and a destination; the baggage questions are yes / no; identification cards are designed to be scanned and matched to people. As a result, these conversations could be encoded into computers built into kiosks, and these kiosks could inexpensively and ceaselessly carry on these conversations with passengers day and night. As mobile technologies and networks spread, these kiosks are now complemented by smartphone apps that carry on these same conversations with you from the palm of your hand.

Still, if you visit a bank of airline check-in kiosks, you will see uniformed airline employees behind the counters and amid the kiosks. As an educator, I am extremely interested in these people—who they are, what they do, and what they are good at. In a sea of automation, what are the tasks being done by the last few people whose jobs could not be automated?

Airline counter staff tackle two general kinds of problems that kiosks and mobile apps don't handle well. First, there are problems that come up periodically that were not anticipated by the designers of the kiosk systems: flights get diverted, payments get mixed up, and other out-of-the-ordinary events occur. Murnane and Levy call these "unstructured problems," problems whose outcomes and solution paths are not immediately clear. Humans have what economists call "a comparative advantage" over computers in these kinds of challenges, meaning that as tasks get more complex and ill structured, the cost of developing and maintaining software to provide a service becomes higher than the cost of hiring people.[3]

Second, people have all kinds of difficulty communicating with the kiosks. They cannot find the right kiosk, or they do not speak a language programmed into the kiosk, or they forgot their glasses, or they are so hopping mad at the airline that they just bang on the kiosk. Human beings are better than computers at "complex communication," problems whose solutions require understanding a task through social interaction, or when the task itself involves educating, persuading, or engaging people in other complex ways.[4]

Complex communication and unstructured problem solving are domains where for the foreseeable future, human beings will outperform computers. David Autor, along with Levy and Murnane, took the list of hundreds of job codes maintained by the United States Department of Labor and labeled each job as routine manual work, routine cognitive work, work requiring complex communication, or work requiring ill-structured problem solving. They found that routine work was disappearing as a proportion of the labor market, and jobs requiring complex communication and expert thinking were expanding. Subsequent studies found that certain kinds of routine jobs were persisting in the service sector, but these were typically jobs that could be performed by any interchangeable person without any particular skills, and they typically paid the state- or federally mandated minimum wage.[5]

This labor market research by Levy and Murnane is the original source for nearly every list of twenty-first-century skills promoted by education reformers over the last two decades. Perhaps the most popular formulation has been the "four Cs" of creativity, critical thinking, communication, and collaboration. The first two of the four Cs (creativity and critical thinking) are derivatives of unstructured problem solving, and the latter two (communication and collaboration) are derivative of complex communication.[6]

Computers Changing Work Up and Down the Labor Force

These kinds of shifts can also be seen within job categories, and the effects are similar across very different kinds of jobs and wage levels. One of my favorite illustrations of this phenomenon comes from a cabin that I own in rural Vermont. My mother bought the cabin thirty-five years ago, and she had a hot-water heater installed by the local plumber. Twenty-five years later, my mother passed, my brother and I inherited the house, and the hot-water heater needed replacing.

The same plumber was still working after all those years, and he installed a beautiful new system. After he finished, he brought me into the utility closet to explain it. The heater had an LED panel that under normal operations displays the word "GOOD." The plumber said that if that panel ever said something other than GOOD, I should hit the reset button and wait a while. If that didn't work, I should toggle the power system on and off and reboot my hot-water heater. I asked him what to do if that didn't work, and he explained that only one plumber in the Upper River Valley of Vermont had flown to Scandinavia to get trained on how to reprogram this kind of heater, and I would have to call him.

Over the years, I have thought about that tradesman in the 1960s and 70s completing his plumbing apprenticeship, learning how to cut and solder pipes, install new appliances, and get frozen houses in rural Vermont up and running again. What would it be like to explain to the young men in that apprenticeship program that fifty years later, plumbers would be computer programmers? Not only that, but the computers inside hot-water heaters can solve the easy problems themselves through rebooting and power cycling. Plumbers with computer programming skills are needed only to solve the uncommon, non-trivial problems that the computer cannot resolve on its own.

There are similar stories on the other end of the economic spectrum. In legal work, a common task is discovery, the request or retrieval of documents from a deposition that may contain evidence of malfeasance. In days gone by, firms might have hired a small army of lawyers to read every document looking for evidence. New services automate part of the discovery process by having computers scan and examine documents to look for keywords or other incriminating patterns. A much smaller subset of documents can then be turned over to a much smaller subset of lawyers for examination.[7]

In every profession in every sector of our economy, enterprising computer programmers are identifying tasks that can be turned into routines and then writing software, developing apps, creating robots, and building kiosks that can replace those elements of human work. Self-driving cars represent one much sought after milestone in the development of automation technologies. In *The New Division of Labor,* published in 2005, Levy and Murnane described a left-hand turn into oncoming traffic as the kind of decision that was so complex, with so many variables of cars, conditions, pedestrians, animals, and so forth that computers could never learn to reliably and safely decide when to turn left. And of course, roboticists, artificial intelligence specialists, machine vision experts, and others are working furiously to program self-driving cars that can turn left against traffic, among many other complex decisions.[8]

As an educator, one of my foremost concerns is whether our educational systems can help all students develop the kinds of skills that computers and robots cannot replicate. Our efforts as educators should have a special focus on domains where humans have a comparative advantage. If computers are changing the demands of the labor market and civic sphere and requiring that students develop proficiency with complex skills, what role can large-scale learning technologies play in addressing those challenges?

As we observed in the previous chapters, the value proposition offered by instructor-guided and algorithm-guided learning at scale is that learners can engage in educational experiences facilitated by computers, and they can advance through those learning materials on the basis of automated assessments. Most MOOCs and adaptive tutoring systems include problems, quiz questions, or other activities that purport to assess learner competencies. On the basis of those assessments, they offer feedback or credentials, or, in the case of personalized tutors, additional problems or learning resources based on those performances.

So what kinds of domains of human performance can we evaluate with computational systems?

(Mis)Understanding Testing: The Reification Fallacy

Before addressing this question, it's worth taking a moment to consider the "reification fallacy," when we uncritically believe that something's name accurately represents what that thing actually is. Psychometricians are statisticians who study testing and all the ways tests and testing data are understood and misunderstood. One of the most common fallacies in evaluating testing systems is believing that the name of a test accurately defines what it tests. In common parlance, we might call something an "algebra test," but just calling it an algebra test doesn't necessarily mean that it's an accurate measure of a person's ability to do algebra. An immigrant student just starting to learn English might understand algebra very well but fail an algebra test that depends on English language fluency. The thing called an "algebra test" isn't just an algebra test, but also an English (or maybe a "mathematical English" or "academic English") test and an evaluation of the knowledge not just of subject matter content but of test-taking strategies.[9]

Also, an algebra test won't evaluate every possible dimension of algebra. All tests are an effort to sample a learner's knowledge within a domain. An algebra test might include many items on rational expressions and very few on reasoning with inequalities, so the test might do a good job of evaluating learners in one part of algebra and a lousy job evaluating in another. The reification fallacy reminds us that something called an "algebra test" is never a universal test of algebra. A well-designed assessment might sample widely from representative domains of algebra while providing enough supports and scaffolds so that the assessment is not also testing English language fluency, or test-taking skills, or other domains. But all assessments are imperfectly designed.[10]

An implication of the reification fallacy is that all tests are better at measuring some parts of what they claim to be testing and worse at others, and tests inevitably also evaluate domains that are not named in the description of the test. When educators and instructional designers use computers to automatically grade assessments, the strengths and limitations of computational tools dramatically shape what parts of a given domain we examine with a test.

Computers, Testing, and Routines

Much as computers out in the world are good at highly routine tasks, computers used in educational systems are good at evaluating human performance when that performance can be defined in highly structured ways or turned into routines with well-defined correct and incorrect answers.

In Chapter 2, I referred to one of the first computer programming languages that was developed exclusively for educational purposes:

the TUTOR language, written in the 1960s for the PLATO computer systems. Over time, PLATO supported a remarkably wide variety of learning experiences, games, and social interactions, but some of its earliest functions were creating computer-assisted instructional lessons in which screens of content delivery alternated with assessments. These assessments used a pattern-matching system. Instructional designers could enter certain words, numbers, or features into an answer bank, PLATO would pose a question to students, students would type in an answer (which appeared immediately on the screen in front of them—a major advance at the time!), and the PLATO systems would evaluate whether there was a match between the learner's answer and the acceptable answers in the bank.[11]

This kind of pattern matching is still the primary way that computers evaluate answers. There is no automated evaluation system that employs reasoning like human reasoning, that evaluates meaning, or that makes any kind of subjective assessment. Rather, computers compare the responses that students submit to "answer banks" that encode the properties of correct and incorrect answers. Computers determine whether or not new answers and the established bank of answers are syntactically or structurally similar. Computers evaluate answers based on syntax and structure because computers understand nothing of substance and meaning.

Over time, we have developed increasingly complex tools for pattern matching. In the early version of the TUTOR programming language, if an instructional designer wanted to accept "5," "five," "fiv," and "3 + 2" as answers to a problem, those alternatives (or rules defining the complete set of alternatives) would all need to be manually programmed into the answer bank. We have increasingly sophisticated answer "parsers" that can evaluate increasingly complex inputs, but at a fundamental level, computational assessment tools match what students submit with what assessment designers have defined as right.[12]

Most automated grading systems can only evaluate structured input. Grading systems can automatically evaluate multiple-choice-type items (if the correct answer is programmed into the system). They can evaluate quantitative questions for which there is a single right answer ("5") or a set of right answers ("5" and "-5"). In chemistry, they can check for balancing of chemical equations, where the inputs aren't strictly numerical but can be converted into numerical systems. When a system can be evaluated through computational logic, like the circuit and electronics systems featured in MIT's first MOOC, 6.002x, instructors can define success criteria even for somewhat open-ended challenges ("using these simulated parts, build a complete circuit that turns this simulated light on"), and computers can identify which student-built systems meet the success criteria.

When considering these capabilities, it is important to remember that even in the most quantitative of subjects and disciplines, not every human performance that we value can be reduced to highly structured input. Consider mathematics. The Common Core State Standards, a set of math and literacy standards widely adopted in the United States, defines the process of mathematical modeling as including five steps: (1) finding a problem in a set of features; (2) arranging that problem into an appropriate model—which could be an equation, table, schematic, graph, or some other representation; (3) resolving computational problems within the model; (4) putting numerical answers in their original context; and (5) using language to explain the reasoning underlying the models and computations.[13] As a field, our autograding tools are good at evaluating the computational component, and of the five parts of mathematical modeling, that component is the one thing we no longer need human beings to do. When I write an academic paper with statistical reasoning, I typically will use a calculator or computer to make every calculation in that paper. The value that I bring as a human into my academic collaboration with computers is that I, not the computers, know what the interesting problems are. My value comes in asking interesting questions, identifying interesting problems, framing those problems for both humans and computers to understand, and then presenting structured equations and inputs that allow computers to compute solutions. Once the computer has (usually instantly) computed a solution, then I take the helm again and explain how the computer's computational answer fits into the context that I initially described, and I craft a written argument to explain the reasoning behind my solution process and what consequences the solution has for my academic field or for human society.

In my collaboration with statistical computing software, my added value comes from doing all of the things that software cannot do—analyzing unstructured data or interesting problems, framing those problems in (subjectively judged) useful ways, and using natural language to explain my process. Computers cannot do those things, and therefore they generally cannot be programmed to evaluate human performance on those kinds of tasks (though I'll come to some advances below). And since we cannot develop autograders for these things, we tend not to evaluate them at scale in math class. Rather, what we evaluate at scale in math class are the computational things that computers are already good at and that we don't need humans to do any more.[14]

Here again, the idea of the reification fallacy is useful. All throughout their careers, students take things called "math tests," but if these math tests are computer graded (or if they are limited to problem types that could be graded by computers), then we know for certain that these tests are only evaluating a portion of the full domain known as "math." A student who scores well on a computer-graded "math test" may be good at computation, but the test has not evaluated his or her ability to find interesting problems, frame those problems, explain his or her reasoning, or any of the other things that we pay professional mathematicians to do.

I do not mean to imply that we should not teach computation in schools. Reasoning about mathematics and writing about mathematics require an understanding of computation, and young people should learn all kinds of computation. Students should still memorize the kinds of mathematical facts—multiplication tables, addends that combine to ten—that are incredibly useful in all kinds of situations where it is advantageous to have faster-than-Google access to those facts. But those computational facts should be building blocks for students' learning how to go beyond quantitative computation into reasoning mathematically.

The trap of routine assessment is that computers can only assess what computers themselves can do, so that's what we teach students. But in our economies and labor markets, we increasingly do not need people to do what computers are already good at. We need students to develop complex communication skills and take on unstructured problems—problem finding and framing rather than problem computing in mathematics—and explain their reasoning. But school systems cannot cheaply test these important domains of mathematics, so school systems do not assess these dimensions at scale, and so teachers, publishers, and others diminish the importance of these dimensions of mathematics in curriculum and teaching. To be sure, there are some fabulous math teachers who do teach a more complete mathematics, but when they do so, they are working against the grain.

Machine Learning and Assessment

If we see improvements in assessment technologies in the decades ahead, where computers develop new capacities to evaluate human reasoning, it will most likely be connected to advances in "machine learning." Machine learning is a field combining algorithms and statistics in which computers are programmed to make determinations without following specific rule sets but by making inferences based on patterns. For assessment, the most relevant branch of machine learning is supervised machine learning, which involves training computer programs to label data or make decisions such that their results are similar to how proficient human beings might label data or make decisions. For instance, native speakers listening to language learners trying to pronounce a series of words would label the words as correctly or incorrectly pronounced. Computer programmers then take these "training" data and try to use them to teach computers how to recognize correctly or incorrectly pronounced words.[15]

The machines doing this learning will not "listen" to the words in any kind of meaningful sense; or at least, they will not listen to words in the same ways that humans do. Rather, computer programmers will instruct the machines to take the audio files of sounds and then break them down into very small audio wave segments and compute certain features of these microsounds, such as pitch and volume. The machine-learning algorithm then calculates which of these quantitative sound properties are more strongly correlated with correct pronunciations and which are more correlated with incorrect pronunciations. When the machine-learning algorithm inputs a new sound that hasn't been labeled as correct or incorrect, it will compare the quantitative properties of the new sound file with existing sound files and produce a probability that the new sound file is more like a correctly pronounced sound file or more like an incorrectly pronounced sound file. Humans can then review these computer-generated assessments and reevaluate them ("No, computer, this sound that you labeled as 'o' for incorrect pronunciation should actually be labeled a '1' for correct pronunciation."). Scoring algorithms can be updated based on these tuning improvements.[16]

Machine-learning-based approaches to improving autograders are most useful when two conditions are true: when a set of rules cannot describe all possible right answers, and when human evaluators can distinguish between right and wrong (or better and worse) answers. If a set of rules can be programmed to describe all possible right answers (as with a circuit simulator or an arithmetic problem), then machine learning is unnecessary; a set of programmed evaluation rules will do. If humans cannot reliably distinguish between correct and incorrect, then humans cannot generate a set of training data that can be used to program computers. Machine-learning approaches to computer-assisted pronunciation training are promising because both of these conditions are true. It is impossible to develop a strict set of rules for correct pronunciation in the same way that computer programmers could develop a strict set of pattern-matching rules for defining the correct answer to an arithmetic problem. At the same time, most native speakers can trivially recognize the difference between a correctly or incorrectly pronounced word. Now, there is "fuzziness" in these human assessments—will a native English speaker from Minnesota recognize my Boston argot of "cah" as an acceptable pronunciation for automobile?—but training data do not need to be labeled with perfect agreement among human beings in order for machine-learning algorithms to develop predictions that work with acceptable levels of reliability.

Through these machine-learning-based pronunciation technologies, you can speak "por favor" into your favorite language-learning app, and the app can make an automated assessment as to whether you are pronouncing the phrase more or less correctly. It is not the case that your phone has "listened" to you saying "por favor" in the same way that your Spanish teacher in middle school did. Instead, your language-learning app took the sound file for your "por favor," broke it down into many tiny sound segments, assessed certain quantitative features of those segments, used those assessments to create a quantitative evaluation of your sound file, and then matched those quantitative assessments against a library of quantitative models of "por," "favor," and "por favor" that had been labeled by humans as correctly or incorrectly pronounced. From that comparison, the pronunciation autograder then made an estimation as to whether the quantitative model of your sound file was more similar to the correctly pronounced sound files or the incorrectly pronounced sound files. This assessment is probabilistic, so a programmer determined the tolerance for false positives and false negatives and decided on a threshold of probabilistic confidence that the language-learning app had to reach in order to assign your sound file a rating of "correct."

All of this is essentially a magnificent kluge of a system to do the same kind of pattern matching that programmers trained the TUTOR language to do with the PLATO system fifty years ago. It takes something as idiosyncratic as the sound of a word and breaks that sound down into a series of quantitative features that can be compared to an "answer bank" of similar quantitative sound models. We have only the tiniest understanding of all the marvelous complexity of what happens inside the sea of neurons and chemicals in the human brain that lets a child instantly recognize a mispronounced word, and our computers take this nuanced, fuzzy assessment that humans can make and transform it into a series of routine computational tasks that can result in a probabilistic assessment.

Training these systems requires vast stores of data. When Google trains its image search engines to classify new images, it can use as training data the enormous corpus of existing images on the internet that have been captioned by human beings. There is no naturally occurring source of data where humans label text as pronounced correctly or not, so companies developing language-learning apps must create these data. As you might imagine, it's relatively inexpensive to have expert humans rate pronunciations for the most common thousand words in the most common pronunciations of a single language, but it becomes much more expensive to develop training sets that include more words and phrases, more variation in acceptable dialect and accent, and more languages. If a pronunciation detector is trained using data from native Spanish language speakers from Spain learning English, the classification algorithms used by the detector will work with decreasing fidelity with Spanish language learners from Latin America, native Portuguese speakers, other Romance language speakers, and native Mandarin speakers. The kinds of errors that native Mandarin speakers make learning to pronounce English are sufficiently different from the kinds of errors that Spanish speakers make that new data are needed to train classifiers that can effectively evaluate the quality of pronunciation from those different speakers. Vast stores of human-labeled data are required for robust pronunciation assessment, and the heterogeneity of the labeled data inputs—such as having novice learners from many different native language backgrounds and experts from many different contemporary dialects of the target language—plays a major role in how effectively the assessments can correctly autograde learners from different backgrounds. The costs of this data collection, labeling, and assessment system training are substantial. Language-learning systems will make steady progress in the decades ahead, but the challenges of recognizing pronunciation demonstrate how far away we are from an adaptive tutor that can listen to natural speech and provide feedback like a native speaker.[17]

Machine Learning and Automated Essay Scoring

Perhaps the most prominent place where machine learning has been applied to advancing autograding is in automated essay scoring. If automated essay scoring worked reliably, then throughout the humanities, social studies, sciences, and professions, we could ask students to demonstrate their understanding of complex topics through writing. Ideally, as essay questions were added to various high-stakes exams and other facets of our testing infrastructure, teachers would need to assign more high-quality writing assignments to help students do well on these gate-keeping experiences. Better tests could allow for better instruction. As in most education technologies, the state of the art does not come close to these majestic hopes. Automated essay scoring provides limited, marginal benefits to assessment systems, benefits that are neither completely trivial nor truly revolutionary. It is possible that in the years ahead, these systems will continue to improve, but gains will probably be incremental.[18]

The mechanics of automated essay scoring strike most educators as weird. In evaluating essays, human scorers examine both syntax—the arrangement of words and punctuation—and semantics, the meaning that emerges from syntax. Just as computers do not understand the sound of words, computers do not understand the meaning of sentences, so computers only parse syntax. An automating essay-scoring tool starts with training data—a large corpus of essays that have been scored by human graders according to a rubric. Then, the computer takes each essay and performs a variety of routines to quantify various characteristics of the text. One such technique is called—and this is a technical term—the *bag of words,* where the software removes all punctuation, spacing, and word order; removes all stop words like *a, an, the,* and *and;* stems all words so that *jumping, jumped,* and *jump* are all the same word; and then produces a list of all remaining words in the document with their frequency counts. Autograders can perform a variety of other similar calculations, such as total word count or n-grams, the frequency with which word pairs or trios occur with each other. The autograder then develops a model of correlations between human scores and the quantized syntactical features of the essay.

With enough training data on a specific essay topic written by a specific target audience, usually hundreds of essays from a particular standardized test essay question, each newly submitted essay is run through the same syntactical algorithms (tossed into a bag of words, counted, weighed, and so on). The autograders can make a prediction, based on feature similarity, of how a human rater would grade an essay with similar syntactic features. Through this process, scores generated by autograders can achieve a level of reliability similar to human graders. Here, reliability refers to the fact that if hundreds of new essays were given to two humans and a computer to be graded, the computer's grade will disagree with the score from any given human rater about as often as any given human disagrees with another human.

The case in favor of this approach to grading is that it allows for more inexpensive grading of natural language writing at scale. The assessment conducted by human graders in these large-scale writing assessments is not particularly good. Raters are typically given only a couple of minutes per essay to provide a holistic assessment with no qualitative feedback for students, but computers can achieve something close to this level of assessment quality and reliability. By using these technologies to increase the number of essays that are included in standardized tests, the hope is that educational systems are more likely to teach writing in their curricula, and even if the assessment is imperfect, it is better than standardized tests without writing.[19]

The case against automated essay grading is that it ignores the essential role of the audience in writing, that it replicates grading that is of low quality to begin with, and that it is difficult to scale. People don't write to have computers dump our craft into a bag of words; we write to reach other people or ourselves. Writing to satisfy the syntactic criteria of a software program drains the meaning out of the activity of writing. The semantic meaning of the grade itself is also somewhat different. A human grade signifies that a person has evaluated the semantic meaning of a piece of writing against a set of criteria and made a claim about quality. A computer grade is a prediction about how the syntactic qualities of a document relate to the syntactic qualities of other documents. Advocates argue that these different means bring about the same grading ends, but critics of autograding argue that the process of these educational activities matters.

Finally, the whole system of standardized test writing is not a crown jewel of our global educational system. The prompts tend to be banal, the time constraints of writing unrealistic, and the quality of human assessment rushed and poor. Developing essay banks and training datasets large enough to reliably autograde new essays is expensive and time consuming, requiring a big investment from students, human raters, assessment designers, and so forth. Importantly, training data from one essay do not allow an autograder to reliably evaluate another essay, so each particular prompt must be trained. Incrementally making this system better by creating ever-so-slightly-less-lousy autograders may not be a productive path to improving teaching and learning.[20]

One clever way to critique essay autograders is to program essay autowriters. Given that computers evaluate patterns in language syntax, if humans can decode those patterns, then they can use computational tools to generate new essays that are semantically meaningless but syntactically adhere to the patterns favored by grading algorithms. Les Perelman, the emeritus director of MIT's Writing across the Curriculum program (now called Writing, Rhetoric, and Communication) and an inveterate critic of automated essay grading, worked with MIT students to develop the Babel Generator, which can produce semantically meaningless essays that nonetheless score highly on automated essay rubrics. Perelman's team used the Educational Testing Service's ScoreItNow! tool to get automated feedback on their autogenerated essays. In an essay about mandatory national school curricula that started with the sentence, "Educatee on an assassination will always be a part of mankind" and concluded, "Therefore, program might engender most of the disenfranchisements," they scored a six, which ScoreItNow! describes as a "cogent, well-articulated analysis of the issue [that] conveys meaning skillfully."[21]

Autowriters probably aren't a threat to proctored standardized exams—though presumably, a determined student could memorize an autogenerated nonsense essay and submit it. But autowriters could be problematic for the grading of un-proctored essays, and they certainly present a striking kind of critique.[22]

When I read about autowriters and autograders, I like to imagine students downloading and running computer programs that automatically write essays while instructors use computers to automatically grade those essays. While the computers instantaneously pass these essays and grades back and forth, students and instructors can retire to a grassy quad, sitting together in the warm sun, holding forth on grand ideas and helping each other learn.

As with many ideas in education technology, this dream is actually quite old. When Sidney Pressey presented the first mechanical teaching machines in the 1930s, students at the Ohio State University student-run publication the *Ohio State University Monthly* wrote that if someone could build a second machine that automatically depressed the correct keys on Pressey's mechanical multiple-choice machine, then the future of education would be "perfect in the eyes of the student."[23]

Autograders in Computer Programming

Perhaps the most complex human performances that we can automatically grade reasonably well are computer programs. The field of computer programming has evolved in part through the development of tools that give feedback to computer programmers on their software. Many computer programmers write in what are called integrated development environments, or IDEs, that perform certain kinds of automated work for computer programmers. For instance, a computing script might include a number of variables that need to be modified and called on through a program, and an IDE might track those variables for programmers and let them select a variable from a list rather than needing to remember the exact right string of characters. Many IDEs have auto-complete functions that let programmers type the first few characters in a string or function and then select the right string or function from a list. Integrated development environments also have features that give programmers feedback on errors that are triggered in running a program; when a program fails to run properly because logic breaks down somewhere, IDEs automatically parse the code to identify possible sources of error. In a sense, every time a computer programmer runs a program, it is a kind of formative assessment task, and good IDEs give programmers feedback about what is working and what is not.

Given that automatically providing feedback on code is central to the development of computer programming as a discipline and profession, it is perhaps no surprise that online education systems have a powerful suite of tools for evaluating computer programs. As assignments, students write computer programs, and then instructors create other computer programs that evaluate the quality of students' programs along a number of dimensions: Does the submission meet engineering requirements? How quickly does it run? How many or how few lines of code are required? Does the code meet design specifications? Even if the code that students are submitting is relatively complex, automated grading tools can evaluate many important dimensions of the quality of that human performance. Computer programming probably represents the pinnacle of computational assessment of complex human performance.

For all that, however, the reification fallacy looms just as large over computer science as over any other domain. Writing computer programs that pass engineering tests is only a fraction of what good computer programmers do. As Hal Abelson, a longtime computer science professor at MIT and collaborator of Seymour Papert, once argued (with collaborators Gerald and Julie Sussman), "We want to establish the idea that a computer language is not just a way of getting a computer to perform operations but rather that it is a novel formal medium for expressing ideas about methodology. Thus, programs must be written for people to read, and only incidentally for machines to execute." Abelson's point is that it is not enough to write a computer program that passes an engineering test; the code should be written in such a way that another reader should be able to understand how the programmer has gone about solving a problem. This information is conveyed in the order of operations, the naming of variables, how the code is structured, and how comments within the code explain how the program proceeds. In Abelson's framing, everything that can be computationally evaluated by autograders is the "incidental" part of programming. Autograders that evaluate for "style" can evaluate whether a given code snippet adheres to certain well-established conventions, but only another human programmer can determine if a given code submission is written in such a way as to be parsable to other human beings as a medium for expressing ideas about methods.[24]

Along the same lines, computer programming is about understanding the needs of human systems, balancing engineering demands with broader societal concerns, collaborating among teams to weigh priorities, and a thousand other concerns that are both common to other engineering disciplines and unique to software engineering. As marvelous as our autograders are for evaluating computer programming, they still can evaluate only a fraction of the knowledge, skills, and dispositions required to be a good software engineer. To say that someone has "aced" a computer-graded exam in a computer programming class doesn't mean that he or she has all the skills to be a good software engineer, only that he or she has demonstrated proficiency in the skills that we can currently assess using autograders.

Escaping the Trap of Routine Assessment, One Innovation at a Time

The trap of routine assessment has two interlocking components: as automation technologies advance, the labor market and civic sphere will put a premium on non-routine skills that computers cannot do. At the same time, computers mostly assess the routine skills that humans no longer need to do. As educators, there is probably little that we can do to stem the tide of automation technologies reshaping the workplace, but it may be possible to continue to develop assessment technologies that slowly expand the range of complex human performances that can be automatically assessed.

As one example, MIT math educators have developed for their calculus MOOCs a new assessment tool for evaluating how students draw curves on a graph. In learning calculus, students are often tasked with evaluating functions and then drawing those functions as curves on a Cartesian plane or drawing their integral or derivative. The goal is not necessarily to perfectly plot these curves but rather to make sure that they cross the x axis and the y axis at roughly the right spot, that they go up or down when they are supposed to go up or down, and that they approach an asymptote at roughly the right point.[25]

Drawing these curves is essential to learning the basics of calculus, so the MOOC team in the Mathematics Department at MIT developed a system to analyze student submissions and evaluate their quality with enough confidence to assign them a grade. Before this innovation, one of the only options for an automated assessment to test students on their conceptual understanding of derivatives and integrals would have been a multiple-choice item displaying four graphs and asking students to recognize the right one. The new tool allows instructors to evaluate students' ability to draw, rather than just recognize, curves. It opens up a wider space for math instructors to computationally assess increasingly complex human performance.

Every assessment involves sampling from a domain. Because no test can cover all the knowledge, skills, and dispositions required for success in a domain, test designers try to choose items that form a representative sample of skills. In this one example, the MIT calculus team expanded the proportion of the full domain of calculus skills and knowledge that could be sampled by test designers relying on autograders. If we go back to our framing of mathematical modeling as consisting of five steps, then this particular advancement stands out because it allows students to demonstrate their proficiency with a dimension of problem representation, not just another form of calculation. It is through these kinds of steady, incremental advances that assessment technologies will allow for a greater range of human performances to be evaluated by machines. And as the field improves its capacity for assessment, these kinds of performances are more likely to appear in curricula, to be taught, and to be learned by more people. The pathway beyond the trap of routine assessment involves developing thousands of other applications like the calculus curve grader, each tackling the evaluation of some new element of complex human performance.

Stealth Assessment

One of the most intriguing lines of research into automated assessment is called "stealth assessment," or assessing students as they go about performing learning tasks rather than during special activities called "assessment." Typical assessment exercises can feel disconnected from the act of learning; learning stops on Friday so that students can take a quiz. What if classroom assessment could look more like formative assessment in apprenticeships? Consider, for instance, an apprentice woodworker turning a chair leg on a lathe while a nearby journeyman offers tips and feedback as the apprentice goes about the task. In this context, assessment naturally is part of the process of building a chair in the woodworking shop.

What might such assessment look like in physics or math? Several researchers, notably Valerie Shute at the University of Florida, have created online games where gameplay requires developing an understanding of mathematical or scientific phenomena, and as players engage in the game, they create log data that can be analyzed for patterns of play that correlate with other measures of scientific understanding. In the game *Newton's Playground,* players engage in tasks that require an understanding of Newtonian motion. In the research study, students do a pre-test about Newtonian motion, play the games, and then do a post-test. These tests effectively serve to "label" the gameplay data, since patterns found in log data can be correlated with scores afterward on a test. The goal is to have the patterns of effective play be identified with sufficient reliability that in the future, it would become unnecessary to give the test. A student who demonstrated sufficient understanding of Newtonian physics through a video game could be evaluated by gameplay rather than a distinct evaluation event.[26]

Though the notion is promising, implementation proves to be quite difficult. Developing playful learning experiences where students demonstrate important mathematical or scientific reasoning skills is quite hard, and substantial investment can be required in developing the game and the associated assessment engine for a handful of content standards. Researchers have explored the promise of using stealth assessment to evaluate competencies that aren't traditionally assessed by tests, such as creativity, patience, or resilience in solving problems. These kinds of assessments might provide a comparative advantage in the future, but as of yet, these systems remain research pilots rather than widely deployed assessment systems.[27]

Perhaps the biggest hurdle is that gameplay data in these virtual assessments often don't reliably correlate with competencies or understanding. When students are tested in a game environment, their behavior is shaped by the novelty of the environment. A student who appears inefficient, hesitant, or confused might understand the content quite well but not the new environment, and their patterns of play might have enough similarities with students who don't understand the content to make distinguishing patterns difficult. It may be possible with more research and development to overcome these kinds of hurdles so that rather than stopping learning to make time for assessment, online learning environments can simply track student problem solving as it happens and make inferences about student learning as the learning is happening.

The Future of Assessment in Learning at Scale

Is the trap of routine assessment a set of temporary hurdles that will be overcome by more advanced technologies or a more permanent and structural feature of automated computer assessment? Techno-optimists will point to the extraordinary gains made by artificial intelligence systems that can identify photos online, play chess or Go at superhuman levels, or schedule an appointment with a hair salon over the phone. These are examples of impressive technological innovation, but each of them has features that are not easily replicated in education.[28] Automated photo classifiers depend upon training data from the billions of photos that have been put online with a caption written by humans. There simply are no equivalent datasets in education where humans naturalistically engage in a labeling activity that distinguishes effective and ineffective teaching practice. The most advanced chess engines use a kind of reinforcement learning whereby the software plays millions of games of chess against itself, and the highly structured nature of the game—pieces with specific movement rules, an 8×8 board, a well-defined winning state—is well suited to automated assessment. Reinforcement learning systems cannot write millions of essays and grade them against other essays, because there is no defined quality state in writing as there is in chess. The advance of computer-voice assistants—such as the kind that can book an appointment at a hair salon over the phone—is impressive, but each individual task that an assistant is trained to do involves extensive data, training, and adjustment. Computer-voice tutors might be developed in limited areas with well-defined right and wrong answers and carefully studied learning progression, but trying to develop such systems for the highly granular goals we have in educational systems—adding 1-digit numbers, adding 2-digit numbers, subtracting 1-digit numbers, and on and on ad infinitum—makes the bespoke nature of those innovations incompatible with systemwide change.[29]

The history of essay autograders in the first part of the twenty-first century is instructive. As natural language-processing software improved, autograders have been more widely adopted by the Graduate Record Exam (for graduate school admissions), state standardized tests, and some limited classroom applications. When MOOCs were at their peak of public discourse in 2013, assessment designers explored implementing essay autograders in courses, and some limited experiments took place. Despite the technological expertise of developers and strong incentives to expand assessment tools, not much progress was made, and today, few MOOCs use automated essay scoring. This activity coincided roughly with the development of the PARCC (Partnership for Assessment of Readiness for College and Careers) and Smarter Balanced testing consortiums, and the Hewlett Foundation funded an automated essay grader competition with eight entrants from research labs and private firms. Since those efforts in the early 2010s, no major changes or advancements in essay-scoring technologies have been implemented in the PARCC or Smarter Balanced assessments. Advocates claiming that massive improvements in automated assessment technologies are just around the corner would need to explain why the last decade has shown such modest progress despite substantial investment by very smart, very devoted teams in academia and in industry.[30]

The problems of assessment are hard. The examples that are featured in this chapter—assessing computer programs, graphical calculus functions, pronunciation, and standardized essays—all represent areas where assessment designers are pushing the boundaries of what can be assessed in human performance. The modest, incremental progress of these innovations and the limited domains where they appear valuable also show how resistant those boundaries are to substantial advancement.

With known technologies, large-scale learning environments will remain bound by the trap of routine assessment in our lifetime. Much of what we can assess at large scale are routine tasks, as opposed to the complex communication and unstructured problem-solving tasks that will define meaningful and valuable human work in the future. Computers can mostly assess what computers are good at doing, and these are things we do not need humans to do in the labor market. Innovations in assessment technology will push gently on these boundaries, and the incremental advances that emerge will make marginal, useful expansions of what can be automatically assessed, but they will not fundamentally reshape automated assessment. There are millions of dollars invested, countless smart and talented people working on this problem, and strong incentives in educational marketplaces for finding new solutions. But progress remains slow, and for the foreseeable future, if we want to assess people on the kinds of performances that are most worthwhile for people to learn, we'll have to depend heavily on bespoke assessments evaluated individually by teachers and other educators. The human-scale limits on the assessment of complex performance will remain one of the most important strict limits on how widely large-scale learning environments can be adopted throughout educational systems.

8

THE TOXIC POWER OF DATA
AND EXPERIMENTS

ALL STORIES HAVE heroes and villains, exemplars and cautionary tales. In this history of the last few decades of learning at scale, the ignoble characters are the charismatic techno-evangelists who promised that technology would lead to revolutionary changes in educational systems. The heroes of this story have been the patient optimists, tinkerers who have been steadily studying one or two of those particular niches and incrementally, iteratively developing technologies that can improve learning for students in specific contexts. Of all these quiet heroes, I most admire technology developers and advocates who subject their designs and interventions to rigorous study, then take the evidence from those studies to improve their products. Improving complex systems through technology will not come via lightning-bolt breakthroughs but rather from these kinds of shoulder-to-the-wheel approaches, especially when conducted in close partnership with practicing educators.

Large-scale learning environments have a series of characteristics that make them well suited for this kind of ongoing investigation and continuous improvement. Across instructor-guided, algorithm-guided, and peer-guided technologies, some unifying features of large-scale learning environments are the data and data structures that underlie these systems. At any given moment, a large-scale learning system must have a model of all possible actions that a learner can take—a model of the system—and a model of a student's state within this system. In Scratch, this might be all of the blocks assembled into a Scratcher's program at that particular moment; in a MOOC, this might mean tracking every assignment a student has completed to date and every assignment that is currently available but not yet completed. All of these data can be harnessed to create a complete record of what every learner has ever done within the system, a longitudinal record collected keystroke by keystroke and click by click for millions of learners around the world. Large-scale learning environments are generating datasets that are orders of magnitude larger than what educational researchers have traditionally studied.

Moreover, learning-at-scale systems are amenable not just to observational data collection, but also to experimentation. As anthropologist Shreeharsh Kelkar has observed, learning scientists (including myself) who are interested in MOOCs and other large-scale platforms are fond of making comparisons between large-scale learning environments and other major software platforms, such as Google, Facebook, and Amazon, that constantly conduct experiments on their users.[1] One way these large internet platforms have improved so rapidly over past decades is by deploying experiments called A/B tests, in which different users are shown slightly different versions of the same website. A "Buy Now" button might be red in one version and blue in another so that retail researchers can incrementally increase their knowledge about designing online environments that encourage more shopping. Large-scale learning platforms can be studied in the same way with pedagogical and content experiments to allow course designers and technology developers to continually improve learning environments.

Data collection and experimentation hold great promise as means by which large-scale learning environments can become ever more effective, efficient, and successful. But with this promise comes risk. To describe this risk, I borrow the term *toxic* from computer security researcher Bruce Schneier. Schneier has described corporate data as a "toxic asset" because simply holding it poses risks for both companies and users.[2] Toxic assets, like radioactive materials—which can both saves lives and cause cancer—must be used with great care. Researchers like me are excited about the power of data and experimentation because it may be possible to use large-scale learning environments to speed up our cycles of continuous improvement and to research online learning while students go about typical activities. Advocates for student privacy and autonomy, however, raise serious, valid concerns about the risks of data breaches, about the dangers of quantifying human performance, about who gets to decide what experiments are conducted and, perhaps most importantly, upon whom. Successfully harnessing the power of data and experiments in learning at scale will involve balancing the potential rewards of research for incrementally improving learning technologies and learning science with the risks and harms that might accompany such research. That navigation starts by understanding these potential risks and rewards.

Large-Scale Learning Data: From Sentences to Stories

Most online learning systems record a history of all user actions. Within MOOCs, the learning management system tracks nearly every action a learner takes in the environment: every page visited, video watched, video paused, problem attempted, and progress status checked. Within Scratch, the system records the state of every Scratch program, including each programming "brick," its location relative to other bricks, comments from other Scratchers on the program, and so on. These data are stored in structured data files in the online servers associated with their respective learning environments, and they are "machine readable" in the sense that they can be systematically manipulated by software programs.[3]

To track an action, learning software often produces a record that functionally operates as a kind of one-sentence description of a learner's action: "On January 6, 2017, at 10:34:17 p.m. UTC, learner number 234,439,009 submitted an answer ('greater than') to problem Unit4Question3, and that answer was incorrect, and a hint was displayed to the learner." The sentences aren't written in English but rather recorded in a structured data format: ["DateTime, UserId, ActionType, ContentID, AnswerCorrect?"]. Researchers can aggregate these "sentences" into different kinds of stories. Some stories might be about individual learners ("User 009 logs in once a week, usually during lunchtime in Egypt, for the duration of a twelve-week course") and others might be stories about elements of the learning experience ("Sixty-three percent of learners answered Unit4Question3 correctly on the first attempt" or "Only 4 percent of learners ever try using one of our new programming bricks).["4]

As millions of learners around the world click their way through various online learning platforms, trillions of these individual data records—these structured sentences about learning—are generated and stored. In platforms with a global reach, these data repositories might include people from nearly every country on Earth, working at all hours of the day and night, in an incredible panoply of patterns: Khan Academy learners who skim a few videos about differential equations and others who plunge in and systematically work their way through problem sets; MOOC participants who dip into a single class and those who complete whole degree programs.

Because these stories are compiled through "structured sentences" of data, they can be aggregated and analyzed in nearly infinite ways. These data logs can also be combined with other datasets, such as self-reported data from learners about their background, goals, or experience in the course. Researchers and developers can then link data about learner characteristics with data about learner behavior and performance to look for patterns. Researchers can also attempt to follow learners across different environments. For instance, researchers at Delft University of Technology in the Netherlands offered a functional programming MOOC on edX and then searched repositories of open-source projects on GitHub (a globally popular software-development platform) to see if learners in their online course made more contributions to open-source projects after taking the class. They did this by looking for people who used the same email in both environments (edX and GitHub). By connecting internal MOOC data logs with publicly available data, the researchers hoped to gain new insights into how learners deploy new skills in real-world contexts.[5]

The data records collected by large-scale learning environments are both wide and deep, and they allow researchers to study learning through "microscopes and telescopes." For the microscopic view, we can examine detailed records from individual students. In 2014, Thomas Mullaney examined learning trajectories of six students who earned certificates in a single MOOC. He identified students whose patterns of behavior varied substantially, from steadily working every week as new content was released, to joining late and catching up, to working in spurts at several instances throughout a course, to waiting until the very last moment.[6] Previously, these kind of individual learner histories could only be captured through close anthropological observation of learners, but now researchers can examine these patterns across millions of learners. A telescopic view is also possible by aggregating data across learners to examine change over time in whole systems. For instance, when the researchers in the Lifelong Kindergarten group add new blocks or features to Scratch, they can aggregate the patterns of many thousands of participants to make claims about how the new activity is being deployed across the whole system.[7]

These new data have inspired new subspecialties of learning science, such as learning analytics and educational data mining. In these subfields, researchers use techniques from computer science, data science, and statistics to analyze data from trillions of entries of individual actions from millions of participants. This analysis can then be used to advance our understanding about learning in large-scale systems and thus how those systems can be improved. For instance, Ryan Baker and colleagues studied the classroom behavior and tracking log data of students using adaptive tutors in order to identify when students were engaged, bored, confused, or frustrated. They then developed "detectors" that could recognize these states based on learner activity. Boredom, confusion, and frustration each call for different kinds of supports for students, and emotion detectors in adaptive tutors might help make learning and practice more engaging and less dreary.[8]

Large-scale learning environments are developed by researchers using very different technologies and implementing very different pedagogical visions, but they can all be studied using the detailed data that systems collect. This data-based analysis may provide a bridge that can unite researchers from the different communities studying instructor-guided, algorithm-guided, and peer-guided learning at scale. It is through these data that diverse researchers can make joint progress toward the as-yet-intractable dilemmas that I have described in the previous three chapters.

A History of Improving Education by Analyzing Data

Almost from the beginning of public schooling in America, schools have compelled students to generate data for the purpose of system evaluation and improvement. In the mid-nineteenth century, Boston's School Committee sent examiners to schools across the district to quiz students about what they were learning. The examiners observed that students "for the most part, learned to recite the words of the textbook, without having had its spirit illustrated, and without having been accustomed to think about the meaning of

what they had learned." Asked "What is History?," eleven of the six-
teen answers quoted the textbook verbatim and without elabora-
tion: "History is a narrative of past events."[9] The examiners asked
students about the date of Thomas Jefferson's embargo and then
asked students to define embargo. Many could produce the date
(which was in the textbook), but didn't know what an embargo was
(which was not in the textbook). Students who took the test gained
no particular advantages themselves. But the data they generated
were used by the visiting committee to recommend improvements
to history instruction, which benefited students generally.[10]

In the middle of the twentieth century, the United States implemented nationwide tests to evaluate the country's education system,
sometimes called the nation's "report card." Under the National Assessment of Educational Progress (NAEP), schools, classes, and
students are randomly sampled from all fifty US states to participate in annual tests of various subjects. Individual students and
teachers are not identified, as the NAEP is an assessment of systems
rather than people. The test dates back to the Elementary and Secondary Education Act of 1965. Senator Robert Kennedy thought that
additional funding for schools should be tied to ongoing monitoring of improvements, including analyses of racial subgroups, so
that policymakers and community members could track whether
additional federal funds and programs were improving learning.
Ever since, the NAEP has been an important tool for understanding
how children from different backgrounds receive unequal educational experiences in the United States.[11]

In some respects, efforts at educational data science build upon
this long history of collecting data from students, classrooms, and
schools to improve educational systems. In previous chapters, I have
described several studies and design research projects that might be
at the top of the list of "Best Outcomes from Education Technology
Research Requiring Large-Scale Data." The development of Carnegie Learning's Cognitive Tutors over more than twenty years and

their promising results on algebra learning outcomes represent one high point in K–12 educational data science. The Open Learning Initiative statistics course, where college students completed introductory statistics in 20 percent less time than students in traditional classes, represents an important benchmark in higher education research. Studies that disprove exaggerated claims about large-scale learning environments also contribute to the literature on education policy. From my own work, I am proud that research with my collaborators on MOOCs helped people question narratives of "democratizing education," recognize the specific fields in higher education where learners were finding success, measure how well learners progressed toward their educational goals, and identify strategies that may help more people achieve their goals. These studies may not have not dramatically improved MOOCs, but they have helped policymakers better understand how MOOCs might or might not fit into educational systems.[12]

As a researcher, I am enthusiastic about these efforts, but I also recognize that evidence for the benefits of data-driven educational research remains less than overwhelming. In 2014, a group of educational researchers and higher education administrators met at Asilomar State Park in California to discuss how to build continued public support for research that would improve online learning and learning science. Several attendees turned to the metaphor of finding a "cure for cancer" (genomic data science enjoys widespread public support because of the potential to find new cures disease). What are the triumphant successes that online learning researchers could trumpet to excite policymakers enough to provide funding? The answer to that question was not obvious to those assembled. Of course, the attendees could brainstorm future goals—completing college in three years instead of four or learning two years of math in one year, for example—but it was not clear what promises or proposals we could make to the public that would obviously justify our stewardship of large quantities of data or what previous studies we could present to the public that would intuitively and compellingly describe what learning analytics research had already accomplished.[13]

Critiques of Student Data Collection: Scope and Compulsion

Putting student data to work to improve education is a worthy goal. Critics, however, raise valid concerns about the current scope of data collection in education systems. In my undergraduate seminars at MIT, I ask students to make a list of all the data that schools collect about them. The discussion often starts with registrar data: name, date of birth, transcript data (courses, grades), placement test scores, address, social security number, and residency. But students rapidly come to understand that schools and their private subcontractors have data far beyond what first comes to mind. Schools collect data from individualized education plans, which have detailed information about student disabilities and accommodation plans. School health systems have personal data about medical visits, diagnoses, medications, and vaccinations. Learning-management systems maintain records of learning activities, assignments, and grades for those assignments. School computers log browser histories and website cookies. School email systems and shared workspaces such as Google Docs track student communications. Identity cards, building entry cards, and Wi-Fi connection points can track a student's movement throughout a campus. As schools provide more digitally mediated services for students and families—such as letting parents log on to portals to see grades or sending notification texts to students when a dryer finishes a run in the college laundry room—schools are choosing to collect ever-growing amounts of data about students.

Critics point out that massive data collection regimes are violations of student privacy because long-term storage of large volumes of student data puts students at risk of disclosure, and students who are compelled to provide their data cannot provide a truly voluntary, informed consent to subsequent research. Intentional, accidental, or criminal release of data about student disabilities, student performance, or other characteristics can also lead to real harms.[14]

Even if worst-case scenarios can be avoided, schools are public institutions that teach students through their actions and procedures as much as they do through their instruction. For critics, forcing students to participate in widespread data collection is training them for docile acceptance of participation in the surveillance capitalism of advertising technology networks and the growing surveillance state. These concerns become increasingly salient in public discourse as social media companies leak, misuse, and illegally share data; as China and other states build widespread online surveillance and citizen-rating systems; and as foreign governments, national security apparatus, commercial data aggregators, and criminal actors buy, steal, sell, and share data.[15]

In the public marketplace of data-based services, individuals nominally have some degree of choice about exchanging access to their data for a company's services. When young people log on to their Instagram accounts, they agree to terms of service and a privacy policy that describes the conditions under which data will be used and shared, though it is widely acknowledged that no one reads those long and unwieldy documents. But students are compelled to attend public schools in the United States and many other countries, and when schools require students to engage in online learning activities, they are requiring students to make data available to schools and their commercial partners. To some extent, students in higher education have more autonomy, but compulsion is a central feature of higher education as well. A student often cannot opt out of an identity card for entering a building if they want to attend classes there; a student choosing a particular major may have to complete the online activities of a required course. A principled student might be able to avoid certain data collection activities, but many academic pathways coerce students to submit to data collection as a condition of attending an institution.[16]

One area in which data collection has become particularly invasive is in technologies to prevent cheating. As online learning in higher education expands, institutions are looking to technology to provide surveillance of students who are taking exams on their own computers at home, with access to textbooks, friends, and the entire internet. Anti-cheating software can record a student's eye movement, body movement, keystrokes, and web use during an exam. Some software prevents a student from opening new browser windows or even from copying and pasting text. Requiring students to install anti-cheating software on their machines is requiring students to install powerful surveillance tools on their personal computers, and some students are vigorously pushing back.

In 2015, Rutgers student Betsy Chao led a campus-wide protest against the anti-cheating software Proctortrack. Chao and her peers in Rutger's online courses were required to download Proctortrack onto their machines, show their face and knuckles for recording and scanning, and have the software running during exams. As Natasha Singer of the *New York Times* wrote, "Once her exam started, Ms. Chao said, a red warning band appeared on the computer screen indicating that Proctortrack was monitoring her computer and recording video of her. To constantly remind her that she was being watched, the program also showed a live image of her in miniature on her screen."[17] Rutgers added the requirement to use Proctortrack mid-semester. Students who had already enrolled in courses on the basis of syllabi and other agreements were told that they now needed to pay $37 for the software, install it, and use it—a particularly egregious form of compulsion for students already invested in their courses. In response to student protest, the university offered to allow students to take human proctored exams for

$40 per exam, an example of a growing trend in many sectors of society where people are charged extra for services that maintain their privacy.

The earlier discussion about the history of data collection demonstrates that not all data collection is pernicious. The NAEP program has been compelling students to take tests as part of data collection exercises for over fifty years, and it has not generated any widespread or volatile public objections during that time. Under the right circumstances, stakeholders in education will consent to compulsory data collection from students. But as the critics point out, emerging technologies raise different questions. New data collection enterprises via large-scale learning technologies are massive, much more so than previous efforts. The time has come to rethink our guidelines for the collection, storage, and use of student data.

Contextual Integrity: A Framework to Reason about Privacy

Information science professor Helen Nissenbaum has developed the idea of *contextual integrity* to provide a new intellectual foundation for setting boundaries around data usage and privacy. Contextual integrity advocates argue that privacy norms should be developed and analyzed while taking the values of users into account. A recent controversy at MIT illustrates some of the potential conflicts between typical uses of data and participant expectations. To better understand students' well-being, the administration asked students to complete an anonymous survey. Some student leaders encouraged their peers to complete the survey to better inform student leadership and the administration about how to support students. The survey did not ask about student housing, and students perceived that decision as protecting student anonymity—certain dorms were perceived as having much higher rates of drug usage and behaviors considered problematic, and some students would not have answered drug questions candidly if they also believed that administrators were asking them about their dorms. But administration researchers had given residence hall information of individual students to the third party administering the study, which allowed residence information to be associated with individual responses without the knowledge of students. Those data were used as part of the evidence in an administrative decision to close a dorm reported to have widespread issues with drug use. Administrators used this information in a good-faith effort to support student well-being, and they did not violate specific agreements about privacy and confidentiality, but students felt that their contextual privacy was violated.[18]

This case illustrates a common challenge for privacy and contextual integrity: information that is not available through a single dataset can be revealed by combining datasets. Thus, a survey about individual health issues provided data to MIT administrators on residence hall–level issues by combining the survey data with residence hall data. Moreover, as new statistical methods are developed, there are new ways of analyzing data that might give survey makers far more information than respondents realize. For instance, in the years ahead, more advanced sentiment analysis techniques might be developed that will allow researchers to estimate student mood or emotional state from snippets of text. What can be learned from surveys when they are distributed is only a portion of what can be learned from the data in the future.

The potential for novel insight, the potential for beneficial new findings, and the potential for privacy risks and violations grow as data are retained over time and combined with other sources of data. Part of the compelling nature of characterizing data as a "toxic asset" is that the toxicity of data grows over time. As time passes, researchers develop more powerful techniques for linking and analyzing large data sources, and thus existing data sources become potentially more revealing.

Studying MOOC Learners through Their Home Address: Balancing Privacy with Advancing Policy Research

In Chapter 1, I described how my colleagues and I used home addresses from MOOC students to better understand how learners from different neighborhoods interacted with MOOCs in different ways. We discovered that in the United States, people from more affluent neighborhoods were more likely to register for and complete courses on HarvardX and MITx than people from less affluent neighborhoods. This study is a useful illustration of the tradeoffs between privacy and research insights.[19]

From the beginning of edX, the process of site registration included an address field where registrants entered their mailing address in open text (rather than through dropdown menus). It has never been clear to me why this information was collected or why it was collected in this format. After entering their name, address, email address, gender, age, and level of education, users agreed to a terms of service and privacy policy that grants researchers wide latitude to use their data. From a legalistic perspective anchored on terms of service agreements, we might say that users consented from that point forward (usually without reading the terms) to researchers like me using any and all of their data to advance research. From the lens of contextual integrity, we might ask, "What would a reasonable person expect that their address would be used for in research by an education technology non-profit (edX) supported by research universities (Harvard and MIT)?"

There cannot be any single answer to that question, as the millions of people from all walks of life from around the world who have entered text in that field assuredly do not share a conception of what the addresses were for. For a residential address, did people expect edX to mail paper certificates? To better understand geographic adoption of the service? To organize local meetups? What fraction of the millions of people who entered the text expected that a researcher would connect their residential address to census databases in order to make inferences about their neighborhood income and level of education? Of those who might expect such behavior, how many would find my behavior acceptable because I'm a researcher, even if they might object to commercial uses? HarvardX, MITx, and edX have all tried, through publications, interactions with the press, and messaging inside HarvardX and MITx courses, to make clear that research is considered a fundamental purpose of edX and that part of the rationale for offering free online learning is to research learning within these environments. Are these communication efforts effective at shaping people's contextual understanding? Contextual integrity theory asks that powerful stakeholders in a system attend to the voices, beliefs, and considerations of users, but users have a range of beliefs that defy easy consensus. In addition, novelty is fundamental to the research enterprise—to conduct research is almost by definition to use data in ways that have not yet been attempted.[20]

As a researcher, I think the risks of violating contextual integrity should be weighed against the potential benefits of the research. The motivation behind my research on MOOC demographics was to understand inequalities in online education and to raise the concern that online learning might expand rather than ameliorate inequality. In my view, our research questions provided important insight on a widespread and potentially misleading public narrative that MOOCs would "democratize education" by disproportionately benefiting folks with limited access to higher education. That claim gave insufficient consideration to how people from different backgrounds used technology differently, and I believed that my research would provide important data about just how that usage varied. I'm confident that my colleagues and I, and our supervisors who supported the research, made the right choice in proceeding with the work.

But the autonomy that I had as an individual research scientist to decide whether and how to use home address data gave me pause then, and it still does. We wrote a deliberately broad research prospectus to Harvard's Committee on the Use of Human Subjects, the Institutional Review Board (IRB) that monitors human subjects research, that asked for wide latitude to use data from edX under the research permissions granted in the terms of service. I remember personally checking with our IRB contact to ask whether we needed any special review to connect our address data with census data. She said that we did not, because we met the criteria for research review guided by federal law and Harvard policy. But that policy could not provide a full set of ethical guidelines in a new field. The decision was up to me. When faced with an ever-growing list of datasets to merge and new techniques to try, I am confident that most of my research colleagues will try to make good decisions that respect learners and learning systems, but without a doubt, our field will make mistakes as well.

Calculating the Cost-Benefit Ratio of Educational Research and Data Collection

Making good judgments about how to collect, store, and analyze educational research data can be understood as a cost-benefit calculation. Can we design a system where harms from disclosure and use are minimized and benefits to students from educational research are assured? Perhaps. But right now, the magnitude of harms and benefits are difficult to measure.

Granting that data from large-scale learning environments have the potential to be beneficial, just how beneficial are they? In previous chapters, I've described how large-scale learning systems have incrementally improved over decades, and log data from these systems are an important part of the research behind that development.

Online learning has unquestionably enriched the lives of many millions of learners of all ages, but education systems are, on their face, not profoundly changed. Humans have been trying to use computers to teach mathematics to other humans for sixty years, and most kids still reach algebra in eighth or ninth grade; we haven't achieved some step-change breakthrough in mathematics instruction such that middle school students are ready for calculus or statistics. We still cannot download kung fu, or anything else, directly into people's brains.

As with the benefits, the risks of data-intensive educational research are not yet wholly clear. People in the networked world are increasingly familiar with massive data breaches: financial and credit data from Equifax, passport data from Marriott, personal data from Facebook, passwords from countless websites. While edtech hasn't yet identified its "cure for cancer" mission, it also has yet to experience an Equifax-level breach where widespread public harm has resulted from a data hack or data exposure. That's not to say substantial breaches, hacks, ransomware attacks, and other assaults on student data haven't occurred. In her "2017 Year in Edtech" roundup, Audrey Watters listed a fraction of the hacks reported in the past year:

> In education, there were breaches at colleges and universities, breaches at K–12 schools, breaches at the Department of Education, breaches at education technology companies, and breaches with software schools commonly use. 77 million users accounts stolen from Edmodo. A file configuration error at Schoolzilla that exposed the data of some 1.3 million students. A ransomware attack at a school system in Maine. A ransomware attack at a community college in Texas. Computers affected by the WannaCry virus at the Massachusetts Institute of Technology, Trinity College, the University of Washington, North Dakota State University, the University of Maine, and

elsewhere. 14 million college email username and passwords for sale on "the dark Web." W2 phishing scams at a school district in Texas. W2 phishing scams at a school district in Connecticut. W2 phishing scams at a school district in Minnesota. Phishing emails posing as Ofsted. Phishing emails posing as the University of California student health plan. $11.8 million scammed from MacEwan University. Keyloggers at the University of Iowa. Keyloggers at the University of Kansas. A hacked school Twitter account in Florida. A privacy breach at Stanford. Data stolen from a community college's health clinic. A data breach at a school board in Ontario. A data breach at the Chicago Public Schools. A malware attack at the University of Alberta. And then there was the ominously named "Dark Overlord," who held the data of multiple school districts for ransom, in one case sending parents text messages threatening to kill their children if they did not pay up.[21]

The magnitude of the harms to students that these breaches caused remains unclear, however. Writing this book from the end of the first Trump term, risks to undocumented students and their families from school data seem particularly acute, and cooperation between school districts and Immigration and Customs Enforcement is bitterly contested in many communities. Broader public outcries against the collection and use of student data, however, have generally not emerged from these incidents; they are mostly treated as nuisances in the digital world rather than acute threats to schools and students.[22]

Harms are possible not just from malicious attacks but also from well-meaning attempts to use data to support student learning. One risk is that software can use algorithms trained on historical data to make recommendations, and these recommendation then reinforce structural biases in the educational system. One place where this risk is acute is in academic counseling services that are based on data and algorithms. For instance, Naviance is a college and postsecondary counseling services platform that is widely adopted in American high schools (used by perhaps 40 percent of high school students). Students in most American high schools are woefully under supported by guidance counselors, with hundreds or thousands of students sharing a single counselor. In the absence of funding for human support to help students prepare for college, schools are turning to computers and algorithmic recommendations. Enter Naviance, which aggregates data about colleges, students, and high schools to provide algorithmically generated advice. Students can query the database to find out how previous applicants with similar characteristics have fared in applying to a wide variety of postsecondary institutions.[23]

In the best of all possible worlds, Naviance would help students discover postsecondary opportunities that they were unfamiliar with, pair students with schools and programs that could advance their interests and opportunities, and provide students with suggestions for schools that could stretch their imagination ("reach" schools and programs) and schools that were likely to admit them ("safety" schools and programs). More realistically but still optimistically, the software could help human counselors serve more students effectively. In the worst-case scenarios, these programs might reinforce and reproduce structural biases in education. The software might detect that students with certain course-taking patterns are unlikely to gain admission to certain programs and steer students away from those opportunities. But course-taking patterns could certainly be correlated with race or other dimensions of socioeconomic status. These kinds of recommendation engines that are based primarily on historical data might offer recommendations that reinforce historically inequitable patterns.

Unfortunately, despite the astounding reach of Naviance, educational research has almost nothing to say about student experiences and outcomes with Naviance or other college recommendation software. Naviance is a strong contender for the most consequential piece of software in American schools. But a search of Google Scholar for the term *Naviance* reveals only a handful of peer-reviewed research studies, leading with a 2017 study called "Increasing College Access through Implementation of Naviance: An Exploratory Study." In a working paper currently under review, Christine Mulhern, a doctoral student at the Harvard Kennedy School, shows that information from Naviance about state colleges increases attendance among disadvantaged students but also deters them from applying to more selective colleges.[24]

In this case as in many others, implementation of large-scale learning tools runs far faster than the research needed to assess them. This makes Naviance a tantalizing illustration of both the benefit and cost of large-scale learning environments. We need data and research to study Naviance to determine if it is a worthy complement to high school counselors or if it is reinforcing structural biases—and if it is reinforcing structural biases, to determine how it could be improved. Without this research, Naviance potentially harms students by posing as a valid substitute for human guidance. And if Naviance suffered a data breach, additional harms could result. Within one product, the potential for both real benefit and significant harm coexist.

Complicating the quest to calculate the cost-benefit ratio of educational research and data collection is the fact that there is limited funding available for education research, and what funding there is tends to go to pilot novel projects rather than analyze existing ones. The National Science Foundation will award millions of dollars this year to support the development of edtech prototypes and small field trials, many of which will engage only a few classes or a handful of students. At the same time, the most widely adopted software tools in schools—learning-management systems, college-recommendation systems, student-information systems—go dramatically understudied. Identifying the cost-benefit or risk-reward ratios of data collection and education technology, and creating sensible policies and practices in response to these assessments, will be almost impossible if education researchers do not study the tools that people and schools actually use.

Maximizing the Value of Learning-at-Scale Data via Experimentation

At the dawn of the MOOC era, a common refrain from computer scientists who were turning their attention to online learning was that education research was poised to make a giant leap forward because "we finally have data." In this view, educational research had been constrained by a lack of robust data about learner behaviors. Now that educational technologies were collecting massive trace logs of learner activity, breakthroughs in our understanding of learning were on the horizon. Computer scientists and data scientists would run new machine-learning algorithms over these vast new data sources, identify correlations between specific instructional practices and student outcomes, and determine which educational practices are most effective.[25]

But as argued in the first half of this book, these observational approaches have not led to breakthrough insights that have revolutionized our understanding of how people learn. Typically, when researchers comb backward over educational data collected during routine learning experiences, they find some version of Reich's Law: "People who do stuff do more stuff, and people who do stuff do better than people who don't do stuff." This is the commonsense observation that people who do more of any type of learning activity—answer problems, watch videos, submit homework, contribute to discussion forums—are more likely to do other types of activities because they are more engaged or more committed to participation. Not surprisingly, these people who complete more learning activities typically do better on measures of learning and persistence. Hoarding data from online platforms in the hopes that new insights will later emerge is a strategy that is incomplete at best and misguided at worst. The much more promising approach to developing powerful large-scale environments is improving them through systematic experimentation.[26]

Online learning environments are particularly well suited to conducting experimental research. They allow researchers to control many aspects of the learning experience since the environment can be held constant in ways that are not possible in physical classrooms. They keep detailed records of how students respond to changes. And in environments where many thousands of learners are engaging online, it is possible to conduct large-scale experiments that are sensitive to detecting small effects that might not make much difference on their own but could be combined with many other small changes to lead to substantial improvements. If large-scale learning leads to substantial breakthroughs in human development, it will be through constant testing, evaluation, and refinement. Though experimentation is not the only way forward—Scratch stands out as a platform on which designers and researchers have systematically introduced design changes without much randomization and with an emphasis on qualitative user research to evaluate results—randomized control trials are among the most promising ways for large-scale learning environments to continuously get better.

My own experiments with MOOCs illustrate the types of insights that this research method can provide. With colleagues, I spent two years investigating how different kinds of interventions inspired by social psychology and behavioral economics affected student persistence and performance in MOOCs. The interventions were short writing exercises to help learners start the course with productive mental frames, such as asking learners to write about how taking the course aligns with their values or how they were planning to complete coursework. After testing our interventions in pilot studies, we implemented them in nearly 250 courses on HarvardX, MITx, and Stanford's OpenEdX, assigning more than 250,000 students to one of our treatment arms. We chose our interventions because they worked well in pilot studies, but early on in our research, we found that when we tested the interventions at larger scales across multiple courses, the average effects tended to be null (sometimes they had positive average effects in courses, and other times they had negative average effects, and there is a good chance that these findings are just sampling error rather than indications of real harm or gains). Over time, however, we found that our interventions did improve average outcomes in certain contexts for certain students. The interventions worked best for students from countries with low scores on the UN Human Development Index (HDI), and they worked only in courses in which there was a substantial gap in completion rates between learners from developed and developing countries (or countries with high and low scores on the HDI). We recognized relatively early on that our interventions seemed to work better on particular students. But it was only after three years and having implemented our approach in hundreds of particular courses that we realized that our interventions worked for certain kinds of people (from developing countries) only in certain kinds of contexts (courses that people from developing courses completed at lower rates than other students). Through these kinds of experiments, we may be able to develop tailored supports for particular students.[27]

Concerns and Critiques of Educational Experiments

For me as a researcher, the phrase "experimenting on students" is a positive one—it means that educators are systematically figuring out how to improve student learning and well-being. Of course, for many people in the public—probably many readers of this book—"experimenting on students" may not sound so great.

In 2018, publishing giant Pearson conducted a study, somewhat similar to the one I described above, to determine whether growth-mindset interventions improve learning in a software product to teach computer science. Mindset theory holds that students learn better when they adopt a growth mindset ("If I keep trying, I can get better at math") rather than a fixed mindset ("I am good/bad at math"). Pearson tested these methods using a randomized controlled trial in which some nine thousand students received a growth-mindset message while a control group of similar students did not. Several observers objected to educational publishers conducting this kind of research. Kate Crawford, the founder of AI Now, a research institute examining the social implications of artificial intelligence, tweeted out, "Ed tech company experiments on 9000 kids without anyone's consent or knowledge to see if they test differently when 'social-psychological' messaging is secretly inserted? HARD NO." Crawford is a brilliant researcher and critic, so her strong objection was a good opportunity for me to reflect on why I see this kind of research differently.[28]

From my point of view, every classroom teacher, educational publisher, and instructional designer implements variation in teaching practices over time to improve teaching. There are virtually no actors in education who do the exact same thing year after year, decade after decade. Instead, they introduce variation, examine whether the variation leads to better outcomes, and make adjustments accordingly. In 2016–2017, students used the old version of the Pearson product, which led to certain educational outcomes. In 2017–2018, Pearson conducted an experiment in which some students were given a new version and some students the old version. If Pearson had rolled out the new version to all the 2017–2018 students, there would still have been a group of students (those from 2016–2017) who had received the old version. But this scenario would not have caused such ire.

I infer two objections in Crawford's comment. The first is an objection to "social-psychological messaging," perhaps because it appears that a publisher is venturing out of its lane by attempting to manipulate students' psychology. But every learning interaction is social-psychological. When a student gets an answer right or wrong in an adaptive tutor, the system needs to somehow inform the student—with a hint, or a symbol (green check, red X), or other feedback. All of these responses are social-psychological to the extent that they both inform students academically and shape, at least in some small way, their self-perception. There is no way to remove the social-psychological from education; rather, we should figure out how to do it well. I thus take Pearson's research goal as a worthy one.

The second objection has to do with randomly assigning kids to different learning experiences. Social science researchers have identified an "experimentation aversion" found in health care, education, and other fields, where "people often approve of untested policies or treatments (A or B) being universally implemented but disapprove of randomized experiments (A/B tests) to determine which of those policies or treatments is superior."[29] When educators use Method A in 2016 and Method B in 2017, it is very hard to figure out which approach is better, because the learners are different from year to year. When researchers use random assignment—testing Method A and Method B each with a random half of students from the same year—we can better control for those kinds of contextual factors; thus, we can make more robust claims about whether changes are improvements. Put another way, educators are constantly introducing variation into classrooms that advantage some students and disadvantage others, but they almost never do so in a way that can tell us which students were advantaged and which were not. Experimental studies are powerful tools for making those kinds of robust inferences, but unfortunately, they also raise serious concerns about student autonomy and the power of institutions—schools, colleges, publishers, tech companies—to un-literally subject students to new experiments.[30]

In my view, Pearson's goal was admirable. They took a well-established line of research (growth-mindset messages have been shown to have small positive effects on student learning, especially for low-achieving students), and before integrating mindset messages with all students, Pearson tested the messages in a particular product to see if they worked in this particular context. The relative technical ease of integrating these kinds of tests into online platforms, the high volume of students participating in large-scale learning projects, and the structure of digital data all combine to make online environments potentially promising places to continue these kinds of experiments that help researchers and educators better understand what kinds of practices support student learning.[31]

If online learning leads to better outcomes from students, it will be through the amalgamation of a thousand or ten thousand studies like this one that incrementally accrete a knowledge base about effective online learning. But if researchers, technology developers, publishers, and educators cannot earn the public trust, if we cannot be trusted to wield the toxic power of data and experimentation wisely, then these kinds of research initiatives will collapse, and some of the potential benefits of learning-at-scale technologies will not be realized.

Mitigating and Managing the Toxic Power of Data and Experiments

The risks of data collection and experimentation in large-scale learning environments are unclear. We know that many data privacy breaches have occurred, but the harms from those breaches are not well documented. No doubt some experimental interventions that have been conducted have disadvantaged some students, but students are regularly advantaged and disadvantaged by the year-to-year unsystematic variation in our education system. Some of the most diffuse long-term risks of large-scale data collection seem quite severe—we don't want public education systems training students for lives in a surveillance state—but they could be avoided with legal and cultural regulations of data usage that balance autonomy and experimental science. We have some studies that show the value of this kind of research for advancing our understanding of learning technology and the science of learning, but no advances have been so dramatic as to make the need for continuing such research self-evident.

Even if as policymakers or citizens we have to make our cost-benefit calculations about education-technology data through a haze of uncertainty, we can still work to mitigate risks and maximize the value of data that we do collect. One of the most unfortunate features of our current infrastructure of educational data is that data collection happens through schools, but then data flow to private subcontractors without the same accountability or incentives. State law and your local school district compel your child to go to school, and then they make that child sign up for a Google education account, a Naviance account, a PowerSchool account to check grades, a Pearson account or Khan Academy account for homework problems and readings—maybe even an account from a single sign-on provider like Clever that helps your student log on to all these different services. Great quantities of data about students—grades, activity in the online platform, performance—are thus accessible to all of those different organizations. The legal protections for student information once it makes its way from the schools out to those companies, which may number in the dozens or hundreds in some school districts, are hazy.[32]

One effort to address this state of affairs was a $100 million Bill and Melinda Gates Foundation initiative called inBloom, funded in 2011 and launched in 2013. The idea of inBloom was to create a trusted non-profit data intermediary between schools and for-profit industry. Schools would partner with inBloom to store student data, firms would partner with inBloom to access data, and inBloom would be responsible for sharing only what firms needed when they needed it. At the same time, by centralizing certain data collection and storage functions, inBloom might also have created new opportunities for research that examined technology use and learning outcomes across schools, districts, and states. But the core value proposition of inBloom was that through its non-profit status, it could strike a better balance between allowing the use of student data for learning and research and protecting students from the risks of disseminating those data widely among firms.[33]

Right from its announcement, inBloom was beset with critics. The Bill and Melinda Gates Foundation is a large, high-profile, and often controversial funder of education policies, and several of their signature initiatives, such as breaking large high schools into smaller ones or creating nationwide curriculum standards—the Common Core—have been critiqued on both their premise and their execution. While the slow accumulation of student data by districts and corporate partners has happened invisibly over the last two decades, inBloom appeared very rapidly, had a controversial funding source, and drew attention to its intentions of accumulating massive stores of student data. Critics raised concerns at the national, state, and local level to this new initiative, with the result that states introduced over four hundred pieces of student-privacy legislation. It is not clear how successful all of these pieces of legislation were or what their effects will be over time, but a little over a year after the launch, inBloom shut down. One feature that favors the status quo in student privacy is that any new effort to address these issues is more likely to raise concerns than the invisible, mostly dysfunctional, but not yet disastrous baseline that already exists.[34]

If a national data repository is not the answer, what could improve data privacy and protections by schools, edtech providers, and researchers? One approach is better contracting between schools and providers that provides explicit limits on what firms can and cannot do with data and how long they can store data. Another approach is to encourage schools to recognize student data as a toxic asset and to delete data regularly while respecting statutory obligations to maintain records. (This would be a loss for researchers interested in longitudinal studies, who use data collected over long periods of time to understand how initiatives in early elementary grades affect students' long-term trajectories.) But these approaches require an expertise that school officials in America's thirteen thousand school districts nearly universally do not have. In an era of constantly tightening budgets, school districts have barely enough administrators to meet the daily requirements of supporting teachers, keeping buildings and vehicles operating, and performing all the other myriad responsibilities necessary to keep schools functioning. Schools are unlikely to be able to develop their own expertise in the nuances of data privacy management and vendor relations. Government regulation might be able to limit the kinds of things that firms can do with student data, and public interest groups—like membership organizations representing school technologists—might be able to pool resources to develop model contracts and terms of service and then pressure edtech firms to adopt best practices.[35]

Another approach is to maintain learning data for long periods but only after stripping the data of identifying information. This is the approach taken in many of the databases maintained in the DataShop repository, from the Pittsburgh Science of Learning Center. Datashop hosts publicly available datasets, primarily from intelligent tutors, that researchers can use to test new theories and conduct new analyses. Some of the datasets have no demographic identifiers, and others that do have access restricted to researchers who can meet standards of data protection. Removing sensitive demographic information does, of course, limit the utility of those datasets; researchers cannot examine important questions of how students from different backgrounds use technology differently. A healthy educational ecosystem will probably have a range of different approaches to storing data and protecting privacy, with different data available for different purposes and stakeholders. The National Center for Education Statistics, for instance, collects large amounts of student data from schools, districts, the NAEP tests, and other initiatives. They make summaries of the data available to the public and datasets with various levels of protection available to researchers, providing one model for how we can protect and use student data. Through a combination of better contracting, regulation, data storage, and retention and deletion practices, schools and systems can reduce some of the risks of data collection while still using data for continuous improvement and long-term research.[36]

Ultimately, the role of experimentation and continuous improvement in edtech development will depend upon public support and public dialogue. Researchers interested in powerful new sources of data and experimentation need to continuously earn the public's trust that they will use that power wisely. As experimental research in learning technologies becomes more common, both transparency and public engagement will be crucial. Publishers, technology developers, and researchers should hold public forums to explain their research interests, gather feedback about how best to protect learner autonomy, and identify the kinds of learning challenges that communities are most interested in seeing progress on. Researchers who conduct experiments should be transparent about their methods and results, reporting positive, negative, or null effects. If this reporting on experimental results leads to public criticism, researchers should lean into that criticism, listen carefully, and consider how concerns can be addressed. Large-scale learning environments have the potential to be powerful sources of new insights about human learning, and public trust will be a crucial resource if the potential benefits of data and experimentation are to be realized.

CONCLUSION

Preparing for the Next
Learning-at-Scale Hype Cycle

The Next Robot Tutor in the Sky

PREDICTIONS OF IMMINENT TRANSFORMATION are among the most reliable refrains in the history of education technology. In 1913, Thomas Edison declared that the age of books was about to give way to the age of motion pictures. He told an interviewer, "Books will soon be obsolete in the public schools. Scholars will be instructed through the eye. It is possible to teach every branch of human knowledge with the motion picture. Our school system will be completely changed inside of ten years." When Edison's ten-year prediction failed to come to pass, he simply gave himself more time. In 1923, speaking before the Federal Trade Commission, Edison explained, "I made an experiment with a lot of pictures to teach children chemistry. I got twelve children and asked them to write down what they had learned, from the pictures. I was amazed that such a complicated subject as chemistry was readily grasped by them to a large extent through pictures. The parts of the pictures they did not understand I did over and over again until they finally understood the entire picture. I think motion pictures have just started and it is my opinion that in 20 years children will be taught through pictures and not through textbooks."[1]

One hundred years after Edison, technologists are still promising that new inventions can instantly solve challenges that education systems have faced for hundreds of years. The 2010s were a banner decade for charismatic technologists, from Knewton founder Jose Ferreira's adaptive robot tutor in the sky to Udacity founder Sebastian Thurn's magic formula for low-cost, global-scale learning with MOOCs. My sense at the end of the decade was that some sobriety had seeped into public conversations about the limits of learning technologies. But even at the nadir of this decade's hype cycle, wishful thinking continued. In 2019, Dan Goldsmith, then the CEO of Instructure, the company that provides the Canvas learning management system, boasted that his company's new learning analytics program would drive student success, make teachers more productive, and increase student retention:

> We have the most comprehensive database on the educational experience in the globe. So, given that information that we have, no one else has those data assets at their fingertips to be able to develop those algorithms and predictive models. What's even more interesting and compelling is that we can take that information, correlate it across all sorts of universities, curricula, etc., and we can start making recommendations and suggestions to the student or instructor in how they can be more successful. Watch this video, read this passage, do problems 17–34 in this textbook, spend an extra two hours on this or that.[2]

As someone who had spent much of the decade on MOOC research, I was taken aback by this particular claim. This prediction of a data-driven revolution in personalized learning was exactly what early MOOC advocates promised. After hundreds of millions of dollars in investments in massive courses and platforms and research across some of the world's leading universities, nothing like what Goldsmith imagined has been accomplished. Despite the examples of the developers of Knewton, Udacity, and other technologists who had to walk back early claims of transformation, here was yet another CEO borrowing the same rhetorical tropes about how massive datasets would be transformed into revolutionary learning insights, like piles of straw spun into gold. In the years ahead, no doubt, entrepreneurs will make these same kinds of promises about artificial intelligence and virtual reality and 5G and whatever new technologies Silicon Valley unleashes upon the world. Educators should be ready.

When new education technologies fail to meet their lofty expectations, a common rhetorical move is to claim that not enough time has passed for the true effects of new technologies to be revealed. The futurist Roy Amara is credited with the claim that "we tend to overestimate the effect of a technology in the short run and underestimate the effect in the long run."[3] Edison's hundred-year-old claims about motion pictures are good test cases for this theory. If we look at learning in its broadest view, some of what Edison predicted has come to pass. Video has become a dominant medium for informal learning, from the crafters of Rainbow Loom to the creators of *Minecraft* and in many fields beyond. But within the complex ecologies of formal educational systems, textbooks remain central to learning experiences and video remains a supplemental resource. I suspect that in the years after 2110 when we celebrate the two-hundredth anniversary of Edison's predictions and the hundredth anniversary of Sal Khan's TED talk "Let's Use Video to Reinvent Education," educational film and video will still play a secondary role in most formal educational systems.

The rhetorical tropes of disruption and charismatic technologies center around a heroic developer creating a new technology that leads to the transformation of educational systems (Edison invents the motion picture, and textbooks are replaced in a decade by more effective instructional films). This doesn't happen. Let me propose three essential shifts to the stories that we tell about how technology can improve learning. First, change won't come from heroic developers or even technology firms, but from communities of educators, researchers, and designers oriented toward innovative pedagogy and a commitment to educational equity. We need villages, not heroes. Second, technology won't transform teaching and learning. Our best hope is that technologies open up new spaces for the work of holistically improving curricula, pedagogy, instructional resources, student support, teacher professional development, policy, and other critical facets of school systems. Technology, at best, has a limited role to play in the broader work of systems change. Finally, we must let go of the hope for the kinds of dramatic shifts that sometimes do happen in consumer technologies and instead envision the work of systems change as a long process of tinkering and continuous improvement.

Promises and predictions for the transformative power of large-scale learning technologies are not going away. The task for educators in the decades ahead will be to examine new technologies as they emerge, to look past overwrought rhetoric and to dismiss egregious hype, while remaining open to possibilities for how new tools might prove useful in specific contexts, for certain subjects, or for particular students. After a century of edtech hype cycles, my dream is that educators will now have enough experience, enough data, and enough history at their disposal to defend against the next wave of overly optimistic claims by crafting their own more realistic, historically grounded predictions for the future of learning at scale.

Four Questions for Probing Learning at Scale

Policymakers, administrators, teachers, and students are asked to predict the future of learning technology all the time. The principal asks, "Are there any new software subscriptions that I can buy for my teachers that would improve student learning?" The policy-maker asks, "What portion of state aid for schools or universities should be designated specifically for technologies in order to improve graduation rates or retention?" The teacher asks, "Will adopting a new technology help my students learn?" The learner asks, "Is it worth spending time on this MOOC, and what will the certificate be worth years later?"

When encountering a new large-scale learning technology, I have found four questions particularly useful in situating a new product in the long history of education technology:

1. What's new?
2. Who is guiding the learning experience—an instructional designer, an adaptive learning algorithm, or a community of peers?
3. Pedagogically, is this attempting to fill pails or kindle flames?
4. What existing technologies does this adopt?

Claims of novelty are central to the charismatic rhetoric of technology evangelists. Canvas's Goldsmith claimed that "no one else" had the data assets that they do, and thus their unique data resources would usher in a new era of personalized learning. The question "What's actually new here?" invites comparisons to related efforts and a skeptical orientation. MOOC researchers have similarly massive datasets, which have proven useful for some policy insights but have not enabled breakthrough research in personalized learning, despite extensive efforts. The Pittsburgh Science of Learning Center's Datashop has reams of data on adaptive tutors; there are researchers using huge datasets from Scratch, Khan Academy, and all kinds of learning management systems. Strictly speaking, it is absolutely true that Canvas is the only company with the exact data assets of Canvas, but plenty of other large datasets of online learning behavior exist. If these older datasets haven't led to a sea change in personalized learning, it is reasonable to expect that Canvas's new data won't either.

Even though edtech evangelists often seem unaware of the long history of education technology, I have found history to be a reliable and useful guide for predicting the future of learning at scale. If you can figure out where a new technology fits in the genealogy of large-scale learning technologies, you have a good chance of predicting how a new technology will operate in schools based on the track records of the ancestors of that new technology. Armed with this understanding, you can then probe the potential value of incremental contributions: Is there anything about Canvas's dataset that differs from prior datasets used for educational data science that might lead to some incremental advance in the field? Answering probing questions like these requires situating new entrants in the long history of education technology.

Most new large-scale learning technologies fit reasonably well into one of the three genres of learning at scale that I described in the first half of this book. After asking, "What's new?," a trio of questions about sequencing, pedagogy, and technology should follow. Ask about who guides the learner's sequence of actions, what pedagogical traditions are enacted in the learning activities, and what technologies are used to engage the learner.

If an instructor determines the sequence of learning for students, if the pedagogy appears instructionist (with experts directly transmitting new knowledge to learners), and if the technology is a combination of a learning management system combined with autograders to assess and track learner progress, then the long history of distance education and the more recent history of MOOCs can provide some useful guidance for predicting the future of a new instructor-guided technology. Since autograders can reliably evaluate human performance only in a few domains where the structure of human performance can be quantified and analyzed by a computer program, then you can predict that the new technology will be most helpful in science, technology, engineering, and math fields and less useful in the humanities and social sciences. If the new system you are examining doesn't include substantial human coaching and advising, then it will probably serve well only a narrow slice of learners—those who have developed the self-regulation skills to navigate and persist through self-paced learning experiences. The students who tend to thrive in these kinds of environments are those who have already demonstrated academic proficiency, since most people develop self-regulated learning through an apprenticeship in the formal educational system. For those learners, self-paced learning can provide powerful, flexible learning experiences at low marginal (per-student) costs. But the risks that these kinds of technologies will accelerate rather than alleviate gaps in educational opportunity are quite high.

If an algorithm decides the sequence of learning activities, then your new specimen may belong in the long history of adaptive tutors and computer assisted instruction. Again, since these systems depend upon autograders, their utility is typically limited to a few fields—in the K–12 system, mostly math, early reading, language acquisition, and computer programming—where domain knowledge is amenable to computer assessment. Meta-analyses of adaptive tutors suggest that they can have positive effects in mathematics, and individual studies have shown benefits in other subjects. In particular, recent studies of Carnegie Learning: Cognitive Tutor and AS-SISTments suggest that individual instruction with adaptive tutors might accelerate math learning; some studies suggest that it may even be possible to use adaptive tutors to address learning gaps between high- and low-achieving students. But because these gains are limited to a few subject areas, there is no realistic pathway to recreating whole-school curricula around these tools.[4]

If a community of peers creates the resources available to learners, the new technology that emerges from their efforts belongs to the peer-guided genre of learning at scale. In the world at large, these communities have dramatically reshaped how people participate in lifelong learning; in schools, the effects of these approaches have been more muted. The most powerful experiences in peer-guided learning at scale tend to be deep, collaborative, sustained, and interest driven. These characteristics, however, are at odds with the pedagogical approach of most schools, which usually require that learning experiences are pursued individually (not collectively), along a set of mandated curriculum guidelines (not determined by students' interests), and for uniform timespans—the class period, the marking period, the semester (not sustained over time). The disjunction between the culture of informal online learning and the culture of formal educational systems means that schools struggle to integrate peer-guided, interest-driven technologies. Programs like Scratch or a Domain of One's Own can gain a toehold in the periphery of educational systems, but the fit is often uneasy. The most powerful implementations tend to be in small pockets of innovation in a few classrooms rather than as part of schoolwide changes. These technologies can introduce new pedagogical ideas to schools, and they can spark dialogue about how best to prepare young people for a future of lifelong learning, but that is at best a starting point. Making open, networked, apprenticeship learning a central part of schooling requires rethinking all aspects of the ecology of schools, from curricula to assessment to schedules to teacher professional development and beyond.

Across all three learning-at-scale genres, predictions of disruption, transformation, and democratizing education through technology have fared poorly over the last decade, and indeed over the last century. Each of these genres has particular technologies that have proven useful in certain fields or for certain students, but new technologies do not disrupt existing educational systems. Rather, existing educational systems domesticate new technologies, and in most cases, they use such technologies in the service of the well-established goals and structures of schools. Two of the most reliable findings from the history of education technology are that educators use new technologies to extend existing practices and that new technologies tend to accrue most of their benefits to already-advantaged learners. With these two fact patterns in mind, and after using the four questions above, the analysis of a new learning technology can usually proceed on solid footing.

Complexity, Unevenness, and Inequality

For all their differences, the three genres of learning at scale all interact with the same formal school system ecology. This intersection, between learning-at-scale technologies and formal education as it exists today, has three reoccurring features: complexity, inequality, and unevenness. These features help explain why learning-at-scale technologies do not simply improve learning for all students in all schools, and they are the source of the thorniest challenges in learning at scale.

Schools are complex systems, and many stakeholders in school systems—teachers, students, parents, administrators, and policymakers—are often quite committed to various aspects of the status quo. The schools that exist today are an assemblage of features designed to balance competing visions of the purpose of schooling: inspiring lifelong learning, helping learners pass through gatekeeping exams, preparing people for their lives as citizens. As a result of these varied purposes, schools are tasked with an almost inconceivable array of often competing functions: to teach people to read, to do math, to understand science, to stay healthy, to abstain from sex before marriage, to practice safe sex, to learn history, to love their country, to question their country, to play sports, to make art, to sing songs, to program computers, to work well with others, to become actualized individuals, and on and on. Each of these goals requires different kinds of curricula, learning environments, schedules, and instructional approaches. All schools choose to invest more resources in some of these goals than others. The utility of new technologies is uneven across these various goals; technologies have more traction in some domains than others. And on top of all of this complexity, our society allocates very different levels of resources to schools serving more and less affluent learners, and our schools all too often offer learning experiences of lesser quality to students from poverty-impacted neighborhoods or from ethno-racial minorities.

When emerging technologies are viewed against this background of social, cultural, political, and pedagogical complexity, it becomes clear why the gains and successes of learning at scale have a mishmash pattern—useful in this subject but not that one, with these learners but not those learners, in some contexts but not others. In most places, these complex forces conspire to limit the impact of emerging technologies. But there are certainly breakthroughs where thoughtful design, careful refinement, public demand, and other factors intersect in just the right way for massive numbers of learners to benefit from learning at scale. The online master of science program in computer science at Georgia Tech—the MOOC-based, asynchronous, online master's that has become the largest computer science degree program in the country—appears to be effectively serving a population of working professional students who by all accounts wouldn't or couldn't pursue a master's otherwise. The Scratch programming community has introduced millions of young people around the world—in schools and beyond—to computational creativity. Findings from large randomized control trials of ASSISTments suggest that it may be a lightweight online math homework helper that can lead to learning gains for all students, especially those who have previously fared poorly in math, with relatively modest investments of technology and time.

These exemplars are useful guides to future success stories in particular niches, but they are not harbingers of a transformation. One MOOC-based master's program in computer science seems to be working, but great success seems far less likely from MOOC-based master's programs in creative writing, nursing, teaching, or many other fields. The Scratch online community has made impressive inroads in schools. There are other online communities where young people develop new skills—the millions of young writers who engage in fan fiction creation stands out as a useful point of comparison—but I think it's unlikely that many of these other online communities will find the same inroads in schools as Scratch has. Even if ASSISTments is a great homework helper for math, it is unlikely that it would work equally well as a homework helper for history, biology, or art class.

These exemplars and other efforts like them are limited by a common set of challenges to improving human well-being through learning at scale. In the second half of this book, I described these "as-yet intractable dilemmas," which can also be framed as a set of questions that designers, policymakers, funders, and educators can use to forecast the challenges of improving learning with technology:

1. How will existing stakeholders in a learning ecosystem see this technology? In particular, how will they use it to extend existing practices?
2. What kinds of learning can and cannot be assessed with this technology?
3. How would learners from different backgrounds and different life circumstances access or use these technologies differently?
4. How could experimentation and data analysis improve this technology, and how might those data collection and experimentation efforts contribute to a culture of surveillance?

The curse of the familiar describes the challenges of introducing novel learning experiences into complex, conservative systems. Technologies that digitize existing school routines are easier to adopt, but they are less likely to meaningfully change schools; technologies that could meaningfully change and improve schools are hard for conservative systems to adopt. ASSISTments works in schools because it is designed to fit in typical schooling routines. But this alignment is also a limit; ASSISTments is helpful to math in schools to the extent that mathematics education is more about rote procedural fluency than more sophisticated mathematical reasoning. When a new learning technology does not reproduce typical schooling routines, educators often have trouble incorporating it into the curriculum. Scratch is designed to help learners and educators imagine computing as something much more creative than the procedure-heavy, syntax-heavy ways it is often taught in schools, but educators struggle to figure out how to make room for passion-driven, playful, time-consuming Scratch projects in the confines of a typical school day. The most promising approaches to these challenges have less to do with scaling technology and more to do with scaling communities of educators who can work together and learn together to do the hard work of reforming complex systems so that technologies can have greater impact.

The fact that large-scale learning technologies have an uneven impact across subjects can be traced to the trap of routine assessment. MOOCs, adaptive tutors, and other technologies that seek to assess and credential learners at scale depend upon autograders to computationally evaluate human performance. Autograders are unevenly useful across the curriculum. They are mostly useful in fields in which desired human performance is sufficiently routine for algorithms to reliably identify the features of high-quality and low-quality performance and to assign grades and scores accordingly—in math, quantitative parts of science, early language acquisition, and computer programming. Much of what we want students to learn, however, cannot be demonstrated through performances that adhere to these kinds of rigid structures. Indeed, in a world where humans are ever more rapidly transitioning routine tasks to robots and AI bots, the premium on creative problem solving and complex communication is growing. Our large-scale learning systems may be growing most rapidly in domains that will be least useful in the future, unless we can develop new ways to expand the subjects, disciplines, and skills that can be assessed meaningfully at scale.

The curse of the familiar and the trap of routine assessment help explain why learning-at-scale technology is difficult to integrate into the complexity of the current education system and why, when it is integrated, its impact is uneven across subjects and disciplines. The edtech Matthew effect helps explain why learning-at-scale technologies have uneven impact across people from different backgrounds. Across all three genres of learning at scale, when researchers evaluate how learners from different backgrounds access and use new technologies, it is common to find that the benefits of new technologies—even free technologies—accrue most rapidly to the already-advantaged. Early adopters of Scratch were likely to have parents who had some experience with computing. MOOC providers have shifted their focus to providing lower-cost master's degrees because students who already have bachelor's degrees are easier to educate than students looking for new pathways into higher education. This fact pattern is not an inevitable destiny, and designers can and should be exploring how to design technologies that are best at serving the students who have the least opportunity. But by the same token, educators should be wary of approaches that claim to rectify deep-seated structural inequalities through new technologies. Perhaps new technologies can play a role in creating more equitable ecologies of learning, but technology alone will not democratize education.

For education researchers, one of the most exciting features of large-scale learning technologies is that they can be changed and improved systematically; we can closely examine and digitally record how learners interact with digital platforms, and we can systematically test instructional variations within those platforms to see how

competing approaches might benefit or harm learners. Yet some of
the most promising approaches to this kind of research raise serious
ethical questions: When should learners or schools consent to participating in educational experiments or assessments? Who should
steward data from digital platforms, and what limits should be put
on their use? Perhaps the most urgent question is, How might these
systems of data collection and experimentation inculcate young
people into accepting a culture of digital surveillance that could ultimately impinge on human autonomy even as it promises new freedoms and benefits? The toxic power of data and experimentation
highlights that even if questions about edtech's possibilities and potential are technical in nature, the questions of what we should
do with technology are irreducibly political. In the long run, the
best future for improving learning technologies through research
will involve greater community involvement in addressing these
tradeoffs.

I view these as-yet intractable dilemmas not as immutable barriers but as challenges for designers, developers, funders, researchers,
and educators to rally around. What are viable design principles for
digital equity? How could new assessment technologies provide
more learners more useful feedback in more domains at scale?
What are effective strategies for building communities of change
agents devoted to improving teaching and learning through new
technologies? How do we balance the possibilities of improving
technology through continuous experimentation with the risks
inherent in large-scale data collection and threats to the autonomy
and dignity of learners? As I examine new announcements from
edtech startups, research projects, and other new forays into learning
at scale, I use these and similar questions as guides to identify what
kinds of projects might be most likely to offer new designs or new
insights that can address complexity, unevenness, and inequality
and therefore could change the direction of learning at scale.

Tinkering Toward the Future of Learning at Scale

Improvements in education very rarely, perhaps never, come by way of dramatic transformations. They come through deep, long-term commitment to the plodding work of building more robust systems. Large-scale learning technologies absolutely can improve learning opportunities both in informal learning and in educational institutions, but lasting and meaningful change is unlikely to emerge through technologies alone, especially for learners with the least opportunity. Nearly all learning is situated in social communities—online networks, community centers, schools, and colleges—and learning improvements in those communities typically come from many interlocking adjustments; a new technology can be of value when schedules are adjusted to accommodate the technology, when goals and assessments are modified to align with what technologies are good at, when community leaders (teachers, moderators, coaches) develop new proficiencies with integrating technologies into their educational practice, and when the developers or peer contributors to a technology improve the product through iterative development cycles.

Consider Wikipedia, one of the most important learning resources in the world, with 18 billion views per month of more than 40 million article entries in 293 languages. It represents one of humanity's most extraordinary achievements, a community-generated repository of global knowledge of almost incomprehensible scale: 27 billion words written, managed, and edited almost entirely by volunteers. When Wikipedia first found its way into schools, usually through students citing it or copying from it for homework, it was treated with deep suspicion; educators didn't know exactly what it was, but they knew they hated it. But over time, reference librarians started peeking at Wikipedia to help address patron questions and sharing their insights with open-minded teachers, and slowly, the world's encyclopedia has been accepted by many educators. The utility of Wikipedia has increased over time as the encyclopedia has grown, but also as communities of educators and learners have better understood how to use the resource.

Educators and experts periodically get together to improve specific elements of Wikipedia. For instance, Mike Caulfield, the director of online learning at Washington State University at Vancouver, recently led an initiative to expand Wikipedia's entries on local and regional papers. Caulfield had observed a surge in viral fake news stories, circulated on Facebook and other social networks, that were crafted to look like stories from local or regional newspapers. Often, those fake news articles were attributed to publications that didn't actually exist. Caulfield decided to strengthen Wikipedia's entries on local newspapers so that citations claiming to be from newspapers that do not actually exist could be more easily and reliably vetted. Through a tiny, volunteer, citizen-educator-led effort, Wikipedia got slightly better, and the US information literacy infrastructure got ever so slightly stronger.[5]

Some communities work on the encyclopedia itself. Others work on curricula and pedagogical approaches to using the encyclopedia. Still others work on professional development for teachers and librarians about how to use the resource or how search engines like Google use Wikipedia as a framing device for many search resources. Through all these efforts, Wikipedia is becoming an increasingly valuable resource for learning and research inside schools and beyond. Whether this represents an educational breakthrough is up for debate—having this quantity of mostly well-edited information available in the pockets of most people in the networked world is an extraordinary achievement—but at the same time, it turns out that learning processes are so complex that having all of these facts in one place does not dramatically accelerate learning. It helps—it's a valuable addition to our global learning ecology, and very few projects are likely to be as incredible a boon to learning globally as Wikipedia—but it is hard to make the case that young people in the

United States or around the world are much smarter, wiser, more ethical, or better prepared for the world because of Wikipedia.

If you are hoping that new technologies will be able to radically accelerate human development, the conclusion that change happens incrementally is probably a disappointment. But if you think that global human development is a game of inches—a slow, complex, maddening, plodding process with two steps back for every three steps forward—then Wikipedia is about as good as it gets. New technologies get introduced into complex learning ecologies, and those complex learning ecologies require multiple changes at multiple levels to take advantage of new technologies. You can give people every fact in the world through Wikipedia, but people cannot make much use of those facts without improvements in instruction in literacy, math, research, self-regulated learning, and information literacy. As a result, changes in educational systems are necessarily incremental, but step change is what continuous, incremental change looks like from a distance.

New technologies can contribute to this ongoing march in two important ways. First, the technologies themselves can aid learning, be it in informal contexts or in formal settings. New technologies are rarely as transformative as we might hope (or as evangelists might promise), but to critique them for bringing only incremental change is not to diminish (all of) their value. If you believe, as I do, that educational improvement is a long, slow journey, it would be unwise to turn away from anything that might take us another step, and another step, and another along the path.

Second, the novelty of education technologies opens space for new conversations about the practice of teaching. The arrival of new learning technologies can be an invitation for communities of educators to look up from their critically important and engrossing day-to-day work and to imagine how a new tool might reinvigorate their practice. Techno-optimists will imagine new ways that learners can interact with content and peers, skeptics will point to the value in practices honed over generations, and in the conversations that emerge, we can find the particular places where specific technologies can provide some additional value and opportunities for learners that were not present before.

I find these kinds of conversations enormously enriching. In the K–12 system, new technologies for learning about computer programming—Scratch, Code.org, and others—have inspired schools and school systems to ask a whole range of important questions about who gets access to educational opportunities around computer programming, where computer science should fit into established curricula, how computer science teachers should be trained and licensed, how non-specialist elementary teachers can be supported in effectively introducing young children to computer programming, and on and on. One of the most generative things to come out of the surge of enthusiasm for MOOCs was a renewed interest in interrogating teaching and learning in higher education. At both Harvard and MIT, the arrival of MOOCs sparked or invigorated organizations such as Harvard's Initiative on Learning and Teaching and MIT's Office of Open Learning. At MIT, I recently helped teach a course called Designing the First Year Experience, in which MIT undergraduates participated in design efforts to reimagine the freshman year at MIT. The new possibilities of technologies opened broader conversations about learning across the institution. My lifelong commitment to understanding education technology is nourished not so much from the technologies themselves, but rather from the dialogue about pedagogy and curriculum that new technologies provoke.

If the energy and excitement generated by new technologies could be applied not just to technology, but to technology and system change combined, that would provide the best possible chance for the field of learning at scale to meaningfully improve how people learn in schools and beyond.

NOTES

ACKNOWLEDGMENTS

INDEX

NOTES

PROLOGUE

1. Dahlia Bazzaz, "Dispatches from Parents: Northshore School District's First Online-Only Day to Prevent Coronavirus Spread," *Seattle Times,* March 9, 2020, https://www.seattletimes.com/seattle-news/education /how-northshore-parents-handled-the-first-day-of-online-learning/.

INTRODUCTION

1. Vanessa Lu and Kristin Rushowy, "Rainbow Loom Bracelet Maker Hot Toy Trend," *Toronto Star,* October 4, 2013.
2. Ashley Rivera, "How to Make a Rainbow Loom Starburst Bracelet," YouTube video, August 1, 2013, https://www.youtube.com/watch?v =RI7AkI5dJzo.
3. Cheong Choon Ng, "Experience: I Invented the Loom Band," *Guardian,* September 26, 2014, https://www.theguardian.com/lifeandstyle/2014 /sep/26/i-invented-the-loom-band-experience.
4. Henry Jenkins, *Confronting the Challenges of Participatory Culture: Media Education for the Twenty-First Century* (Cambridge, MA: MIT Press, 2009).
5. Mizuko Ito, Crystle Martin, Rachel Cody Pfister, Matthew H. Rafalow, Katie Salen, and Amanda Wortman, *Affinity Online: How Connection and Shared Interest Fuel Learning* (New York: New York University Press, 2018).
6. Clayton M. Christensen, Michael B. Horn, and Curtis W. Johnson, *Disrupting Class: How Disruptive Innovation Will Change the Way the World Learns* (New York: McGraw-Hill, 2008), 101.

7. Salman Kahn, "Let's Use Video to Reinvent Education," TED talk, March 1, 2011, https://www.youtube.com/watch?v=nTFEUsudhfs.

8. Michael Noer, "One Man, One Computer, 10 Million Students: How Khan Academy Is Reinventing Education," *Forbes,* November 19, 2012, https://www.forbes.com/sites/michaelnoer/2012/11/02/one-man-one-computer-10-million-students-how-khan-academy-is-reinventing-education/#7c96110644e0; Clive Thompson, "How Khan Academy Is Changing the Rules of Education," *Wired,* July 15, 2011, https://www.wired.com/2011/07/ff_khan/; Kayla Webley, "Reboot the School," *Time,* July 2012.

9. Salman Khan, *The One World Schoolhouse: Education Reimagined* (Boston: Grand Central, 2012).

10. Laura Pappano, "The Year of the MOOC," *New York Times,* November 2, 2012.

11. David Carr, "Udacity CEO Says MOOC 'Magic Formula' Emerging," *InformationWeek,* August 19, 2013, https://www.informationweek.com/software/udacity-ceo-says-mooc-magic-formula-emerging/d/d-id/1111221. Three good brief histories of MOOCs are Audrey Watters, "MOOCs: An Introduction," *Hack Education* (blog), August 26, 2014, http://hackeducation.com/2014/08/26/introduction-to-moocs; Fiona Hollands and Devayani Tirthali, *MOOCS: Expectations and Reality, Full Report* (New York: Center for Benefit-Cost Studies of Education, 2014), https://files.eric.ed.gov/fulltext/ED547237.pdf; and Barbara Means, Marianne Bakia, and Robert Murphy, *Learning Online: What Research Tells Us about Whether, When, and How* (New York: Routledge, 2014). On Sebastian Thrun's prediction, see Steven Leckart, "The Stanford Education Experiment Could Change Higher Learning Forever," *Wired,* March 30, 2012, https://www.wired.com/2012/03/ff_aiclass/. For a critical response, see Audrey Watters, "A Future with Only Ten Universities," *Hack Education* (blog), October 15, 2013, http://hackeducation.com/2013/10/15/minding-the-future-openva.

12. On Thrun's reversal, see Max Chafkin, "Udacity's Sebastian Thrun, Godfather of Free Online Education, Changes Course," *Fast Company,* November 14, 2013, https://www.fastcompany.com/3021473/udacity-sebastian-thrun-uphill-climb. For contemporaneous criticism of the

comments, see Rebecca Schuman, "The King of MOOCS Abdicates the Throne," *Slate*, November 19, 2013, https://slate.com/human-interest /2013/11/sebastian-thrun-and-udacity-distance-learning-is -unsuccessful-for-most-students.html.

13. Emily Ann Brown, "Sal Khan Envisions a Future of Active, Mastery-Based Learning," *District Administration*, January 31, 3019, https:// districtadministration.com/sal-khan-envisions-a-future-of-active -mastery-based-learning/. There is no robust published evidence to validate Khan's claims about the magnitude of learning gains.

14. Kenneth R. Koedinger, John R. Anderson, William H. Hadley, and Mary A. Mark, "Intelligent Tutoring Goes to School in the Big City," *International Journal of Artificial Intelligence in Education* 8 (1997): 30–43.

15. Philip Wesley Jackson, *Life in Classrooms* (New York: Teachers College Press, 1990), 166–167; Larry Cuban, *The Flight of a Butterfly or the Path of a Bullet? Using Technology to Transform Teaching and Learning* (Cambridge, MA: Harvard Education Press, 2018).

16. Justin Reich and Mizuko Ito, "Three Myths about Education Technology and the Points of Light Beyond," *Connected Learning Alliance Blog*, October 30, 2017, https://clalliance.org/blog/three-myths-education -technology-points-light-beyond/.

17. Morgan G. Ames, *The Charisma Machine: The Life, Death, and Legacy of One Laptop per Child* (Cambridge, MA: Harvard University Press, 1995).

18. David Tyack and Larry Cuban, *Tinkering toward Utopia: A Century of Public School Reform* (Cambridge, MA: MIT Press, 2019).

19. For an example of my teaching, see Justin Reich, "Conflict and Identity: Using Contemporary Questions to Inspire the Study of the Past," *World History Connected*, last modified February 2007, https://world historyconnected.press.uillinois.edu/4.2/reich.html.

20. UNESCO Global Education Monitoring Report, "Six Ways to Ensure Higher Education Leaves No One Behind," Policy Paper 30, April, 2017, https://unesdoc.unesco.org/ark:/48223/pf0000247862.

21. Victoria Lee and Constance Lindsey, "Access to Calculus Could Hinder Low-Income and Black Students," *Urban Wire* (blog), March 6, 2018, https://www.urban.org/urban-wire/unequal-access-calculus-could -hinder-low-income-and-black-students.

I. INSTRUCTOR-GUIDED LEARNING AT SCALE

1. Audrey Watters, "MOOCs: An Introduction," Modernlearners.com, n.d., https://modernlearners.com/moocs-an-introduction; Fiona M. Hollands and Devayani Tirthali, *MOOCs: Expectations and Reality* (New York: Center for Benefit-Cost Studies, Teachers College, Columbia University, 2014); Barbara Means, *Learning Online: What Research Tells Us about Whether, When and How* (New York: Taylor and Francis, 2014); John Naughton, "Welcome to the Desktop Degree," *Guardian,* February 4, 2012, https://www.theguardian.com/technology/2012/feb/05/desktop -degree-stanford-university-naughton.

2. "Press Conference: MIT, Harvard Announce edX," YouTube video, May 3, 2012, https://www.youtube.com/watch?v=7pYwGpKMXuA; Laura Pappano, "The Year of the MOOC," *New York Times,* November 2, 2012.

3. 1999–2000 online learning numbers are from Anna Sikora and C. Dennis Carroll, *A Profile of Participation in Distance Education: 1999–2000* (Washington, DC: National Center for Educational Statistics, 2002), https://nces.ed.gov/pubs2003/2003154.pdf. For background on early HarvardX and MITx MOOCs, see Andrew Ho, Justin Reich, Sergiy Nesterko, Daniel Seaton, Tommy Mullaney, James Waldo, and Isaac Chuang, "HarvardX and MITx: The First Year of Open Online Courses, Fall 2012–Summer 2013 (HarvardX and MITx Working Paper No. 1)," *SSRN* (2014), https://ssrn.com/abstract=2381263.

4. "Clayton Christensen Interview with Mark Suster at Startup Grind 2013," YouTube video, 06:40, "Startup Grind," February, 20, 2013, https://www.youtube.com/watch?v=KYVdf5xyD8I. For more on the idea of "super-professors," see Justin Reich, "Personalized Learning, Backpacks Full of Cash, Rockstar Teachers, and MOOC Madness: The Intersection of Technology, Free-Market Ideology, and Media Hype in U.S. Education Reform," lecture, Berkman Klein Center for Internet and Society at Harvard University, May 7, 2013, https://cyber.harvard.edu/events/luncheon /2013/05/reich. For a related perspective on how online learning would remake higher education, see Kevin Carey, *The End of College: Creating the Future of Learning and the University of Everywhere* (New York: Riverhead Books, 2016); and Steven Leckart, "The Stanford Education Experiment

Could Change Higher Learning Forever," *Wired*, March 28, 2012, https://www
.wired.com/2012/03/ff_aiclass/.

5. Daphne Koller, "What We're Learning from Online Education," filmed
June 2012 at TEDGlobal 2012, Edinburgh, Scotland, video, https://www
.ted.com/talks/daphne_koller_what_we_re_learning_from_online_edu
cation?language=en.

6. Koller, "What We're Learning."

7. The Quote Investigator website has an excellent investigation into this
framing, often misattributed to Yeats; see "The Mind Is Not a Vessel
That Needs Filling, but Wood That Needs Igniting," *Quote Investigator*,
last modified March 28, 2013, https://quoteinvestigator.com/2013/03/28
/mind-fire/. The Loeb Classical Library translation has the full quote
as, "For the mind does not require filling like a bottle, but rather, like
wood, it only requires kindling to create in it an impulse to think independently and an ardent desire for the truth"; see Bill Thayer, "Plutarch,
Moralia: On Listening to Lectures," last modified April 1, 2018, http://
penelope.uchicago.edu/Thayer/E/Roman/Texts/Plutarch/Moralia/De
_auditu*.html. The first known usage of the translation that I use comes
from James Johnson Sweeney, *Vision and Image: A Way of Seeing* (New York:
Simon and Schuster, 1968), 119. The Lagemann quotation, definitively,
is from Ellen Lagemann, "The Plural Worlds of Educational Research,"
History of Education Quarterly 29, no. 2 (1989): 185–214, https://doi.org/10
.2307/368309. Lagemann's goal in the essay is to highlight how these different pedagogical traditions led to different traditions among different scholarly communities in the late twentieth century; part of the
task of this book is to show that these fractures continue in the digital
age, and I share Lagemann's enthusiasm for bridging these divides.

8. John Dewey, "My Pedagogic Creed," *School Journal* 54, no. 3 (1897): 77–80,
http://dewey.pragmatism.org/creed.htm.

9. One early entry point into Thorndike's work is Edward Thorndike, *The
Psychology of Learning* (New York: Teachers College, 1913).

10. For research on MOOC instructional quality, see Anoush Margaryan,
Manuela Bianco, and Allison Littlejohn, "Instructional Quality of Massive Open Online Courses (MOOCs)," *Computers & Education* 80 (2015):
77–83. The literature of MOOC criticism is extensive and thoughtful.

An early response was from the faculty of the Philosophy Department of San Jose State University, when the university proposed requiring students to use Harvard's JusticeX for an introductory course; "An Open Letter to Professor Michael Sandel from the Philosophy Department at San Jose State U," *Chronicle of Higher Education,* May 2, 2013, https://www.chronicle.com/article/The-Document-an-Open-Letter/138937. Elizabeth Losh has a monograph and an edited volume that are useful starting points for critique; Elizabeth Losh, *The War on Learning: Gaining Ground in the Digital University* (Cambridge, MA: MIT Press, 2014); and Elizabeth Losh, *MOOCs and Their Afterlives: Experiments in Scale and Access in Higher Education* (Chicago: University of Chicago Press, 2017). Jonathan Rees is another thoughtful critic through his *More or Less Bunk* blog; a starting point is a piece in *Slate:* Jonathan Rees, "The MOOC Racket," *Slate,* July 25, 2013, https://slate.com/technology/2013/07/moocs-could-be-disastrous-for-students-and-professors.html.

11. James Becker, *Toward Automated Learning. A Professional Paper* (Pittsburgh: Research for Better Schools, 1968); William Cooley and Robert Glaser, "The Computer and Individualized Instruction," *Science* 166, no. 3905 (1969): 574–582; James Becker and Robert Scanlon, *Applying Computers and Educational Technology to Individually Prescribed Instruction* (Pittsburgh: Research for Better Schools, 1970).

12. On feature convergence, see Carl Straumsheim, "Where Does the LMS Go from Here?" *Inside Higher Ed,* September 23, 2014, https://www.insidehighered.com/news/2014/09/23/educause-gates-foundation-examine-history-and-future-lms.

13. For the relationship between MOOC platform and pedagogy, see Shreeharsh Kelkar, "Engineering a Platform: The Construction of Interfaces, Users, Organizational Roles, and the Division of Labor," *New Media & Society* 20, no. 7 (2018): 2629–2646.

14. For an early description of the storefront metaphor, see Michael Feldstein, "Is Coursera Facebook, Amazon, or Pets.com?," *e-Literate,* November 14, 2012, https://mfeldstein.com/is-coursera-facebook-amazon-or-petscom-2/. Coursera and edX weren't the first to directly market online courses—Udemy had been marketing direct-to-consumer online courses since 2010, as one example—but they were the first to my knowledge to do so with elite university partners.

15. For a recent review, see Draylson M. Souza, Katia R. Felizardo, and Ellen F. Barbosa, "A Systematic Literature Review of Assessment Tools for Programming Assignments," presentation, International Conference on Software Engineering Education and Training, Dallas, TX, April 2016, IEEE, https://ieeexplore.ieee.org/document/7474479. For an example, see the check50 program developed by Harvard's CS50 team: https://cs50.readthedocs.io/check50/.

16. An early iteration of websim, the circuits simulator used in the first MITx course, is online at http://euryale.csail.mit.edu/.

17. Test developers sometimes argue that multiple-choice questions can test critical thinking or reasoning. Stanford researcher Mark Smith contests this claim, demonstrating that high-performing students on history assessments do not use complex reasoning to take multiple-choice tests, but rather use "three construct-irrelevant processes: factual recall / recognition, reading comprehension, and test-taking strategies." Mark D. Smith, "Cognitive Validity: Can Multiple-Choice Items Tap Historical Thinking Processes?" *American Educational Research Journal* 54, no. 6 (2017): 1256–1287.

18. On evaluating writing with peer grading and automated essay scoring, see Stephen P. Balfour, "Assessing Writing in MOOCs: Automated Essay Scoring and Calibrated Peer Review™," *Research & Practice in Assessment* 8 (2013): 40–48. For peer and self-assessment in MOOCs, see Chinmay Kulkarni, Koh Pang Wei, Huy Le, Daniel Chia, Kathryn Papadopoulos, Justin Cheng, Daphne Koller, and Scott R. Klemmer, "Peer and Self Assessment in Massive Online Classes," *ACM Transactions on Computer-Human Interaction (TOCHI)* 20, no. 6 (2013): 1–31.

19. The literature and commentary on MOOCs' low completion rates are extensive. One interesting voice making this point was Larry Bacow (along with Michael McPherson), who went on to become Harvard University president; Michael S. McPherson and Lawrence S. Bacow, "Online Higher Education: Beyond the Hype Cycle," *Journal of Economic Perspectives* 29, no. 4 (2015): 135–154. The most comprehensive early study of MOOCs and completion rates is Katy Jordan, "Massive Open Online Course Completion Rates Revisited: Assessment, Length and Attrition," *International Review of Research in Open and Distributed Learning* 16, no. 3 (2015): 341–358. Early reports on completion rates include Gayle

Christensen, Andrew Steinmetz, Brandon Alcorn, Amy Bennett, Deirdre Woods, and Ezekiel Emanuel, "The MOOC Phenomenon: Who Takes Massive Open Online Courses and Why?" *SSRN* (2013), https://ssrn.com/abstract=2350964; René F. Kizilcec, Chris Piech, and Emily Schneider, "Deconstructing Disengagement: Analyzing Learner Subpopulations in Massive Open Online Courses," presentation, International Conference on Learning Analytics and Knowledge, Leuven, Belgium, April 2013; Ho et al., "The First Year of Open Online Courses." On completion rates of students who intend to complete, see Justin Reich, "MOOC Completion and Retention in the Context of Student Intent," *EDUCAUSE Review Online*, December 8, 2014, https://er.educause.edu/articles/2014/12/mooc-completion-and-retention-in-the-context-of-student-intent. On completion rates of learners pursing verified certificates, see Justin Reich and José A. Ruipérez-Valiente, "The MOOC Pivot," *Science* 363, no. 6423 (2019): 130–131.

20. Zach Lam, Kathy Mirzae, Andreas Paepcke, Krystal Smith, and Mitchell Stevens, "Doing Things with MOOCs: Utilization Strategies of Stanford's California MOOC Learners," MIT Office of Digital Learning x-Talks, October 16, 2018, https://openlearning.mit.edu/events/doing-things-moocs-utilization-strategies-learners-massively-open-online-courses.

21. "Open edX Conference 2018 with Zvi Galil Keynote: Georgia Tech's Online MOOC-based Master Program," YouTube video, "Open edX," June 13, 2018, https://www.youtube.com/watch?v=-ETTblOvH6w; Joshua Goodman, Julia Melkers, and Amanda Pallais, "Can Online Delivery Increase Access to Education?" *Journal of Labor Economics* 37, no. 1 (2019): 1–34.

22. Joshua Littenberg-Tobias and Justin Reich, *Evaluating Access, Quality, and Equity in Online Learning: A Case Study of a MOOC-Based Blended Professional Degree Program*, pre-print retrieved from doi:10.31235/osf.io/8nbsz.

23. Littenberg-Tobias and Reich, "Evaluating Access."

24. NanoDegrees have much in common with earlier forms of non-degree technical certificates, such as the Microsoft Certified Technician programs. On the 1990s history of Microsoft and related information tech-

nology non-degree certifications, see Clifford Adelman, "A Parallel Universe: Certification in the Information Technology Guild," *Change: The Magazine of Higher Learning* 32, no. 3 (2000): 20–29.

25. For more on for-profit higher education and the role of credentials in higher education, see Tressie McMillan Cottom, *Lower Ed: The Troubling Rise of For-Profit Colleges in the New Economy* (New York: New Press, 2017).

26. Phil Hill, "Coursera CEO Interview: Betting on OPM Market and Shift to Low-Cost Masters Degrees," *E-literate,* December 6, 2018, https://mfeldstein.com/coursera-ceo-interview-betting-on-opm-market-and-shift-to-low-cost-masters-degrees/. For a critique of OPMs, see Kevin Carey, "The Creeping Capitalist Take Over of Higher Education," *Highline: Huffington Post,* April 1, 2019, https://www.huffpost.com/highline/article/capitalist-takeover-college/.

27. Laura Pappano, "The Boy Genius of Ulan Bator," *New York Times,* September 13, 2013, https://www.nytimes.com/2013/09/15/magazine/the-boy-genius-of-ulan-bator.html.

28. Justin Reich and Ruipérez-Valiente, "MOOC Pivot"; John D. Hansen and Justin Reich, "Democratizing Education? Examining Access and Usage Patterns in Massive Open Online Courses," *Science* 350, no. 6265 (2015): 1245–1248; René F. Kizilcec, Andrew J. Saltarelli, Justin Reich, and Geoffrey L. Cohen, "Closing Global Achievement Gaps in MOOCs," *Science* 355, no. 6322 (2017): 251–252; Ezekiel J. Emanuel, "Online Education: MOOCs Taken by Educated Few," *Nature* 503, no. 7476 (2013): 342. For more recent data, see Isaac Chuang and Andrew Ho, "HarvardX and MITx: Four Years of Open Online Courses—Fall 2012–Summer 2016," December 23, 2016, https://ssrn.com/abstract=2889436.

29. The initial report on the SJSU Plus experiment was Ellaine D. Collins, "SJSU Plus Augmented Online Learning Environment Pilot Project Report," *Research and Planning Group for California Community Colleges* 38 (2013): 45. A subsequent analysis put results in a somewhat more favorable light, especially for courses run twice with refinements between iterations. Erin L. Woodhead, Preston Tim Brown, Susan Snycerski, Sean Laraway, Nicholas G. Bathurst, Greg Feist, and Ronald F. Rogers, "An Examination of the Outcomes of a Brief and Innovative Partnership: SJSU and Udacity," *Innovative Higher Education* 42, no. 5–6 (2017): 463–476,

DOI: 10.1007/s10755-017-9400-4; Lindsay McKenzie, "Arizona State Moves on from Global Freshman Academy," *Inside Higher Ed,* September 17, 2019, https://www.insidehighered.com/digital-learning/article/2019/09/17/arizona-state-changes-course-global-freshman-academy.

30. For self-regulated learning and MOOCs, see Allison Littlejohn, Nina Hood, Colin Milligan, and Paige Mustain, "Learning in MOOCs: Motivations and Self-Regulated Learning in MOOCs," *Internet and Higher Education* 29 (2016): 40–48; René F. Kizilcec, Mar Pérez-Sanagustín, and Jorge J. Maldonado, "Self-Regulated Learning Strategies Predict Learner Behavior and Goal Attainment in Massive Open Online Courses," *Computers and Education* 104 (2017): 18–33; and M. Elena Alonso-Mencía, Carlos Alario-Hoyos, Jorge Maldonado-Mahauad, Iria Estévez-Ayres, Mar Pérez-Sanagustín, and Carlos Delgado Kloos, "Self-Regulated Learning in MOOCs: Lessons Learned from a Literature Review," *Educational Review* (2019): 1–27. For how people develop self-regulated learning skills, see Scott G. Paris and Alison H. Paris, "Classroom Applications of Research on Self-Regulated Learning," *Educational Psychologist* 36, no. 2 (2001): 89–101; and Barry J. Zimmerman, "Becoming a Self-Regulated Learner: An Overview," *Theory into Practice* 41, no. 2 (2002): 64–70.

31. Reich and Ruipérez-Valiente, "MOOC Pivot."

32. Reich, "Rebooting MOOC Research."

33. Justin Reich, "Big Data MOOC Research Breakthrough: Learning Activities Lead to Achievement," *EdTech Researcher* (blog), March 30, 2014, http://www.edtechresearcher.com/2014/03/big_data_mooc_research_breakthrough_learning_activities_lead_to_achievement/. For a variant, see Kenneth R. Koedinger, Jihee Kim, Julianna Zhuxin Jia, Elizabeth A. McLaughlin, and Norman L. Bier, "Learning Is Not a Spectator Sport: Doing Is Better Than Watching for Learning from a MOOC," presentation, ACM Conference on Learning at Scale, Vancouver, BC, Canada, March 14–15, 2015; Jennifer DeBoer, Andrew D. Ho, Glenda S. Stump, and Lori Breslow, "Changing 'Course': Reconceptualizing Educational Variables for Massive Open Online Courses," *Educational Researcher* 43, no. 2 (2014): 74–84.

34. For a case study of OLI development, see Candace Thille, Emily Schneider, René F. Kizilcec, Christopher Piech, Sherif A. Halawa, and Daniel K.

Greene, "The Future of Data-Enriched Assessment," *Research & Practice in Assessment* 9 (2014): 5–16.

35. For the OLI statistics study, see William G. Bowen, Matthew M. Chingos, Kelly A. Lack, and Thomas I. Nygren, "Interactive Learning Online at Public Universities: Evidence from a Six-Campus Randomized Trial," *Journal of Policy Analysis and Management* 33, no. 1 (2014): 94–111. David Pritchard's introductory physics MOOC at MIT is probably the best studied xMOOC; Kimberly F. Colvin, John Champaign, Alwina R. Liu, Qian Zhou, Colin Fredericks, and David E. Pritchard, "Learning in an Introductory Physics MOOC: All Cohorts Learn Equally, Including an On-Campus Class," *International Review of Research in Open and Distributed Learning* 15, no. 4 (2014). On the high costs of effective online learning, also see McPherson and Bacow, "Beyond the Hype Cycle."

36. Justin Reich and Elizabeth Huttner-Loan, *Teaching Systems Lab MOOCs in Review: 2017–2019* (Cambridge, MA: Teaching Systems Lab, 2019), doi:10.35542/osf.io/c3bhw.

37. The total number of MOOC learners has increased at a lower rate than the total number of MOOC courses, so that each course now has many fewer people in it. See Chuang and Ho "HarvardX and MITx Year 4"; and Reich and Ruiperez-Valiente, "MOOC Pivot."

38. On credit recovery, see Carolyn J. Heinrich, Jennifer Darling-Aduana, Annalee Good, and Huiping Cheng, "A Look Inside Online Educational Settings in High School: Promise and Pitfalls for Improving Educational Opportunities and Outcomes," *American Educational Research Journal* 56, no. 6 (2019): 2147–2188. For state-level studies of virtual schools, see June Ahn and Andrew McEachin, "Student Enrollment Patterns and Achievement in Ohio's Online Charter Schools," *Educational Researcher* 46, no. 1 (2017): 44–57; Brian R. Fitzpatrick, Mark Berends, Joseph J. Ferrare, and R. Joseph Waddington, "Virtual Illusion: Comparing Student Achievement and Teacher and Classroom Characteristics in Online and Brick-and-Mortar Charter Schools," *Educational Researcher* 49, no. 3 (2020): 161–175, https://doi.org/10.3102/0013189X20909814. One exception to the bleak research on K-12 virtual schools comes from the Florida Virtual Schools: Guido Schwerdt and Matthew M. Chingos, "Virtual

Schooling and Student Learning: Evidence from the Florida Virtual School," Beiträge zur Jahrestagung des Vereins für Socialpolitik 2015, Ökonomische Entwicklung–Theorie und Politik–Session: ICT in Educational Production, No. B24-V2, ZBW–Deutsche Zentralbibliothek für Wirtschaftswissenschaften, Leibniz Informationszentrum Wirtschaft, https://www.econstor.eu/bitstream/10419/113202/1/VfS_2015_pid_39 .pdf. Notably, Florida Virtual Schools is one of the only K–12 providers to be based within the state educational system rather than provisioned by a for-profit provider.

39. Chris Dede and John Richards proposed a name for LMSs that are prepopulated with content but intended for use by teachers in small classes: digital teaching platforms; Christopher Dede and John Richards, eds., *Digital Teaching Platforms: Customizing Classroom Learning for Each Student* (New York: Teachers College Press, 2012). On Summit Learning, see Joanne Jacobs, "Pacesetter in Personalized Learning: Summit Charter Network Shares Its Model Nationwide," *Education Next* 17, no. 4 (2017): 16–25; and Matt Barnum, "Summit Learning, the Zuckerberg-Backed Platform, Says 10% of Schools Quit Using It Each Year. The Real Figure is Higher," *Chalkbeat,* May 23, 2019, https://www .chalkbeat.org/posts/us/2019/05/23/summit-learning-the-zuckerberg -backed-platform-says-10-of-schools-quit-using-it-each-year-the-real -figure-is-higher/.

40. John Daniel, Asha Kanwar, and Stamenka Uvalić-Trumbić, "Breaking Higher Education's Iron Triangle: Access, Cost, and Quality," *Change: The Magazine of Higher Learning* 41, no. 2 (2009): 30–35. The metaphor comes from the project management field; Dennis Lock, *Project Management Handbook* (Aldershot, Hants, England: Gower Technical Press, 1987).

41. Patrick McAndrew and Eileen Scanlon, "Open Learning at a Distance: Lessons for Struggling MOOCs," *Science* 342, no. 6165 (2013): 1450–1451.

2. ALGORITHM-GUIDED LEARNING AT SCALE

1. In the late 2000s and early 2010s, some other common reform efforts in schools involved alignment with the new Common Core curriculum, using data from standardized tests to improve instruction, adopting differentiated instruction approaches like "response to intervention" and addressing issues of social and emotional learning.

2. Benjamin S. Bloom, "The 2 Sigma Problem: The Search for Methods of Group Instruction as Effective as One-to-One Tutoring," *Educational Researcher* 13, no. 6 (1984): 4–16. Bloom's thought-piece was inspired by two doctoral dissertations. Subsequent investigations of human tutoring have demonstrated less than two standard deviation effects; see Kurt VanLehn, "The Relative Effectiveness of Human Tutoring, Intelligent Tutoring Systems, and Other Tutoring Systems," *Educational Psychologist* 46, no. 4 (2011): 197–221.

3. R. C. Atkinson and H. A. Wilson, "Computer-Assisted Instruction," *Science* 162, no. 3849 (1968): 73–77.

4. Brian Dear, *The Friendly Orange Glow: The Untold Story of the PLATO System and the Dawn of Cyberculture* (New York: Pantheon, 2017). R. A. Avner and Paul Tenczar, "The TUTOR Manual" (Washington, DC: Education Resources Information Center, 1970), https://eric.ed.gov/?id=ED050583.

5. Michael Horn and Heather Staker, *Blended: Using Disruptive Innovation to Improve Schools* (New York: Wiley, 2014).

6. Eric Westervelt, "Meet the Mind Reading Robo Tutor in the Sky," *NPRed,* October 13, 2015, https://www.npr.org/sections/ed/2015/10/13/437265231/meet-the-mind-reading-robo-tutor-in-the-sky.

7. Anya Kamenetz, "5 Doubts about Data Driven Schools," *NPRed,* June 3, 2016, https://www.npr.org/sections/ed/2016/06/03/480029234/5-doubts-about-data-driven-schools. The largest dataset in DataShop, a public repository of data from computer-assisted learning systems, has 2.4 million transactions, which were collected from 628 students over a period of six months, several orders of magnitude less than millions of data points per student per day. https://pslcdatashop.web.cmu.edu/DatasetInfo?datasetId=428.

8. "The Mismeasure of Students: Using Item Response Theory instead of Traditional Grading to Assess Student Proficiency," *Knewton Blog,* June 7, 2012, https://medium.com/knerd/the-mismeasure-of-students-using-item-response-theory-instead-of-traditional-grading-to-assess-b55188707ee5.

9. For a history and introduction to item response theory, see W. J. van der Linden, "Item Response Theory," in *International Encyclopedia of Education,* 3rd ed., eds. Penelope Peterson, Eva Baker, and Barry McGaw (Oxford, UK: Elsevier, 2010), 81–89.

10. Among the most important variants to IRT are a set of algorithms developed at Carnegie Mellon University called "knowledge tracing." For an introduction, see John R. Anderson, Albert T. Corbett, Kenneth R. Koedinger, and Ray Pelletier, "Cognitive Tutors: Lessons Learned," *The Journal of the Learning Sciences* 4, no. 2 (1995): 167–207; Kenneth R. Koedinger and Albert T. Corbett, "Cognitive Tutors: Technology Bringing Learning Sciences to the Classroom," in *The Cambridge Handbook of the Learning Sciences,* ed. R. K. Sawyer (New York: Cambridge University Press, 2006), 61–77.

11. Tony Wan, "Jose Ferreira Steps Down as Knewton CEO, Eyes Next Education Startup," *EdSurge,* December 21, 2016, https://www.edsurge.com /news/2016-12-21-jose-ferreira-steps-down-as-knewton-ceo-eyes-next -education-startup; Jeffrey Young, "Hitting Reset, Knewton Tries New Strategy: Competing with Textbook Publishers," *EdSurge,* November 30, 2017, https://www.edsurge.com/news/2017-11-30-hitting-reset-knewton -tries-new-strategy-competing-with-textbook-publishers; Lindsay McKenzie, "End of the Line for Much-Hyped Tech Company," *Inside Higher Ed,* May 7, 2019, https://www.insidehighered.com/digital-learning/article /2019/05/07/wiley-buys-knewton-adaptive-learning-technology-company.

12. Maciej Cegłowski. "The Internet with a Human Face," presentation at Beyond Tellerrand, Düsseldorf, Germany, May 20, 2014, https://idlewords .com/talks/internet_with_a_human_face.htm.

13. For further discussion, see Justin Reich, "Personalized Learning, Backpacks Full of Cash, Rockstar Teachers, and MOOC Madness: The Intersection of Technology, Free-Market Ideology, and Media Hype in U.S. Education Reform," May 7, 2013, presentation at Berkman Klein Center, Harvard University, https://cyber.harvard.edu/events/luncheon/2013/05/reich. For an example of advocating for market-based reforms through technological changes, see Chester E. Finn, Jr. and Daniela R. Fairchild, eds., *Education Reform for the Digital Era,* https://files.eric.ed.gov/fulltext/ED532508.pdf.

14. Emily Ann Brown, "Sal Khan Envisions a Future of Active, Mastery-Based Learning," *District Administration,* January 31, 3019, https:// districtadministration.com/sal-khan-envisions-a-future-of-active -mastery-based-learning/; Salman Kahn, *The One World Schoolhouse: Education Reimagined* (New York: Grand Central, 2012), 12.

15. Audrey Watters, *Teaching Machines* (Cambridge, MA: MIT Press, forthcoming), citing Simon Ramo, "A New Technique of Education," *Engineering and Science* 21 (October 1975): 372.

16. Clayton M. Christensen, Curtis W. Johnson, and Michael B. Horn, *Disrupting Class: How Disruptive Innovation Will Change the Way the World Learns* (New York: McGraw-Hill, 2008).

17. Jill Lepore, "The Disruption Machine," *New Yorker* 23 (2014): 30–36. Audrey Watters, "The Myth and Millennialism of 'Disruptive Innovation,'" *Hack Education,* May 24, 2013, http://hackeducation.com/2013/05/24/disruptive-innovation.

18. Alex Molnar, Gary Miron, Najat Elgeberi, Michael K. Barbour, Luis Huerta, Sheryl Rankin Shafer, and Jennifer King Rice, "Virtual Schools in the U.S., 2019," National Education Policy Center, May 28, 2019, https://nepc.colorado.edu/publication/virtual-schools-annual-2019; Jeff Wulfson, "Commonwealth of Massachusetts Virtual Schools—Funding and Amendment of Certificates for Greenfield Commonwealth Virtual School and for TEC Connections Academy Commonwealth Virtual School," December 8, 2017, http://www.doe.mass.edu/bese/docs/fy2018/2017-12/item5.html; Christian Wade, "Virtual Schools Grow, along with Costs to Districts," *The Daily News of Newburyport,* March 25, 2019, https://www.newburyportnews.com/news/regional_news/virtual-schools-grow-along-with-costs-to-districts/article_be168543-ae01-5bfa-8ac3-d3c6db09eb49.html.

19. Mark Dynarski, Roberto Agodini, Sheila Heaviside, Timothy Novak, Nancy Carey, Larissa Campuzano, Barbara Means, et al., "Effectiveness of Reading and Mathematics Software Products: Findings from the First Student Cohort," *National Center for Education Evaluation and Regional Assistance* (2007); Saiying Steenbergen-Hu and Harris Cooper, "A Meta-analysis of the Effectiveness of Intelligent Tutoring Systems on K–12 Students' Mathematical Learning," *Journal of Educational Psychology* 105, no. 4 (2013): 970.

20. Eric Taylor, "New Technology and Teacher Productivity" (unpublished manuscript, January 2018), Cambridge, MA, Harvard Graduate School of Education, available at https://scholar.harvard.edu/files/erictaylor/files/technology-teachers-jan-18.pdf. Taylor's literature review has an

excellent overview and set of references for the history of evaluation of computer-assisted instruction.

21. John F. Pane, Beth Ann Griffin, Daniel F. McCaffrey, and Rita Karam, "Effectiveness of Cognitive Tutor Algebra I at Scale," *Educational Evaluation and Policy Analysis* 36, no. 2 (2014): 127–144.

22. Interpreting effect sizes is the topic of vigorous discussion in education research. Cohen proposed a set of guidelines whereby a 0.2 standard deviation improvement would be considered small, 0.5 medium, and 0.8 large; in Jacob Cohen, *Statistical Power Analysis for the Behavioral Sciences* (New York: Academic Press, 1977). Since then, it has been more widely agreed in education research that these large effect sizes are almost never found in well-conducted randomized control trials. Lipsey argues for evaluating the magnitude of effect size based on prior research about gains in typical conditions; Carolyn J. Hill, Howard S. Bloom, Alison Rebeck Black, and Mark W. Lipsey, "Empirical Benchmarks for Interpreting Effect Sizes in Research," *Child Development Perspectives* 2, no. 3 (2008): 172–177. Kraft suggests that based on more recent evidence, appropriate guidelines might be 0.05 standard deviation as small, 0.1 as medium, and 0.2 as large; Matthew A. Kraft, "Interpreting Effect Sizes of Education Interventions," *Educational Researcher* (forthcoming), available at https://scholar.harvard.edu/files/mkraft/files/kraft_2018_interpreting _effect_sizes.pdf.

23. Steve Ritter, Michael Yudelson, Stephen E. Fancsali, and Susan R. Berman, "How Mastery Learning Works at Scale," in *Proceedings of the Third (2016) ACM Conference on Learning at Scale* (Association of Computing Machinery Digital Library, 2016), 71–79.

24. Neil T. Heffernan and Cristina Lindquist Heffernan, "The ASSISTments Ecosystem: Building a Platform that Brings Scientists and Teachers Together for Minimally Invasive Research on Human Learning and Teaching," *International Journal of Artificial Intelligence in Education* 24, no. 4 (2014): 470–497; Jeremy Roschelle, Mingyu Feng, Robert F. Murphy, and Craig A. Mason, "Online Mathematics Homework Increases Student Achievement," *AERA Open* 2, no. 4 (2016), https://doi.org/10.1177 /2332858416673968.

25. Early evidence of Teach to One was more positive; Douglas D. Ready, Katherine Conn, Elizabeth Park, and David Nitkin, "Year-One Impact and Process Results from the I3 Implementation of Teach to One: Math" (New York: Consortium for Policy Research Education, Teachers College, Columbia University, 2016), https://www.classsizematters.org/wp-content/uploads/2018/11/Ready-1st-year-Teach-to-One-Elizabeth-evaluation-Nov.-2016.pdf. The last study was Douglas D. Ready, Katherine Conn, Shani Bretas, and Iris Daruwala, "Final Impact Results from the i3 Implementation of Teach to One: Math" (New York: Consortium for Policy Research Education, Teachers College, Columbia University, 2019), https://www.newclassrooms.org/wp-content/uploads/2019/02/Final-Impact-Results-i3-TtO.pdf.

3. PEER-GUIDED LEARNING AT SCALE

1. For an example of where lines blur between algorithmic personalization and "whole child" learning, see Tom Vander Ark, "Chan Zuckerberg Backs Personalized Learning R&D Agenda," *Getting Smart,* November 17, 2017, https://www.gettingsmart.com/2017/11/chan-zuckerberg-backs-personalized-learning-rd-agenda.

2. Antonio Fini, "The Technological Dimension of a Massive Open Online Course: The Case of the CCK08 Course Tools," *International Review of Research in Open and Distributed Learning* 10, no. 5 (2009); David Cormier, "What Is a MOOC?," YouTube video, December 8, 2010, https://www.youtube.com/watch?v=eW3gMGqcZQc. The CCK08 course had several antecedents, including courses developed by Alec Couros, David Wiley, and Cathy Davidson. See Cathy Davidson, "What Was the First MOOC?," *HASTAC,* September 27, 2013, https://www.hastac.org/blogs/cathy-davidson/2013/09/27/what-was-first-mooc.

3. George Siemens, "Connectivism: A Learning Theory for the Digital Age," *International Journal of Instructional Technology and Distance Learning* 2, no. 1 (2005), http://www.itdl.org/Journal/Jan_05/article01.htm; Stephen Downes, "Places to Go: Connectivism and Connective Knowledge," *Innovate: Journal of Online Education* 5, no. 1 (2008): 6; David Weinberger, *Too Big to Know: Rethinking Knowledge Now That the Facts*

Aren't the Facts, Experts Are Everywhere, and the Smartest Person in the Room Is the Room (New York: Basic Books, 2011).

4. Detailed technical plans for developing these kinds of learning environments can be found at Kim Jaxon and Alan Levine, "Staking Your Claim: How the Open Web Is Won for Teaching and Learning," University of California Irvine, 2017, http://connectedcourses.stateu.org/.

5. Downes, "Places to Go"; Fini "The Technological Dimension."

6. Stephen Downes, "The Rise of MOOCs," April 23, 2012, https://www.downes.ca/cgi-bin/page.cgi?post=57911.

7. Jean Lave and Etienne Wenger, *Situated Learning: Legitimate Peripheral Participation* (Cambridge, UK: Cambridge University Press, 1991). For other connections from connectivism to prior pedagogical theory, see Rita Kop and Adrian Hill, "Connectivism: Learning Theory of the Future or Vestige of the Past?," *The International Review of Research in Open and Distributed Learning* 9, no. 3 (2008), http://www.irrodl.org/index.php/irrodl/article/view/523/1103. For Downes on physicists, see Stephen Downes, "'Connectivism' and Connective Knowledge," *Huffington Post,* January 5, 2011, https://www.huffpost.com/entry/connectivism-and-connecti_b_804653.

8. On DS106, see Howard Rheingold, "DS106: Enabling Open, Public, Participatory Learning," *Connected Learning Alliance,* https://clalliance.org/resources/ds106-enabling-open-public-participatory-learning/. Alan Levine, "A MOOC or Not a MOOC: DS106 Questions the Form," in *Invasion of the MOOCs: The Promise and Perils of Massive Open Online Courses,* eds. Steven D. Krause and Charles Lowe (Anderson, SC: Parlor Press, 2014), 29–38, available online at https://parlorpress.com/products/invasion-of-the-moocs. For the origins of edupunk, see Jim Groom, "The Glass Bees," *bavatuesdays,* May 25, 2008, https://bavatuesdays.com/the-glass-bees/. Some history is also discussed in Anya Kamenetz, *DIY U: Edupunks, Edupreneurs, and the Coming Transformation of Higher Education* (New York: Chelsea Green, 2010).

9. A discussion of the Daily Create is in Abram Anders, "Theories and Applications of Massive Online Open Courses (MOOCs): The Case for Hybrid Design," *International Review of Research in Open and Distributed Learning* 16, no. 6 (2015): 39–61.

10. W. Ian O'Byrne and Kristine E. Pytash, "Becoming Literate Digitally in a Digitally Literate Environment of Their Own," *Journal of Adolescent & Adult Literacy* 60, no. 5 (2017): 499–504, http://thinq.studio/wp-content /uploads/2018/02/JAAL-article-Becoming-Literate-Digitally-Domain -of-OnesOwn.pdf.

11. I discuss some of my own efforts along these lines at Justin Reich, "Techniques for Unleashing Student Work from Learning Management Systems," *KQED Mindshift,* February 13, 2015, https://www.kqed.org /mindshift/39332/techniques-for-unleashing-student-work-from -learning-management-systems.

12. Alexandra Juhasz and Anne Balsamo, "An Idea Whose Time Is Here: FemTechNet–A Distributed Online Collaborative Course (DOCC)," *Ada: A Journal of Gender, New Media, and Technology* 1, no. 1 (2012); Robinson Meyer, "5 Ways of Understanding the New, Feminist MOOC That's Not a MOOC," *Atlantic,* August 20, 2013, https://www.theatlantic.com /technology/archive/2013/08/5-ways-of-understanding-the-new -feminist-mooc-thats-not-a-mooc/278835/.

13. For the shift from the open web to walled gardens maintained by oligopolist technology companies see David Weinberger, "The Internet That Was (and Still Could Be)," *Atlantic,* June 22, 2015, https://www .theatlantic.com/technology/archive/2015/06/medium-is-the-message -paradise-paved-internet-architecture/396227/. For similar patterns in higher education, see Jim Groom and Brian Lamb, "Reclaiming Innovation," *EDUCAUSE Review Online,* May 13, 2014. https://www.educause .edu/visuals/shared/er/extras/2014/ReclaimingInnovation/default .html. As of 2019, the Connected Learning MOOC, CLMOOC, stands out, along with DS106, as one of the few remaining ongoing facilitated cMOOC learning experiences; see Chad Sansing, "Your Summer of Making and Connecting," *English Journal* 103, no. 5 (2014): 81.

14. Mitchel Resnick, John Maloney, Andrés Monroy-Hernández, Natalie Rusk, Evelyn Eastmond, Karen Brennan, Amon Millner, Eric Rosenbaum, Jay Silver, Brian Silverman, and Yasmin Kafai, "Scratch: Programming for All," *Communications of the ACM* 52, no. 11 (2009): 60–67.

15. Mitchel Resnick, *Lifelong Kindergarten: Cultivating Creativity through Projects, Passion, Peers, and Play* (Cambridge, MA: MIT Press, 2017).

16. Seymour Papert, *Mindstorms: Children, Computers, and Powerful Ideas* (New York: Basic Books, 1980).

17. For Scratch usage statistics, see https://scratch.mit.edu/statistics/.

18. Mizuko Ito, Kris Gutiérrez, Sonia Livingstone, Bill Penuel, Jean Rhodes, Katie Salen, Juliet Schor, Julian Sefton-Green, and S. Craig Watkins, *Connected Learning: An Agenda for Research and Design* (Irvine, CA: Digital Media and Learning Research Hub, 2013), https://dmlhub.net/wp -content/uploads/files/Connected_Learning_report.pdf, 7.

19. Mitchel Resnick, " Let's Teach Kids to Code," TEDx Beacon Street, November 2012, https://www.ted.com/talks/mitch_resnick_let_s_teach _kids_to_code/transcript?language=en.

20. Mitchel Resnick, "The Next Generation of Scratch Teaches Much More Than Coding," *EdSurge,* January 3, 2019, https://www.edsurge.com/news /2019-01-03-mitch-resnick-the-next-generation-of-scratch-teaches -more-than-coding.

21. Jal Mehta and Sarah Fine, *In Search of Deeper Learning* (Cambridge, MA: Harvard University Press, 2019).

22. Ito et al., *Connected Learning.*

23. Resnick et al., "Scratch"; Papert, "Mindstorms."

24. Paul A. Kirschner, John Sweller, and Richard E. Clark, "Why Minimal Guidance during Instruction Does Not Work: An Analysis of the Failure of Constructivist, Discovery, Problem-Based, Experiential, and Inquiry-Based Teaching," *Educational Psychologist* 41, no. 2 (2006): 75–86.

25. Sigal Samuel, "Canada's 'Incel Attack' and Its Gender-Based Violence Problem," *Atlantic,* April 28, 2018, https://www.theatlantic.com/inter national/archive/2018/04/toronto-incel-van-attack/558977/.

26. danah boyd, "Media Manipulation, Strategic Amplification, and Responsible Journalism," *Points,* September 14, 2018, https://points .datasociety.net/media-manipulation-strategic-amplification-and -responsible-journalism-95f4d611f462.

27. Alice Marwick and Rebecca Lewis, "Media Manipulation and Disinformation Online," *Data and Society,* May 5, 2017, https://datasociety.net /library/media-manipulation-and-disinfo-online/.

28. Zeynep Tufekci, "YouTube: The Great Radicalizer," *New York Times,* March 10, 2018.

29. Richard Hofstadter, *The Paranoid Style in American Politics* (New York: Vintage, 2012). On Lewin, see MIT News Office, "MIT Indefinitely Removes Online Physics Lectures and Courses by Walter Lewin," December 8, 2014, http://news.mit.edu/2014/lewin-courses-removed-1208.

30. On confusion in cMOOCs, see Rita Kop, "The Challenges to Connectivist Learning on Open Online Networks: Learning Experiences during a Massive Open Online Course," *The International Review of Research in Open and Distributed Learning* 12, no. 3 (2011): 19–38; Colin Milligan, Allison Littlejohn, and Anoush Margaryan, "Patterns of Engagement in Connectivist MOOCs," *Journal of Online Learning and Teaching* 9, no. 2 (2013): 149–159. For "getting stuck" in classrooms in Scratch and solutions for educators, see Paulina Haduong and Karen Brennan, "Helping K–12 Teachers Get Unstuck with Scratch: The Design of an Online Professional Learning Experience," in *Proceedings of the 50th ACM Technical Symposium on Computer Science Education* (Association for Computing Machinery Digital Library, 2019), 1095–1101; Karen Brennan, "Beyond Right or Wrong: Challenges of Including Creative Design Activities in the Classroom," *Journal of Technology and Teacher Education* 23, no. 3 (2015): 279–299.

31. Anton Barua, Stephen W. Thomas, and Ahmed E. Hassan, "What Are Developers Talking About? An Analysis of Topics and Trends in Stack Overflow," *Empirical Software Engineering* 19, no. 3 (2014): 619–654.

4. TESTING THE GENRES OF LEARNING AT SCALE

1. Games researcher Jane McGonigal estimated in 2010 that people across the world played 3 billion hours of video games per week. Jane McGonigal, "Gaming Can Make a Better World," TED talk, February 2010, https://www.ted.com/talks/jane_mcgonigal_gaming_can_make_a_better_world.

2. See, for instance, Larry Johnson, Samantha Adams Becker, Victoria Estrada, and Alex Freeman, *NMC Horizon Report: 2014 K–12 Edition* (Austin, TX: New Media Consortium, 2014), https://files.eric.ed.gov/fulltext/ED559369.pdf.

3. For games as powerful sites of learning, see James Gee, *What Video Games Have to Teach Us about Learning and Literacy* (New York: St. Martin's Press, 2007).

4. Federal Trade Commission, *Lumosity to Pay $2 Million to Settle FTC Deceptive Advertising Charges for Its "Brain Training" Program*, January 5, 2016, https://www.ftc.gov/news-events/press-releases/2016/01/lumosity-pay-2-million-settle-ftc-deceptive-advertising-charges.

5. Daniel J. Simons, Walter R. Boot, Neil Charness, Susan E. Gathercole, Christopher F. Chabris, David Z. Hambrick, and Elizabeth A. L. Stine-Morrow, "Do 'Brain-Training' Programs Work?," *Psychological Science in the Public Interest* 17, no. 3 (2016): 103–186. Thomas S. Redick, Zach Shipstead, Elizabeth A. Wiemers, Monica Melby-Lervåg, and Charles Hulme, "What's Working in Working Memory Training? An Educational Perspective," *Educational Psychology Review* 27, no. 4 (2015): 617–633.

6. Robert S. Woodworth and E. L. Thorndike, "The Influence of Improvement in One Mental Function upon the Efficiency of Other Functions (I)," *Psychological Review* 8, no. 3 (1901): 247. For a recent piece on the origins of transfer research, see Daniel Willingham, "Critical Thinking: Why Is It So Hard to Teach?," *American Educator,* Summer 2007, https://www.aft.org/sites/default/files/periodicals/Crit_Thinking.pdf.

7. Giovanni Sala and Fernand Gobet, "Does Far Transfer Exist? Negative Evidence from Chess, Music, and Working Memory Training," *Current Directions in Psychological Science* 26, no. 6 (2017): 515–520. The research on memory and chess is quite extensive. An important early contribution is William G. Chase and Herbert A. Simon, "Perception in Chess," *Cognitive Psychology* 4, no. 1 (1973): 55–81. A more recent study is Yanfei Gong, K. Anders Ericsson, and Jerad H. Moxley, "Recall of Briefly Presented Chess Positions and Its Relation to Chess Skill," *PloS one* 10, no. 3 (2015): https://doi.org/10.1371/journal.pone.0118756. Giovanni Sala, and Fernand Gobet, "Experts' Memory Superiority for Domain-Specific Random Material Generalizes across Fields of Expertise: A Meta-analysis," *Memory & Cognition* 45, no. 2 (2017): 183–193.

8. Douglas B. Clark, Emily E. Tanner-Smith, and Stephen S. Killingsworth, "Digital Games, Design, and Learning: A Systematic Review and Meta-analysis," *Review of Educational Research* 86, no. 1 (2016): 79–122. Pieter Wouters, Christof van Nimwegen, Herre van Oostendorp, and Erik D. van der Spek, "A Meta-analysis of the Cognitive and Motivational Effects of Serious Games," *Journal of Educational Psychology* 105, no. 2 (2013): 249–265, https://doi.org/10.1037/a0031311.

9. Brenda Laurel, *Utopian Entrepreneur* (Cambridge, MA: MIT Press, 2001).

10. David B. Tyack and Larry Cuban, *Tinkering toward Utopia* (Cambridge, MA: Harvard University Press, 1995).

11. Frederic Lardinois, "Duolingo Hires Its First Chief Marketing Officer as Active User Numbers Stagnate but Revenue Grows," *Techcrunch,* August 1, 2018, https://techcrunch.com/2018/08/01/duolingo-hires-its-first -chief-marketing-officer-as-active-user-numbers-stagnate/.

12. Hermann Ebbinghaus, *Memory,* trans. H. A. Ruger and C. E. Bussenius (New York: Teachers College, 1913); Nicholas Cepeda, Harold Pashler, Edward Vul, John T. Wixted, and Doug Rohrer, "Distributed Practice in Verbal Recall Tasks: A Review and Quantitative Synthesis," *Psychological Bulletin* 132, no. 3 (2006): 354.

13. Burr Settles and Brendan Meeder, "A Trainable Spaced Repetition Model for Language Learning," in *Proceedings of the 54th Annual Meeting of the Association for Computational Linguistics,* vol. 1, *Long Papers* (Stroudsburg, PA: Association for Computational Linguistics, 2016), 1848–1858; Roumen Vesselinov and John Grego, "Duolingo Effectiveness Study" (City University of New York, 2012), https://s3.amazonaws.com/duolingo-papers /other/vesselinov-grego.duolingo12.pdf.

14. Eric Klopfer, Jason Haas, Scot Osterweil, and Louisa Rosenheck, *Resonant Games* (Cambridge, MA: MIT Press, 2018).

15. Alex Calhoun, "*Vanished* Helps Kids Save the Future with Science," *Wired,* November 28, 2011, https://www.wired.com/2011/11/vanished-helps-kids -save-the-future-with-science/; Eric Klopfer, Jason Haas, Scott Osterweil, and Louisa Rosenheck, "I Wish I Could Go On Here Forever," in *Resonant Games: Design Principles for Learning Games that Connect Hearts, Minds, and the Everyday* (Cambridge, MA: MIT Press, 2018), https://www .resonant.games/pub/8w3uihyo.

16. For an introduction to the game and an optimistic take on educational possibilities, see Steve Nebel, Sascha Schneider, and Günter Daniel Rey, "Mining Learning and Crafting Scientific Experiments: A Literature Review on the Use of Minecraft in Education and Research," *Journal of Educational Technology & Society* 19, no. 2 (2016): 355. Sales and user participation data at https://en.wikipedia.org/wiki /Minecraft.

17. Stampylonghead's *Minecraft* introductions can be found at https://www.youtube.com/watch?v=cMsQlTkpQMM&list=UUj5i58mCkAREDqFWlhaQbOw.

18. Katie Salen, "10 Life Skills Parents Can Nurture through Minecraft," *Connected Camps Blog,* September 16, 2017, https://blog.connectedcamps.com/10-life-skills-parents-nurture-in-minecraft/.

19. Samantha Jamison, "Computer Game a Building Block for Engineers," *Carnegie Mellon University News,* July 26, 2017, https://www.cmu.edu/news/stories/archives/2017/july/minecraft-course.html; Sarah Guthals and Beth Simon, "Minecraft, Coding, and Teaching," https://www.edx.org/course/minecraft-coding-and-teaching.

20. For some recent research on *Zoombinis* gameplay, see Elizabeth Rowe, Jodi Asbell-Clarke, Santiago Gasca, and Kathryn Cunningham, "Assessing Implicit Computational Thinking in Zoombinis Gameplay," in *Proceedings of the 12th International Conference on the Foundations of Digital Games* (Association for Computing Machinery, 2017), https://par.nsf.gov/servlets/purl/10061931. The Wikipedia page for Zoombinis provides a helpful overview of the game: https://en.wikipedia.org/wiki/Logical_Journey_of_the_Zoombinis. See also Chris Hancock and Scot Osterweil, "Zoombinis and the Art of Mathematical Play," *Hands On!* Spring 1996, https://external-wiki.terc.edu/download/attachments/41419448/zoombinisandmathplay.pdf?api=v2; and Eric Klopfer, Jason Haas, Scot Osterweil, and Louisa Rosenheck, "In a Game, You Can Be Whoever You Want," in *Resonant Games: Design Principles for Learning Games that Connect Hearts, Minds, and the Everyday* (Cambridge, MA: MIT Press, 2018), https://www.resonant.games/pub/wkrjlp3o.

5. THE CURSE OF THE FAMILIAR

1. Judith Haymore Sandholtz, Cathy Ringstaff, and David C. Dwyer, *Teaching with Technology: Creating Student-Centered Classrooms* (New York: Teachers College Press, 1997).

2. A comment on Class Central, a review site for MOOCs, captures some of the critiques of the Neuroscience course: "Material & topic seemed interesting. Kind of silly way of presenting it, in my opinion, but quality of the videos was frankly good. Instructor tried to be funny too hard. I dropped; too much posh design & annoying music as background dis-

traction for me in a neuroscience course," https://www.classcentral.com
/course/edx-fundamentals-of-neuroscience-part-1-the-electrical
-properties-of-the-neuron-942. For a response to the critiques of DAL-
MOOC, see George Siemens, "Students Need to Take Ownership of
Their Own Learning," *Online Educa Berlin,* November 19, 2014, https://oeb
.global/oeb-insights/george-siemens-moocs-elearning-online-educa
-berlin/. For more on the "two-track" DALMOOC, see Shane Dawson,
Srecko Joksimović, Vitomir Kovanović, Dragan Gašević, and George Siemens, "Recognising Learner Autonomy: Lessons and Reflections from
a Joint x/c MOOC," *Proceedings of Higher Education Research and Development Society of Australia 2015* (2015).

3. Tom Page, "Skeuomorphism or Flat Design: Future Directions in Mobile Device User Interface (UI) Design Education," *International Journal
of Mobile Learning and Organisation* 8, no. 2: 130–142; David Oswald and
Steffen Kolb, "Flat Design vs. Skeuomorphism–Effects on Learnability
and Image Attributions in Digital Product Interfaces," in *DS 78: Proceedings of the 16th International Conference on Engineering and Product Design
Education* (Design Education and Human Technology Relations, University of Twente, The Netherlands, May 4, 2014), 402–407.

4. Matthew Glotzbach, "A New Monthly Milestone for Quizlet: 50 Million
Monthly Learners," *Quizlet Blog,* October 29, 2018, https://quizlet.com
/blog/a-new-milestone-for-quizlet-50-million-monthly-learners.

5. One useful source for understanding why structural elements of schools
are so inimical to new innovations is David K. Cohen and Jal D. Mehta,
"Why Reform Sometimes Succeeds: Understanding the Conditions That
Produce Reforms That Last," *American Educational Research Journal* 54,
no. 4 (2017): 644–690.

6. From 2012 to 2018, Audrey Watters tracked and commented on venture
investments in the edtech sector. For the 2018 example, see Audrey
Watters, "The Business of 'EdTech Trends,'" *Hack Education,* December 31,
2018, http://hackeducation.com/2018/12/31/top-ed-tech-trends-money.
For another critical view of venture capitalism and philanthropy in
education, see Ben Williamson, "Silicon Startup Schools: Technoc-
racy, Algorithmic Imaginaries and Venture Philanthropy in Corporate Education Reform," *Critical Studies in Education* 59, no. 2 (2018):
218–236.

7. John B. Diamond, "Where the Rubber Meets the Road: Rethinking the Connection between High-Stakes Testing Policy and Classroom Instruction," *Sociology of Education* 80, no. 4 (2007): 285–313; Christopher Lynnly Hovey, Lecia Barker, and Vaughan Nagy, "Survey Results on Why CS Faculty Adopt New Teaching Practices," in *Proceedings of the 50th ACM Technical Symposium on Computer Science Education* (Association for Computing Machinery Digital Library, 2019), 483–489.

8. Seymour Papert, *Mindstorms: Children, Computers, and Powerful Ideas* (New York: Basic Books, 1980); Mitchel Resnick, Brad Myers, Kumiyo Nakakoji, Ben Schneiderman, Randy Pausch, Ted Selker, and Mike Eisenberg, "Design Principles for Tools to Support Creative Thinking," National Science Foundation workshop on Creativity Support Tools (Washington, DC, 2005), http://www.cs.umd.edu/hcil/CST/Papers/designprinciples.htm; Moran Tsur and Natalie Rusk, "Scratch Microworlds: Designing Project-Based Introductions to Coding," in *Proceedings of the 49th ACM Technical Symposium on Computer Science Education* (Association for Computing Machinery Digital Library, 2018), 894–899.

9. Natalie Rusk and Massachusetts Institute of Technology Media Laboratory, *Scratch Coding Cards: Creative Coding Activities for Kids* (San Francisco: No Starch Press, 2017).

10. Tsur and Rusk, "Scratch Microworlds"; Phillip Schmidtt, Mitchel Resnick, and Natalie Rusk, "Learning Creative Learning: How We Tinkered with MOOCs," P2PU, http://reports.p2pu.org/learning-creative-learning/.

11. Karen Brennan, Sarah Blum-Smith, and Maxwell M. Yurkofsky, "From Checklists to Heuristics: Designing MOOCs to Support Teacher Learning," *Teachers College Record* 120, no. 9 (2018): n9; Paulina Haduong and Karen Brennan, "Getting Unstuck: New Resources for Teaching Debugging Strategies in Scratch," in *Proceedings of the 49th ACM Technical Symposium on Computer Science Education*, 1092 (Association for Computing Machinery Digital Library, 2018), https://doi.org/10.1145/3159450.3162248; see also https://gettingunstuck.gse.harvard.edu/about.html.

12. For an example of Desmos integration into College Board tests, see https://digitaltesting.collegeboard.org/pdf/about-desmos-calculator.pdf. For an example of integration into the Smarter Balanced consortium tests, see Tony Wan, "Desmos Passes the Smarter Balanced Tests

(and Hopes to Save Students $100)," *EdSurge,* May 8, 2017, https://www
.edsurge.com/news/2017-05-08-desmos-passes-the-smarter-balanced
-test-and-hopes-to-save-math-students-100.

13. Dan Meyer, "Math Class Needs a Makeover," TED talk (2010), https://
www.ted.com/talks/dan_meyer_math_class_needs_a_makeover
?language=en; "The Three Acts of a Mathematical Story," *Mr. Meyer*
(blog), May 11, 2011, http://blog.mrmeyer.com/2011/the-three-acts-of-a
-mathematical-story/; "Missing the Promise of Mathematical Modeling," *Mathematics Teacher* 108, no. 8 (2015): 578–583.

14. Dan Meyer, "Video and Multiple Choice: What Took Us So Long?" *Desmos*
(blog), October 27, 2016, https://blog.desmos.com/articles/video-multiple
-choice-what-took-us-so-long/.

15. Ibid.

16. Larry Cuban. *Hugging the Middle: How Teachers Teach in an Era of Testing
and Accountability* (New York: Teachers College, Columbia University,
2009); Larry Cuban, *Inside the Black Box of Classroom Practice: Change
without Reform in American Education* (Cambridge, MA: Harvard Education Press, 2013).

17. Cohen and Mehta, "Why Reform."

18. For the connections between Dewey's pragmatism and Web 2.0, see Michael Glassman and Min Ju Kang "The Logic of Wikis: The Possibilities of the Web 2.0 Classroom," *International Journal of Computer-Supported
Collaborative Learning* 6, no. 1 (2011): 93–112, https://doi.org/10.1007/s11412
-011-9107-y. Another example of the idea of technology as the tool that
allows Dewey's pedagogy to come to life is Chris Lehmann, "The True
Promise of Technology," *Whole Child Blog,* February 25, 2011, http://www
.wholechildeducation.org/blog/the-true-promise-of-technology.

6. THE EDTECH MATTHEW EFFECT

1. This chapter is adapted from Justin Reich and Mizuko Ito, *From Good
Intentions to Real Outcomes: Equity by Design in Learning Technologies* (Irvine,
CA: Digital Media and Learning Research Hub, 2017), https://clalliance
.org/wp-content/uploads/2017/11/GIROreport_1031.pdf, which was released under a Creative Commons 3.0 license. I am particularly in-
debted to Mimi for the "three myths" discussed later in the chapter. In

the iPad era when tablet computers were first released, I wrote a book with Tom Daccord highlighting how iPads might easily be used to extend existing practices and exploring what some of these pockets of excellence looked like then and could look like in the future; see Tom Daccord and Justin Reich, *iPads in the Classroom: From Consumption and Curation to Creation* (Dorchester, MA: EdTech Teacher, 2014); and Tom Daccord and Justin Reich, "How to Transform Teaching with Tablets," *Educational Leadership* 72, no. 8 (2015): 18–23.

2. Matthew 25:29 (New International Version).

3. Larry Cuban, *Teachers and Machines: The Classroom Use of Technology since 1920* (New York: Teachers College Press, 1986), 23.

4. Jeannie Oakes, *Keeping Track: How Schools Structure Inequality* (New Haven: Yale University Press, 2005).

5. Paul Attewell, "Comment: The First and Second Digital Divides," *Sociology of Education* 74, no. 3 (2001): 252–259.

6. Harold Wenglinsky, "Does It Compute? The Relationship between Educational Technology and Student Achievement in Mathematics" (Princeton, NJ: Educational Testing Services, 1998), https://www.ets.org /research/policy_research_reports/publications/report/1998/cneu, 3.

7. Ulrich Boser, "Are Schools Getting a Big Enough Bang for Their Education Buck?," *Center for American Progress Blog,* June 14, 2013, https://www .americanprogress.org/issues/education-k-12/reports/2013/06/14/66485 /are-schools-getting-a-big-enough-bang-for-their-education -technology-buck; Matthew H. Rafalow, "Disciplining Play: Digital Youth Culture as Capital at School," *American Journal of Sociology* 123, no. 5 (2018): 1416–1452.

8. I describe the hopes for education in the Web 2.0 era in "Reworking the Web, Reworking the World: How Web 2.0 Is Changing Our Society," *Beyond Current Horizons* (2008), https://edarxiv.org/hqme5/, https://doi .org/10.35542/osf.io/hqme5. Another perspective is Christine Greenhow, Beth Robelia, and Joan E. Hughes, "Learning, Teaching, and Scholarship in a Digital Age: Web 2.0 and Classroom Research: What Path Should We Take Now?," *Educational Researcher* 38, no. 4 (2009): 246–259.

9. Justin Reich, Richard Murnane, and John Willett, "The State of Wiki Usage in US K–12 Schools: Leveraging Web 2.0 Data Warehouses to As-

sess Quality and Equity in Online Learning Environments," *Educational Researcher* 41, no. 1 (2012): 7-15.

10. John D. Hansen and Justin Reich, "Democratizing Education? Examining Access and Usage Patterns in Massive Open Online Courses," *Science* 350, no. 6265 (2015): 1245-1248.

11. Justin Reich, "The Digital Fault Line: Background," *EdTech Researcher,* May 3, 2013, https://blogs.edweek.org/edweek/edtechresearcher/2013/05/the_digital_fault_line_background.html; S. Craig Watkins and Alexander Cho, *The Digital Edge: How Black and Latino Youth Navigate Digital Inequality* (New York: NYU Press, 2018); Vikki S. Katz and Michael H. Levine, "Connecting to Learn: Promoting Digital Equity among America's Hispanic Families," Joan Ganz Cooney Center at Sesame Workshop, 2015, https://eric.ed.gov/?id=ED555584; Vikki S. Katz, Meghan B. Moran, and Carmen Gonzalez, "Connecting with Technology in Lower-Income US Families," *New Media & Society* 20, no. 7 (2018): 2509-2533.

12. René F. Kizilcec, Andrew J. Saltarelli, Justin Reich, and Geoffrey L. Cohen, "Closing Global Achievement Gaps in MOOCs," *Science* 355, no. 6322 (2017): 251-252.

13. Kizilcec et al., "Closing."

14. Rene Kizilcec, Justin Reich, Michael Yeomans, Christoph Dann, Emma Brunskill, Glenn Lopez, Selen Turkay, Joseph Williams, and Dustin Tingley, "Scaling Up Behavioral Science Interventions in Online Education," in *Proceedings of the National Academy of Science* (forthcoming).

15. Kizilcec et al. "Closing."

16. Tressie McMillan Cottom, "Intersectionality and Critical Engagement with the Internet" (February 10, 2015). Available at *SSRN,* https://ssrn.com/abstract=2568956, 9.

17. Reich and Ito, "From Good intentions."

18. Betsy James DiSalvo, "Glitch Game Testers: The Design and Study of a Learning Environment for Computational Production with Young African American Males," PhD diss., Georgia Institute of Technology, 2012; Betsy James DiSalvo, Mark Guzdail, Tom Mcklin, Charles Meadows, Kenneth Perry, Corey Steward, and Amy Bruckman, "Glitch Game Testers: African American Men Breaking Open the Console," in *Proceedings*

of the 2009 DiGRA International Conference: Breaking New Ground: Innovation in Games, Play, Practice and Theory, http://www.digra.org/digital-library/publications/glitch-game-testers-african-american-men-breaking-open-the-console/.

19. Digital Promise, *IT Best Practices Toolkits: Student Tech Teams,* 2018, https://verizon.digitalpromise.org/toolkit/student-tech-teams/.

20. Ricarose Roque, "Family Creative Learning," *Makeology: Makerspaces as Learning Environments* 1 (2016): 47. For research on Scratchers and their parents, see Karen Brennan and Mitchel Resnick, "Imagining, Creating, Playing, Sharing, Reflecting: How Online Community Supports Young People as Designers of Interactive Media," in *Emerging Technologies for the Classroom,* eds. Chrystalla Mouza and Nancy Lavigne (New York: Springer, 2013), 253–268. In the One Laptop Per Child deployment in Paraguay, similar evidence emerged that constructionist tools like Scratch were primarily taken up in homes where parents could support learning about computing; see Morgan Ames, *The Charisma Machine: The Life, Death, and Legacy of One Laptop per Child* (Cambridge, MA: MIT Press, 2019).

21. See, *Tech Goes Home 2018 Annual Report,* https://static.wixstatic.com/ugd/6377ee_1a8d7ab992c94c3da08f0dc4a5d56e49.pdf.

22. Sarah Kessler, "How Jim McKelvey's Launchcode Is Helping Unconventional Tech Talent," *Fast Company,* April 18, 2016, https://www.fastcompany.com/3058467/how-jim-mckelveys-launchcode-is-helping-unconventional-tech-talent; Carl Straumsheim, "One Course, Three Flavors," *Inside Higher Ed,* January 21, 2014, https://www.insidehighered.com/news/2014/01/21/harvard-u-experiments-three-versions-same-course.

23. Mizuko Ito, Kris Gutiérrez, Sonia Livingstone, Bill Penuel, Jean Rhodes, Katie Salen, Juliet Schor, Julian Sefton-Green, and S. Craig Watkins, "Connected Learning: An Agenda for Research and Design" (Irvine, CA: Digital Media and Learning Research Hub, 2013), https://dmlhub.net/wp-content/uploads/files/Connected_Learning_report.pdf.

24. Moran Tsur and Natalie Rusk, "Scratch Microworlds: Designing Project-Based Introductions to Coding," in *Proceedings of the 49th ACM Technical Symposium on Computer Science Education* (Association for Computing Machinery Digital Library, 2018), 894–899.

25. Nichole Pinkard, Sheena Erete, Caitlin K. Martin, and Maxine McKinney de Royston, "Digital Youth Divas: Exploring Narrative-Driven Curriculum to Spark Middle School Girls' Interest in Computational Activities," *Journal of the Learning Sciences* 26, no. 3 (2017): 477–516.

26. Rebecca Pitt, "Mainstreaming Open Textbooks: Educator Perspectives on the Impact of Openstax College Open Textbooks," *International Review of Research in Open and Distributed Learning* 16, no. 4 (2015); David Ruth, "OpenStax Announces Top 10 Schools That Have Adopted Free College Textbooks," *OpenStax,* February 21, 2019, https://openstax.org /press/openstax-announces-top-10-schools-have-adopted-free-college -textbooks.

27. Benjamin L. Castleman, and Lindsay C. Page, *Summer Melt: Supporting Low-Income Students through the Transition to College* (Cambridge, MA: Harvard Education Press, 2014).

28. Benjamin L. Castleman and Lindsay C. Page, "Summer Nudging: Can Personalized Text Messages and Peer Mentor Outreach Increase College Going among Low-Income High School Graduates?," *Journal of Economic Behavior & Organization* 115 (2015): 144–160; Benjamin L. Castleman and Lindsay C. Page, "A Response to 'Texting Nudges Harm Degree Completion,'" *EducationNext,* January, 28, 2019, https://www.educationnext .org/response-texting-nudges-harm-degree-completion/.

7. THE TRAP OF ROUTINE ASSESSMENT

1. An early version of the argument in this chapter is in Justin Reich, "Will Computers Ever Replace Teachers?," *New Yorker: Elements,* July 8, 2014, https://www.newyorker.com/tech/annals-of-technology/will-computers -ever-replace-teachers.

2. One of the most readable summaries of how computers are changing labor market demands is Frank Levy and Richard J. Murnane, *Dancing with Robots: Human Skills for Computerized Work* (Washington, DC: Third Way NEXT, 2013). Two of the researchers who have continued research along similar lines are David Autor and David Deming; see Autor's *Work of the Past, Work of the Future* (Cambridge, MA: National Bureau of Economic Research, 2019); and Deming's "The Growing Importance of Social Skills in the Labor Market," *Quarterly Journal of Economics* 132, no. 4

(2017): 1593-1640. See also Morgan R. Frank, David Autor, James E. Bessen, Erik Brynjolfsson, Manuel Cebrian, David J. Deming, Maryann Feldman, et al., "Toward Understanding the Impact of Artificial Intelligence on Labor," *Proceedings of the National Academy of Sciences* 116, no. 4 (2019): 6531-6539.

3. Levy and Murnane "Dancing with Robots."

4. Frank Levy and Richard J. Murnane, *The New Division of Labor: How Computers Are Creating the Next Job Market* (Princeton, NJ: Princeton University Press, 2005).

5. David H. Autor, Frank Levy, and Richard J. Murnane, "The Skill Content of Recent Technological Change: An Empirical Exploration," *The Quarterly Journal of Economics* 118, no. 4 (2003): 1279-1333; Deming, "Social Skills."

6. On various skill frameworks, see Chris Dede, "Comparing Frameworks for 21st Century Skills," in *21st Century Skills: Rethinking How Students Learn,* eds. James Bellanca and Ron Brandt (Bloomington, IN: Solution Tree Press, 2010), 51-76.

7. Dana Remus and Frank S. Levy, "Can Robots Be Lawyers?," *Computers, Lawyers, and the Practice of Law* (November 27, 2016), available at *SSRN*: https://ssrn.com/abstract=2701092 or http://dx.doi.org/10.2139/ssrn.2701092.

8. Levy and Murnane, "New Division."

9. Henry I. Braun and Robert Mislevy, "Intuitive Test Theory," *Phi Delta Kappan* 86, no. 7 (2005): 488-497.

10. Daniel M. Koretz, *Measuring Up* (Cambridge, MA: Harvard University Press, 2008).

11. Brian Dear, *The Friendly Orange Glow: The Untold Story of the PLATO System and the Dawn of Cyberculture* (New York: Pantheon, 2017).

12. R. A. Avner and Paul Tenczar, "The TUTOR Manual" (US Department of Education, Education Resources Information Center [ERIC], 1970), https://eric.ed.gov/?id=ED050583.

13. See Common Core State Standards Initiative, http://www.corestandards.org/.

14. For another argument in favor of focusing education on what computers can't do, see Conrad Wolfram, "Teaching Kids Real Math with Com-

puters," TED talk (2010), https://www.ted.com/talks/conrad_wolfram
_teaching_kids_real_math_with_computers/transcript?language=en.

15. Unsupervised machine learning, where algorithms classify documents
into clusters based on feature similarity, is another branch of machine
learning, which thus far has limited applications to assessment. With
colleagues, I've proposed ways of using natural language processing and
unsupervised machine learning to aid human assessment; see Justin
Reich, Dustin Tingley, Jetson Leder-Luis, Margaret E. Roberts, and
Brandon Stewart, "Computer-Assisted Reading and Discovery for
Student Generated Text in Massive Open Online Courses," *Journal
of Learning Analytics* 2, no. 1 (2015): 156–184; Researchers at the University
of Illinois at Urbana-Champaign have proposed using unsupervised
learning models as inputs to supervised algorithms for assessment; see Saar Kuzi, William Cope, Duncan Ferguson, Chase Geigle,
and ChengXiang Zhai, "Automatic Assessment of Complex Assignments Using Topic Models," *Proceedings of the 2019 ACM Learning at Scale
Conference* (Association for Computing Machinery Digital Library,
2019), 1–10.

16. For an overview of machine-evaluated pronunciation, see Silke M. Witt,
"Automatic Error Detection in Pronunciation Training: Where We Are
and Where We Need to Go," *Proceedings of the International Symposium on
Automatic Detection on Errors in Pronunciation Training* (2012): 1–8.

17. For a paper that offers some sense of the amount of data required for
various pronunciation training tasks, see Wenping Hu, Yao Qian, and
Frank K. Soong, "A New DNN-based High Quality Pronunciation Evaluation for Computer-Aided Language Learning (CALL)," *Interspeech*
(2013): 1886–1890, https://pdfs.semanticscholar.org/ef29/bfcf0fcf71496b
2c6a09ae415010c5d7a2dc.pdf.

18. For an optimistic argument for the state of automated essay grading,
see Mark D. Shermis, "State-of-the-Art Automated Essay Scoring: Competition, Results, and Future Directions from a United States Demonstration," *Assessing Writing* 20 (2014): 53–76. For a more pessimistic view,
see Les Perelman, "When 'the State of the Art' Is Counting Words," *Assessing Writing* 21 (2014): 104–111.

19. Shermis, "State-of-the-Art."

20. Perelman, "State"; Randy Elliot Bennett, "The Changing Nature of Educational Assessment," *Review of Research in Education* 39, no. 1 (2015): 370–407, https://doi.org/10.3102/0091732X14554179.

21. Quotations from https://secureservercdn.net/45.40.149.159/b56.e17 .myftpupload.com/wp-content/uploads/2019/12/R.pdf. As cited in Les Perelman, "Babel Generator" (n.d.), http://lesperelman.com/writing -assessment-robo-grading/babel-generator/.

22. Steven Kolowich, "Writing Instructor, Skeptical of Automated Grading, Pits Machine vs. Machine," *Chronicle of Higher Education* 28 (2014), https://www.chronicle.com/article/Writing-Instructor-Skeptical /146211.

23. The excerpt is found in Audrey Watters *Teaching Machines* (Cambridge, MA: MIT Press, forthcoming), and the quotation is from "Exams by Machinery," *Ohio State University Monthly* (May 1931): 339. The quotation is also cited in Stephen Petrina, "Sidney Pressey and the Automation of Education, 1924–1934," *Technology and Culture* 45, no. 2 (2004): 305–330.

24. Harold Abelson, Gerald Jay Sussman, and Julie Sussman, *Structure and Interpretation of Computer Programs* (Cambridge, MA: MIT Press, 1996), xxii.

25. Jennifer French, Martin A. Segado, and Phillip Z. Ai, "Sketching Graphs in a Calculus MOOC: Preliminary Results," in *Frontiers in Pen and Touch: Impact of Pen and Touch Technology on Education* (Cham, Switzerland: Springer, 2017), 93–102.

26. Valerie Jean Shute and Matthew Ventura, *Stealth Assessment: Measuring and Supporting Learning in Video Games* (Cambridge, MA: MIT Press, 2013). Jennifer S. Groff, "The Potentials of Game-Based Environments for Integrated, Immersive Learning Data," *European Journal of Education* 53, no. 2 (2018): 188–201.

27. Groff, "The Potentials of Game-Based Environments for Integrated, Immersive Learning Data."

28. For one example of a rapidly developing AI / machine-learning-based technological system in the game of Go, see David Silver, Aja Huang, Chris J. Maddison, Arthur Guez, Laurent Sifre, George Van Den Driessche, Julian Schrittwieser, et al., "Mastering the Game of Go with Deep Neural Networks and Tree Search," *Nature* 529, no. 7587 (2016): 484.

29. David Pogue, "I'll Have My AI Call Your AI," *Scientific American* 319, no. 2 (2018): 26, https://www.scientificamerican.com/article/googles-duplex-ai -scares-some-people-but-i-cant-wait-for-it-to-become-a-thing/.

30. An early description of edX efforts at autograding is Piotr Mitros, Vikas Paruchuri, John Rogosic, and Diana Huang, "An Integrated Framework for the Grading of Freeform Responses," in *The Sixth Conference of MIT's Learning International Networks Consortium,* 2013, https://linc.mit.edu /linc2013/proceedings/Session3/Session3Mit-Par.pdf. Another early evaluation is Erin Dawna Reilly, Rose Eleanore Stafford, Kyle Marie Williams, and Stephanie Brooks Corliss, "Evaluating the Validity and Applicability of Automated Essay Scoring in Two Massive Open Online Courses," *International Review of Research in Open and Distributed Learning* 15, no. 5 (2014), http://www.irrodl.org/index.php/irrodl/article/view/1857.

8. THE TOXIC POWER OF DATA AND EXPERIMENTS

1. On the analogies between online learning platforms and experimentation in consumer technology, see Shreeharsh Kelkar, "Engineering a Platform: The Construction of Interfaces, Users, Organizational Roles, and the Division of Labor," *New Media & Society* 20, no. 7 (2018): 2629–2646.

2. Bruce Schneier, "Data Is a Toxic Asset," *Schneier on Security Blog,* March 4, 2016, https://www.schneier.com/blog/archives/2016/03/data_is_a_toxic .html.

3. A detailed description of a publicly available dataset with five years of Scratch data is Benjamin Mako Hill and Andrés Monroy-Hernández, "A Longitudinal Dataset of Five Years of Public Activity in the Scratch Online Community," *Scientific Data* 4 (2017): 170002, https://doi.org/10.1038 /sdata.2017.2. Research involving extensive uses of Scratch data includes Sayamindu Dasgupta, William Hale, Andrés Monroy-Hernández, and Benjamin Mako Hill, "Remixing as a Pathway to Computational Thinking," in *Proceedings of the 19th ACM Conference on Computer-Supported Cooperative Work and Social Computing* (Association for Computing Machinery Digital Library, 2016), 1438–1449; and Seungwon Yang, Carlotta Domeniconi, Matt Revelle, Mack Sweeney, Ben U. Gelman, Chris Beckley, and Aditya Johri, "Uncovering Trajectories of Informal Learning

in Large Online Communities of Creators," in *Proceedings of the Second (2015) ACM Conference on Learning at Scale* (Association for Computing Machinery Digital Library, 2015), 131–140. A detailed description of a publicly available HarvardX and MITx dataset is at Jon P. Daries, Justin Reich, Jim Waldo, Elise M. Young, Jonathan Whittinghill, Andrew Dean Ho, Daniel Thomas Seaton, and Isaac Chuang, "Privacy, Anonymity, and Big Data in the Social Sciences," *Communications of the ACM* 57, no. 9 (2014): 56–63.

4. For an example of treating learning records like text documents, see Cody A. Coleman, Daniel T. Seaton, and Isaac Chuang, "Probabilistic Use Cases: Discovering Behavioral Patterns for Predicting Certification," in *Proceedings of the Second (2015) ACM Conference on Learning at Scale* (Association for Computing Machinery Digital Library, 2015), 141–148.

5. Guanliang Chen, Dan Davis, Claudia Hauff, and Geert-Jan Houben, "Learning Transfer: Does It Take Place in MOOCs? An Investigation into the Uptake of Functional Programming in Practice," in *Proceedings of the Third (2016) ACM Conference on Learning at Scale* (Association for Computing Machinery Digital Library, 2016), 409–418. In a related study that connected MOOC learning to new behaviors, researchers investigated whether participation in a MOOC about learning analytics led to greater involvement in the scholarly society for learning analytics or submissions to learning analytics conferences; see Yuan Wang, Luc Paquette, and Ryan Baker, "A Longitudinal Study on Learner Career Advancement in MOOCs," *Journal of Learning Analytics* 1, no. 3 (2014): 203–206.

6. Tommy Mullaney, "Making Sense of MOOCs: A Reconceptualization of HarvardX Courses and Their Students," *SSRN* (2014), https://papers.ssrn.com/sol3/papers.cfm?abstract_id=2463736.

7. For another take on using large-scale data to zoom in and zoom out on learner behavior, see Jennifer DeBoer, Andrew D. Ho, Glenda S. Stump, and Lori Breslow, "Changing 'Course': Reconceptualizing Educational Variables for Massive Open Online Courses," *Educational Researcher* 43, no. 2 (2014): 74–84. For research on how changes in the Scratch environment lead to changes in behavior, see Sayamindu Dasgupta and Benjamin Mako Hill, "How 'Wide Walls' Can Increase Engagement: Evi-

dence from a Natural Experiment in Scratch," in *Proceedings of the 2018 CHI Conference on Human Factors in Computing Systems* (Association for Computing Machinery Digital Library, 2018), 1–11.

8. Ryan Baker, Sidney D'Mello, Merecedes Rodrigo, and Arthur Graesser, "Better to be Frustrated Than Bored: The Incidence, Persistence, and Impact of Learners' Cognitive-Affective States during Interactions with Three Different Computer-Based Learning Environments," *International Journal of Human-Computer Studies* 68, no. 4 (2010), 223–241, https://www.sciencedirect.com/science/article/pii/S1071581909001797.

9. Boston School Committee, *Reports of the Annual Visiting Committees of the Public Schools of the City of Boston, (1845)*, City Document no. 26 (Boston: J. H. Eastburn), 12.

10. Justin Reich, "'Compass and Chart': Millenarian Textbooks and World History Instruction in Boston, 1821–1923," *SSRN* (2009), https://papers.ssrn.com/sol3/papers.cfm?abstract_id=2193129.

11. Lorrie Shepard, "A Brief History of Accountability Testing, 1965–2007," in *The Future of Test-Based Educational Accountability*, eds. Katherine Ryan and Lorrie Shepard (New York: Routledge. 2008), 25–46.

12. For two studies with promising results for education technology at scale, see John F. Pane, Beth Ann Griffin, Daniel F. McCaffrey, and Rita Karam, "Effectiveness of Cognitive Tutor Algebra I at Scale," *Educational Evaluation and Policy Analysis* 36, no. 2 (2014): 127–144; and William G. Bowen, Matthew M. Chingos, Kelly A. Lack, and Thomas I. Nygren, "Interactive Learning Online at Public Universities: Evidence from a Six-Campus Randomized Trial," *Journal of Policy Analysis and Management* 33, no. 1 (2014): 94–111. On the risk/benefit calculation from data-intensive educational research, see Rebecca Ferguson and Doug Clow, "Where Is the Evidence? A Call to Action for Learning Analytics," *Proceedings of the Seventh International Learning Analytics and Knowledge Conference* (2017), 56–65.

13. For the official statement from the meeting, see Asilomar Convention for Learning Research in Higher Education, 2014, http://asilomar-highered.info/.

14. For an introduction to some of these concerns, see Elana Zeide, "Education Technology and Student Privacy," in *The Cambridge Handbook of*

Consumer Privacy, eds. Evan Selinger, Jules Polonetsky, and Omer Tene, 70–84, *SSRN* (2018), https://ssrn.com/abstract=3145634.

15. A landmark text of how surveillance and data capture is reshaping the world is Shoshana Zuboff, *The Age of Surveillance Capitalism: The Fight for a Human Future at the New Frontier of Power* (New York: Public Affairs, 2019).

16. For an overview of K–12 legal issues related to student data and privacy, see Leah Plunkett, Alicia Solow-Niederman, and Urs Gasser, "Framing the Law and Policy Picture: A Snapshot of K–12 Cloud-Based Ed Tech and Student Privacy in Early 2014," *Berkman Center Research Publication 2014-10* (2014). For the yawning gaps between current law and much needed ethical guidelines, see Elana Zeide, "Unpacking Student Privacy," in *Handbook of Learning Analytics,* eds. Charles Lang, George Siemens, Alyssa Wise, and Dragan Gasevic (Society for Learning Analytics Research, 2017), 327–335.

17. Natasha Singer, "Online Test-Takers Feel Anti-cheating Software's Uneasy Glare," *New York Times,* April 5, 2015, https://www.nytimes.com/2015/04/06/technology/online-test-takers-feel-anti-cheating-softwares-uneasy-glare.html.

18. Helen Nissenbaum, *Privacy in Context: Technology, Policy, and the Integrity of Social Life* (Stanford, CA: Stanford University Press, 2009). For the theory of contextual integrity applied to MOOCs and virtual learning environments, see Elana Zeide and Helen F. Nissenbaum, "Learner Privacy in MOOCs and Virtual Education," *Theory and Research in Education* 16, no. 3 (2018): 280–307, available at https://ssrn.com/abstract=3303551 or http://dx.doi.org/10.2139/ssrn.3303551; Charlie Moore, Vivian Zhong, and Anshula Gandhi, "Healthy Minds Study Survey Data Informed 2016 Senior House Decisions," *Tech,* July 26, 2017, https://thetech.com/2017/07/26/healthy-minds-data-used-in-2016-senior-house-decisions. See also Cynthia Barnhart, *Senior House Decision Process FAQ,* http://chancellor.mit.edu/sites/default/files/sh-decisionprocess-faq.pdf; and Elizabeth Glaser, "MIT Misused Survey Data to Take Action against Senior House," *Tech,* July 26, 2017, https://thetech.com/2017/07/26/healthy-minds-survey-misuse.

19. John D. Hansen and Justin Reich, "Democratizing Education? Examining Access and Usage Patterns in Massive Open Online Courses," *Science* 350, no. 6265 (2015): 1245–1248.

20. Two efforts to share the role of research in the edX consortium are the edX page on research, https://www.edx.org/about/research-pedagogy, and the HarvardX research statement, https://harvardx.harvard.edu/research-statement, which is attached to many course registration pages.

21. Audrey Watters, "The Weaponization of Education Data," *Hack Education*, December 11, 2017, http://hackeducation.com/2017/12/11/top-ed-tech-trends-weaponized-data.

22. On school cooperation with Immigration and Customs Enforcement, see Erica Green, "For Immigrant Students, a New Worry: Call to ICE," *New York Times*, May 30, 2018, https://www.nytimes.com/2018/05/30/us/politics/immigrant-students-deportation.html.

23. James Murphy, "The Undervaluing of School Counselors," *Atlantic*, September 16, 2016, https://www.theatlantic.com/education/archive/2016/09/the-neglected-link-in-the-high-school-to-college-pipeline/500213/; Douglas J. Gagnon and Marybeth J. Mattingly, "Most U.S. School Districts Have Low Access to School Counselors: Poor, Diverse, and City School Districts Exhibit Particularly High Student-to-Counselor Ratios," *Carsey Research* (2016), https://scholars.unh.edu/cgi/viewcontent.cgi?article=1285&context=carsey. The claim that Naviance is used in 40 percent of high schools is from the company's website; see https://www.naviance.com/solutions/states.

24. David Christian, Amy Lawrence, and Nicole Dampman, "Increasing College Access through the Implementation of Naviance: An Exploratory Study," *Journal of College Access* 3, no. 2 (2017): 28–44; Christine Mulhern, "Changing College Choices with Personalized Admissions Information at Scale: Evidence on Naviance," April 2019, https://scholar.harvard.edu/files/mulhern/files/naviance_mulhern_april2019.pdf.

25. A Learning at Scale keynote, unrecorded but with a short published abstract, provides one example of this position: Peter Norvig, "Machine Learning for Learning at Scale," in *Proceedings of the Second (2015) ACM*

Conference on Learning at Scale (Association for Computing Machinery Digital Library, 2015), 215. See also Daphne Koller, "What We're Learning from Online Education," filmed June 2012 at TEDGlobal 2012, Edinburgh, Scotland, video, https://www.ted.com/talks/daphne_koller_what_we_re_learning_from_online_education?language=en.

26. Justin Reich "Engineering the Science of Learning," *Bridge* 46, no. 3 (2016), https://www.nae.edu/162627/Engineering-the-Science-of-Learning.

27. Rene Kizilcec, Justin Reich, Michael Yeomans, Christoph Dann, Emma Brunskill, Glenn Lopez, Selen Turkay, Joseph Williams, and Dustin Tingley, "Scaling Up Behavioral Science Interventions in Online Education," in *Proceedings of the National Academy of Science* (forthcoming).

28. Benjamin Harold, "Pearson Tested 'Social-Psychological' Messages in Learning Software, with Mixed Results," *Education Week: Digital Education,* April 17, 2018, https://blogs.edweek.org/edweek/DigitalEducation/2018/04/pearson_growth_mindset_software.html. Kate Crawford (@katecrawford), "Ed tech company experiments on 9000 kids without anyone's consent or knowledge to see if they test differently when 'social-psychological' messaging is secretly inserted? HARD NO," https://twitter.com/katecrawford/status/986584699647791104. On mindset theory, see David Scott Yeager and Carol S. Dweck, "Mindsets That Promote Resilience: When Students Believe That Personal Characteristics Can Be Developed," *Educational Psychologist* 47, no. 4 (2012): 302–314.

29. Michelle N. Meyer, Patrick R. Heck, Geoffrey S. Holtzman, Stephen M. Anderson, William Cai, Duncan J. Watts, and Christopher F. Chabris, "Objecting to Experiments That Compare Two Unobjectionable Policies or Treatments," *Proceedings of the National Academy of Sciences* 116, no. 22 (2019): 10723–10728.

30. For Pearson's response, see Valerie Strauss, "Pearson Conducts Experiment on Thousands of College Students without Their Knowledge," *Washington Post: Answer Sheet Blog,* April 23, 2018, https://www.washingtonpost.com/news/answer-sheet/wp/2018/04/23/pearson-conducts-experiment-on-thousands-of-college-students-without-their-knowledge/?utm_term=.9efe30965b57.

31. For more thoughts on my cautious optimism on these experiments, see Justin Reich, "Can Text Messages and Interventions Nudge Students

through School?" *KQED Mindshift,* June 3, 2015, https://www.kqed.org/mindshift/40719/can-text-messages-and-interventions-nudge-students-through-school.

32. Zeide, "Unpacking."

33. Monica Bulger, Patrick McCormick, and Mikaela Pitcan, "The Legacy of inBloom," *Data & Society Research Institute,* 2017, https://datasociety.net/library/the-legacy-of-inbloom/.

34. Bulger, McCormick, and Pitcan "The Legacy of inBloom."

35. Leah Plunkett, Alicia Solow-Niederman, and Urs Gasser, "Framing the Law and Policy Picture: A Snapshot of K–12 Cloud-Based Ed Tech and Student Privacy in Early 2014," presentation at Harvard Law School, June 3, 2014, available at https://papers.ssrn.com/sol3/papers.cfm?abstract_id=2442432.

36. Kenneth R. Koedinger, Ryan S.J.d. Baker, Kyle Cunningham, Alida Skogsholm, Brett Leber, and John Stamper, "A Data Repository for the EDM Community: The PSLC DataShop," *Handbook of Educational Data Mining* 43 (2010): 43–56.

CONCLUSION

1. Frederick James Smith, "The Evolution of the Motion Picture: VI—Looking into the Future with Thomas A. Edison," *New York Dramatic Mirror,* July 9, 1913, 24, column 3, as analyzed in https://quoteinvestigator.com/2012/02/15/books-obsolete/; "Edison Predicts Film Will Replace Teacher, Books," Associated Press, May 15, 1923, available at https://virginiachronicle.com/cgi-bin/virginia?a=d&d=HR19230518.2.11.

2. Phil Hill, "Instructure: Plans to Expand Beyond Canvas LMS into Machine Learning and AI," *e-Literate,* March, 2019, https://eliterate.us/instructure-plans-to-expand-beyond-canvas-lms-into-machine-learning-and-ai/.

3. "Roy Amara: 1925–2007, American Futurologist," *Oxford Essential Quotations,* 4th ed., ed. Susan Ratcliffe, 2016, https://www.oxfordreference.com/view/10.1093/acref/9780191826719.001.0001/q-oro-ed4-00018679.

4. John F. Pane, Beth Ann Griffin, Daniel F. McCaffrey, and Rita Karam, "Effectiveness of Cognitive Tutor Algebra I at Scale," *Educational Evaluation*

and Policy Analysis 36, no. 2 (2014): 127–144; Jeremy Roschelle, Mingyu Feng, Robert F. Murphy, and Craig A. Mason, "Online Mathematics Homework Increases Student Achievement," *AERA Open* 2, no. 4 (2016), https://doi.org/10.1177/2332858416673968.

5. For statistics on Wikipedia size, see https://en.wikipedia.org/wiki /Wikipedia:Size_comparisons#cite_note-wikistatsall-2. For the Newspapers on Wikipedia Projects, see Mike Caulfield, "Announcing the Newspapers on Wikipedia Project (#NOW)," Hapgood.us, May 29, 2018, https://hapgood.us/2018/05/29/announcing-the-local-historical -newspapers-project-lhnp/. See also Emma Lurie and Eni Mustafaraj, "Investigating the Effects of Google's Search Engine Result Page in Evaluating the Credibility of Online News Sources," in *Proceedings of the 10th ACM Conference on Web Science* (Association for Computing Machinery Digital Library, 2018), 107–116, https://dl.acm.org/doi/10.1145 /3201064.3201095. On early distaste for Wikipedia and some argument for how it might be useful to educators, see Justin Reich and Tom Daccord, *Best Ideas for Teaching with Technology: A Practical Guide for Teachers, by Teachers* (New York: Routledge, 2015).

ACKNOWLEDGMENTS

My first thanks go to my agent Karen Gantz, who reached out to me in July 2014 after reading some of my research on MOOCs. She suggested that I write a book on the topic and provided encouragement throughout. Andrew Kinney at Harvard University Press provided excellent editorial guidance, and he had great patience during the slow years of writing. I apologize to both for the long incubation; it took me years to realize that the trick was to schedule all my classes and meetings on Mondays, Wednesdays, and Fridays and then to earnestly write two days a week.

Many people generously read drafts or sections of the manuscript in process: Neil Heffernan, Eric Klopfer, Jal Mehta, Jim Paradis, and Ed Schiappa convened an enormously helpful review workshop at MIT; Tressie McMillan Cottom, Fiona Holland, Andrew Ho, Mimi Ito, David Joyner, René Kizilcec, Meira Levinson, Nannette Napier, Audrey Watters, Ethan Zuckerman, members of the Berkman-Klein book authors club, and the anonymous reviewer from Harvard University Press also provided valuable insights along the way. Several semesters' worth of students in my Learning, Media, and Technology seminar have read draft chapters of the book and offered good questions, rebuttals, and feedback. My colleagues in the Teaching Systems Lab not only read and offered feedback on the chapters, but also kept the rest of our research agenda on track to give me time to finish. Rachel Slama deserves special thanks for building and leading the lab with me. I am grateful for the collaborations with my other research coauthors, whose work is cited throughout.

The manuscript benefited enormously from developmental editing by Lisa Camner McKay and my dear colleague Alyssa Napier; together, they strengthened some chapters and rescued others. Alison Fang, in her first year at MIT, did a wonderful job doing a final pass over references and sleuthing some hard-to-confirm facts. Julia Kirby of Harvard University Press shepherded the production of the book, and Richard Feit provided the final editing; both offered an energizing jolt of editorial guidance on the way to the finish line. Despite all these efforts, the errors that remain are my own.

The staff at Kickstand Café kept me fed and caffeinated, and Yo-Yo Ma, Edgar Meyer, and Mark O'Connor's "Appalachia Waltz" provided the soundtrack for my writing. I'm grateful to Harvard and MIT for supporting my career, though nothing in the preceding pages represents the official positions of either university.

The list of teachers, students, and research participants who contributed to this work and to my life is overwhelming; literally millions of people have answered survey items that I have designed for MOOC research. Every time I open those files or review those data, I do so with a moment of gratitude for their time and with the hope that the research that my colleagues and I do with these data is worthy of their effort. So many teachers, school leaders, and university administrators have opened their doors to me over the years, and if we've talked, tweeted, or corresponded about technology and learning, you have my thanks. I'm particularly grateful to my first teaching mentor, Tom Daccord; our work together with EdTechTeacher has shaped much of how I understand technology in schools. My life in schools has been blessed by four decades of extraordinary educators. At the front end, Sharon Jackson started my learning in daycare, and Jo Truesdell launched a love of schooling in kindergarten; as I was passing through high school and college, Tom Heise and Ed Russell believed that what I wrote was worthy of other's attention—and here we are.

INDEX

Abelson, Hal, 190–191

academic counseling services, 215–217

access to higher education, 20–21, 45–46

access to technology, 3, 71; digital divide and, 150, 153–155; edtech and, 11; gaps in broadband access, 156; social and cultural barriers and, 155–160. *See also* edtech Matthew effect; inequality; opportunity; resources; socioeconomic status

achievement gap: computer-assisted instruction and, 66; global, 158. *See also* socioeconomic status

adaptive tutors, 47, 235; adopting, 48–50; assessment in, 176; Duolingo, 113–114, 122; goal of education and, 93; in K–12 schools, 43; learning outcomes and, 64–73. *See also* algorithm-guided learning at scale systems

adoption of new technologies, 48–50; challenges to, 133–134; community of teachers and, 136–137, 147; familiarity and, 136; process of, 130–132. *See also* change; curse of the familiar; domestication of new technologies; implementation of innovations; technology integration

advantage. *See* access to higher education; edtech Matthew effect; inequality; socioeconomic status

affinity networks, 2–3, 7

Agarwal, Anant, 17–18, 22

AI Now, 221

algorithm-guided learning at scale systems, 7–8, 47–76, 235; ASSIST-ments, 70–72, 235, 238, 239, 240; Cognitive Tutor, 67–73, 204–205, 235; compared with other genres, 91–93; content sequencing in, 52–53; costs of implementing, 74;